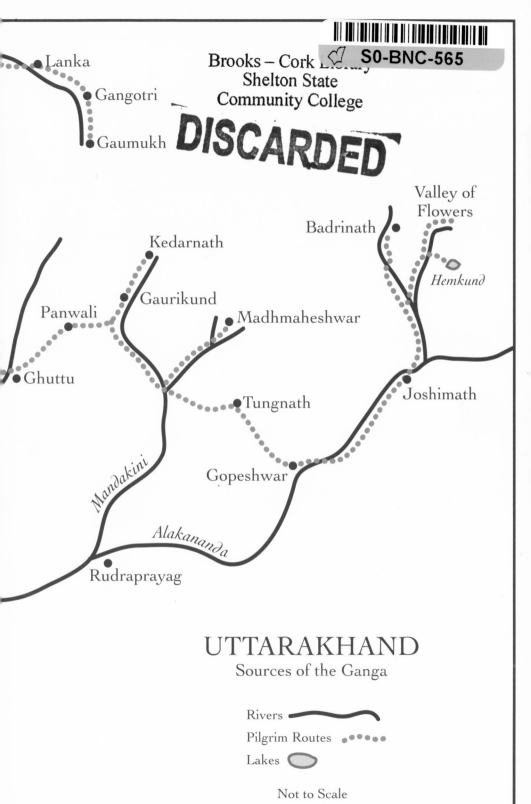

Lanka

Gangotri

Gaumukh

Valley of
Flowers

Badrinath

Hemkund

Kedarnath

Gaurikund

Panwali

Madhmaheshwar

Ghuttu

Tungnath

Joshimath

Mandakini

Gopeshwar

Alakananda

Rudraprayag

# UTTARAKHAND
Sources of the Ganga

Rivers

Pilgrim Routes

Lakes

Not to Scale

# SACRED
# WATERS

# SACRED
# WATERS

## A PILGRIMAGE UP THE GANGES RIVER
## TO THE SOURCE OF HINDU CULTURE

### STEPHEN ALTER

HARCOURT, INC.
New York   San Diego   London

www.HarcourtBooks.com

Library of Congress Cataloging-in-Publication Data

Alter, Stephen.
Sacred waters: a pilgrimage up the Ganges river to the source of the Hindu culture /
Stephen Alter. — 1st U.S. ed.
p.   cm.
ISBN  0-15-100585-0
1. India — Description and travel.   2. Alter, Stephen — Journeys — India.
3. India — Religious life and customs.   I. Title.
DS414.2 .A557 2001
954.05'2 — dc21      2001024954

Text set in Cochin
Designed by Linda Lockowitz
First U.S. edition
A C E G I K J H F D B

Printed in the United States of America

*For my brothers,*
*Joseph and Andrew Alter*

*When one sees Eternity in things that pass away*
*and Infinity in finite things, then one has pure knowledge.*

*But if one merely sees the diversity of things,*
*with their divisions and limitations, then one has impure knowledge.*

*And if one selfishly sees a thing as if it were everything,*
*independent of the ONE and the many, then one is in the darkness*
*of ignorance.*

BHAGAVAD GITA


*A man's life should be as fresh as a river.*
*It should be the same channel but a new water every instant.*

HENRY DAVID THOREAU

# CONTENTS

# III
# REFLECTION
### GANGOTRI — KEDARNATH

# IV
# TRANSCENDENCE
### KEDARNATH — BADRINATH

# ACKNOWLEDGMENTS

Travel and research for this book was supported in part by the grant program of the Banff Centre for Mountain Culture and by MIT's School of Humanities, Arts and Social Sciences. My thanks to André Bernard, Jill Grinberg, David Hough, Meredith Phillips, Kevin McConeghey, and Arun Sanon.

The following passages are reproduced by permission of Penguin Books Ltd.: *The Bhagavad Gita*, translated by Juan Mascaro (v. 20-22, p. 81), *The Upanishads*, translated by Juan Mascaro ("Katha Upanishad" part 3, p. 61), ("Isa Upanishad" v. 6, p. 49), and *The Rig Veda*, translated by Wendy Doniger O'Flaherty ("The Funeral Fire" v. 10.16, p. 49 and "The Waters, Who Are Goddesses" v. 7.49, p. 232).

# SACRED
# WATERS

# SRAVAN

A MONTH OF WARM RAIN.

Season of fertility and germination.

Humid shadows beneath a mango tree. Its roots are littered with seeds, like hairy cocoons, their flesh sucked clean. Discarded peels lie rotting in the black mud. There are so many seeds it looks as if the tree must have spawned them all at once, shedding mangoes from its limbs in unison, ripe fruit cascading to the ground like heavy drops of rain.

I sit here, under the eaves of a temple roof, where I have taken shelter from a sudden downpour. A lone boy comes by, his bookbag dangling from one shoulder, blue shirt untucked, walking home from school in the rain. He stops beneath the tree, studying its dense canopy of leaves, then takes a stone and hurls it into the branches. Once. Twice. On the third try he knocks a mango to the ground and with the casual self-consciousness of youth, he turns around to see if anyone has observed his aim. The schoolboy does not know that I am watching him, half hidden behind a pillar that supports the temple roof. He steps forward, picks up the fallen mango, and bites at its green skin hungrily. Squeezing the juicy sweetness into his mouth the boy continues on his way toward home.

When the rain subsides I come out from under cover. The air feels cooler now, a fresh breeze skimming off the river. But beneath the mango tree the shadows are still heavy with unspent moisture. The decomposing peels emit a cloying, unhealthy fragrance. Mosquitoes swarm around my legs as I stare down at the carpet of mango seeds, strewn about like the eggs of a giant fly, waiting to hatch in the fecund soil. Some of the seeds have already split open, their fibrous hulls breaking apart. Inside I can see the bright new shapes of mango seedlings, their leaves unfolding like the wings of luminous green moths.

On my office wall is a map of Garhwal, printed by the Survey of India in the 1920s. It is a family heirloom, handed down to me from my parents and grandparents who used it when they hiked through these mountains, long before I was born. The paper is now yellowed and cracked, held together by a frayed cloth backing, the same kind of cotton gauze that is used for bandages. A year ago I had the map framed, wanting to preserve its abstract beauty, the faint contour lines like fingerprints, the weathered colors of an old man's skin. Stained and dog-eared from having been carried in rucksacks, the map looks well used, some of the routes traced over in pencil or red ink, altitudes and destinations underlined. It reminds me of an antique parchment, documenting journeys taken years ago. Through the center of the map flows the Ganga, or Ganges, as it was labeled by British cartographers, a series of blue veins that converge in the creased folds of the Himalayas.

The four main sources of this river are located in Garhwal, or Uttarakhand as it is also known, a mountainous region of northern India that borders Tibet. Each year, monsoon storms deposit more than a hundred and fifty centimeters of rain on these precipitous slopes. The water runs into ravines and valleys. High-altitude lakes and springs spill over rocks and waterfalls. Snowfields and glaciers melt into ice-fed streams.

Tributaries are formed and each confluence adds to the cumulative force of the river until it becomes a single current, cutting its way through a maze of ridges.

The map on my wall was printed before most of the motor roads were built in Garhwal. It depicts the walking trails as a network of lines that connect the scattered towns and villages, an intricate web of footpaths that cross the ridges and follow the valleys. Here in Uttarakhand there are no straight lines, no symmetrical patterns, no level ground. Just as streams and rivers carve their own circuitous route through the rugged terrain, these trails seem to follow a winding course that reaches back into the mountains, toward a secret and inaccessible point of origin.

JULY 28, 1999

The thirteenth day of Sravan in the year 1920 (Saka) or 2055 (Vikrami), according to the Hindu calendars. I have no idea whether or not this is an auspicious day to start my pilgrimage. Just after dawn I woke up to the drumming of rain on a corrugated tin roof. It continued until late afternoon, a steady shower that soaked my clothes before I had walked the first kilometer. I could have waited, postponing my departure until a drier moment, but it seemed appropriate to set off in the rain. My umbrella provided little protection, errant drops blowing in from all sides and the air saturated with moisture, humidity condensing on my skin.

In the colorful oleographs that decorate religious calendars, Ganga appears as a demure goddess streaming from the monsoon clouds. Daughter of Himavant, lord of the mountains, she is a celestial river that fell to earth. The fluid pleats of her purple sari blend into the brush strokes of a torrential storm that rains down upon the meditating figure of Shiv. For a thousand years

Ganga flowed through the matted locks of his hair, forming countless tributaries. Most powerful of deities—creator and destroyer—Shiv absorbed the violent impact of Ganga's descent from heaven. In the form of a rishi, the blue-throated god remains impassive and undisturbed in his immortal meditation, seated cross-legged on a tiger skin, white snow peaks in the background.

At Hardwar, one of India's holiest cities, the Ganga passes through a gap in the Siwalik Hills. Named after the hair of Shiv (Shiv Alak), these crumbling ridges are all that remain of a primordial chain of mountains, older than the Himalayas. Compared to the higher peaks of Garhwal, thirty kilometers to the north, the Siwalik Hills are nothing more than a minor ripple in the landscape. Their summits have eroded over time until they are barely taller than the sal trees that forest these slopes. Worn down by centuries upon centuries of monsoon storms, the Siwaliks are a reminder of the tenuous provenance of nature.

Known as the gateway of the gods, Hardwar marks the point at which the Ganga enters the plains of northern India and sets its course for the sea. The river carries with it a rich lode of sediment washed down from the high Himalayas. Like the Siwalik Hills, these mountains are also in the process of being eroded by the Ganga, its current scouring away the soil.

During the month of Sravan, from late July to early August, which coincides with the monsoon, over a million pilgrims descend upon Hardwar. These kavar, as they are called, collect vessels of Gangajal (water from the Ganga) and carry them to a Shiv temple at Garh Mukteshwar, over a hundred kilometers downstream. Some of the more ambitious kavar walk all the way from Gaumukh Glacier above Gangotri, an added distance of three hundred kilometers. Traveling on foot, the kavar transport their bottles of Gangajal in a pair of wicker baskets, suspended from a bamboo yoke that rests upon their shoulders.

The water is never allowed to touch the ground and the pilgrims travel for weeks, stopping at roadside shelters erected by pious benefactors along their route. Ultimately, when the kavar reach their destination, the Gangajal is presented as an offering to Shiv, a rite of worship that reenacts the myth of Ganga's descent to earth.

In recent years this pilgrimage has become so popular that most of the highway between Hardwar and Delhi is closed for several weeks to allow the kavar to complete their journey. Walking together, like an army on the march, they form a human river, carrying the sacred water on their shoulders. The majority of these pilgrims are men in their twenties and thirties, who abandon their fields, their jobs, or their businesses, and leave behind the comforts of home to perform a ritual that runs parallel to the natural course of the Ganga, as it flows out of the mountains and across the land.

There is something both fascinating and disturbing about this mass migration of devout Hindus. The kavar form a colorful procession, their baskets decorated with gold and silver tinsel, saffron scarves, garlands of marigolds, framed pictures of Shiv and Hanuman. Many of them walk barefoot, a seemingly endless line of men stretching along the side of the highway, exhausted faces staring straight ahead, some of them hobbling with canes. Pale pink elastic bandages are wrapped around knees or ankles, evidence of pain and exertion, their skin glistening with sweat in the muggy sunlight. The kavar seem so single-minded in their communal passion, a relentless determination in their stride.

"Bam Bam Bholey!"

They chant in unison.

"Jai Bholey!"—another name for Shiv.

In their numbers, the kavar seem unstoppable, like the swollen current of the Ganga itself. Their devotion reflects an unquestioning faith in God and a uniformity of belief. The ritual itself is innocent enough, carrying water from a river to a temple, but the symbolic force of all these men walking together gives the impression of a parade, a collective demonstration of power. It is impossible to ignore connections between the threatening floodwaters of Hindu chauvinism and this annual march of the kavar, a crowd of celebrants herded together by an exclusive current of beliefs.

My own pilgrimage takes me in the opposite direction. While the kavar carry their precious loads of water away from the mountains, I am traveling upstream to the four main sources of the Ganga—a journey known as the Char Dham Yatra. According to popular Hindu belief, anyone who traverses the watershed of the Ganga, walking from Yamnotri in the west to Badrinath in the east, achieves moksha, or salvation. This is the route that was followed by the five Pandav brothers and their wife, Draupadi, at the end of the Mahabharata. After renouncing their kingdom the Pandavs wandered through the Himalayas on their way to heaven. These mountains are perhaps the most sacred topography on earth and Garhwal is often called Dev Bhoomi, land of the gods. Every snow peak and glacier, every confluence and village temple, is invested with mythology. The stories that permeate this region are part of a religious narrative that inspires millions of pilgrims every year.

Until the middle of the twentieth century, when motor roads began to penetrate Garhwal, the Char Dham Yatra was always completed on foot. Beginning at Hardwar, pilgrims followed the river up to Devprayag, the confluence of the Alakananda and Bhagirathi tributaries. From there most pilgrims headed west to Yamnotri, then walked eastward across the ridges to Gangotri, Kedarnath, and Badrinath. This route was clearly defined, with rest stops and dharamshalas at regular intervals.

Originally, the Char Dham Yatra was completed in anywhere from two to four months but with the construction of motor roads, the pilgrimage has become less of a challenge. Today the vast majority of yatris travel in buses or cars, which carry them from point to point in a matter of days. Both Badrinath and Gangotri can be reached directly by motor road. At Yamnotri and Kedarnath, only the final stage of the walking route remains, the last fourteen kilometers, which must be completed on foot. Unlike the kavar, who choose to carry out their pilgrimage as an act of physical penance and devotion, most yatris who visit the four main sources of the Ganga complete their journey in relative comfort. Public bus routes connect all of the major towns in Garhwal while air-conditioned coaches or private cars and taxis ferry the wealthier devotees across these mountains.

The ultimate destinations remain the same but the spirit and objectives of this pilgrimage have changed. Whereas the Char Dham Yatra used to involve a demanding commitment of time and energy, it now costs little more than the price of a bus ticket. What has been lost is the slow progress of a spiritual journey, the physical challenge of the walking trail, and the many opportunities for reflection a pilgrim encounters in the forests and mountains of Uttarakhand.

Every pilgrimage begins with a question.

It is a journey in search of answers, not just spiritual but physical, emotional, personal, and sometimes even scientific. One could just as easily stay at home and meditate on the conundrums of existence, but setting out on a pilgrimage involves a different form of inquiry, committing body as well as mind and soul to the rigors of a quest that is both internal and external. For this reason our most important discoveries are likely to be those that transcend both rationality and religion, taking us beyond the conventions of ordinary belief and revealing the essential connection between man and nature. From Gilgamesh to Gandhi, centuries of thought have been expended on the basic question, "What is it that makes us human?" Perhaps we should have asked instead: "What is it that links us to a rock, a blade of grass, the stature of an elm?" For questions like these there is no surety of a single truth, no scientific formula or dogmatic creed, but instead the enigmas and mysteries of the natural world, of which we are inseparably a part.

In many ways it would be so much easier to possess the kind of faith that the kavar carry with them as they transport their bottles of Gangajal, a shared conviction that overcomes any obstacles in your path and satisfies every question with a concrete answer. Sometimes I wonder what it would be like to have an absolute sense of purpose that propelled me forward, without hesitation, without fear, without concern for past or future. On the other hand, doubt can often be as powerful a motive as belief.

I have never been on a pilgrimage before. Organized religion holds no appeal for me and I resist the idea of undertaking this journey as an act of devotion. Despite my Christian upbringing, I have no faith in God. If asked, I usually admit to being an atheist. At the same time, there is something in me that responds to the spiritual elements in nature. I can easily understand how the force of a river or the shape of a rock might be interpreted as something larger than itself. Ritual has always fascinated me and though I offer no allegiance to the deities and doctrines of any one religion, I cannot help but be intrigued by the gestures of different faiths.

In preparation for the Char Dham Yatra, I remove my wristwatch and cowhide belt, leaving them coiled together in a dresser drawer at home. For the duration of this journey I will forsake the pleasures of alcohol, tobacco, sex, and meat. From childhood the mythology of Garhwal has been a part of my imagination, though I would never claim to be a Hindu. Instead, I see myself as a pilgrim who does not follow the prescribed tenets of any particular faith, but seeks to find the subtle and mysterious connections between human experience, mythological narratives, and natural history.

Near the bathing ghats in Hardwar and Rishikesh lives a species of fish called the mahseer, which pilgrims feed with scraps of bread and puffed rice. Growing as large as four feet in length and weighing up to a hundred pounds, mahseer are a golden green color with large heads and streamlined bodies. At Hardwar and Rishikesh these fish are considered sacred and nobody is permitted to catch or harm them in the vicinity of the temples that line the riverbank. As a result, many of the mahseer are so tame they come right up to the steps of the bathing ghats. Sometimes they even swim between a pilgrim's legs. Years ago the priests at the temples used to put gold rings through the lips of the largest fish, though this practice is no longer observed. Whenever a handful of puffed rice is thrown into the river, dozens of fish surge to the surface, mouths agape, tails slapping the water furiously.

Most of the year these mahseer live near Hardwar and Rishikesh but at the height of the monsoon, they migrate up the Ganga and into smaller side streams and tributaries to lay their eggs. Following an instinct, as predictable as the seasons, they swim against the current. For fish of this size the shallower streams are inaccessible during much of the year but with the monsoon floods mahseer are able to make their way up into the higher valleys, where they will leave their roe clustered between sand and rocks. Even for these powerful swimmers it is a difficult journey. The water is clouded with sediment and their gills are choked with silt. Struggling against the full force of the

Ganga these fish are drawn upriver by an inner current that takes them back to a distant point of origin.

The mahseer seem to carry an instinctual map in their memory, knowing exactly where they must go to lay their eggs. It is as if the course of the river were imprinted in their genes along with the impulse to swim upstream and reproduce their own kind. For several weeks each year the mahseer leave the quiet backwaters of the bathing ghats, the sanctuary of the temples, the free handouts from pilgrims, to struggle against the floodwaters of the Ganga. For these fish it is a matter of survival, fighting exhaustion and hunger to propagate their species. Only when the water begins to recede do they return to the bathing ghats at Hardwar and Rishikesh, leaving their eggs behind to hatch.

The rain is still falling and my cotton T-shirt clings to my skin as I tug it over my head. White rocks that rim the banks of the Ganga are glistening in the dull light. The sand has been compacted by the rain and I leave only the faintest footprints as I walk to the water's edge. A branch floats by on the current. I can feel the rain against my shoulders, a gentle, intimate sensation. The air is warm and close around me, my hair dripping, water trickling down the back of my legs. I am alone, upstream from the temples and bathing ghats at Rishikesh, a secluded bend in the river.

The constant sound of the Ganga echoes between the ridges, a monotonous roar that obliterates the whisper of the rain. Racing out of the mountains, the river seems to crush itself in a stampede of water, whirlpools and rapids, brown waves tumbling one upon the other in a violent torrent—the goddess Ganga in all her fury. Drops of rain vanish into the muddy current as they sprinkle the surface. Wading into the water, I can feel the icy grasp of glaciers that lie two hundred kilometers upstream. To keep from being swept away, I dig my feet into the sand and submerge myself in the cleansing current, a ritual of purification that every pilgrim must undertake.

Having been born in Uttarakhand, I have always felt a strong personal connection to this river. Our family often went on camping trips along the tributaries of the Ganga. Since childhood the river has been an integral part of my imagination, a constant stream of stories that flows through my dreams. It also reminds me of my own mortality.

When I was nine years old I nearly drowned in the Ganga, at a place called Shivpuri, twenty kilometers above Rishikesh. We had gone there for a day trip with my aunt and uncle, an Easter picnic. Playing in the river, my cousins, my brother, and I made a raft of logs and tried to float a short distance down the Ganga. When the logs we'd wedged together began to fall apart, I was swept into the water. If it hadn't been for my aunt and cousin who rescued me, I would have drowned. This is the closest I have ever come to dying and for that reason the Ganga has always held an uneasy fascination for me. Each time I step into its current to bathe, I can recall the frightening sensation of tumbling over and over in the rapids, coming up for air, then going down again. In nightmares I can still see the submerged rocks below my kicking feet and taste the water as it sucks me under, a helpless feeling of being pulled downstream, unable to resist the river's flow.

Death and rebirth are symbolized in the Ganga's current, which has always been the eternal resting place for Hindus. At Hardwar and Rishikesh there are cremation ghats on the riverbank, where pyres burn in perpetuity. Farther up the Ganga, along the pilgrim route, villagers bring their dead to its shores and perform last rites.

To witness these cremations is to experience a profound understanding of our place in nature. The corpse is wrapped in a shroud of white cotton and carried to the water's edge on a bamboo bier. Each of the mourners collects dry branches and driftwood from the surrounding forest and riverbank. When the pyre is finally set alight it blazes up with a startling brilliance that blossoms like the orange petals on a semal tree. The four elements of nature come together in this ceremony of death — the fire that consumes the body, the wind that whips the smoke in circles, the earth that bears the weight of the bier, and the water that will carry away the charred remains. A cremation can take four to five hours before the corpse is reduced to ash. As the mourners sit and wait they watch their grief reflected in the dancing flames. These final rites serve to reaffirm a belief in the cycle of rebirth. When the pyre eventually burns out and the last ember is extinguished, the mourners collect the ash in their hands and release it into the swift waters of the Ganga. Through this process the river absorbs our physical remains and we become part of an eternal current that constantly renews itself.

The first episode of the Mahabharata contains a story about the goddess Ganga that emphasizes the immortal properties of her waters. Assuming the form of a beautiful woman, Ganga appeared before King Santanu of Hastinapur, who immediately fell in love with her and proposed marriage. The goddess, keeping her true identity hidden, agreed to wed the king on one condition: He was never to stand in the way of anything she did or question her actions. Entranced by Ganga's beauty and chaste demeanor, Santanu readily agreed. The marriage was celebrated and they lived together in a palace by the riverbank. The king was delighted with his bride, for she was everything he had expected her to be and fulfilled all of his desires. Soon Ganga became pregnant with their first child and Santanu made preparations to announce the birth of an heir. However, immediately after the baby boy was born, Ganga carried her child to the river's edge and threw him into the water. When he heard that his newborn son had been drowned, King Santanu was distraught but remembering his vow, he did not ask Ganga to explain herself. Soon she became pregnant once again and bore him another son, which she also drowned in the river. This happened seven times in succession, until Santanu could no longer bear his grief. When the eighth son was born, the king rushed to the riverbank and refused to let Ganga throw the baby into the water.

The queen turned to Santanu sadly and reminded him of his broken promise. Ganga said that she would spare the child but could no longer be his wife. Revealing her divine form, she explained that each of their sons were incarnations of the eight Vasus, attendants of the god Indra and celestial agents of natural phenomena. The Vasus had been born into the world of men because of a curse put on them by the great sage Vasishtha. Terrified of their fate on earth, the Vasus had prayed to Ganga, asking her to become their mother. They also pleaded with her to drown them immediately after birth, while they were still innocent of sin. This was the only way the Vasus could be released from the cycle of suffering and rebirth. Ganga agreed to do as they asked and, in this manner, all but one of Indra's attendants were liberated from the curse. Holding the newborn child in her arms, Ganga promised Santanu that once the boy was older she would return his son to him. Saying this she and the baby disappeared into the river.

The king was overwhelmed with sadness and for the next few years he ruled Hastinapur as an ascetic, renouncing all sensual pleasures. One day, however, he was walking along the riverbank and saw a handsome youth playing in the water. The boy had built a dam of arrows across the Ganga and seemed to have no fear of the flooded river. As Santanu approached in amazement the goddess appeared and introduced him to his son. She told the king that the boy's name was Devavrata and that one day he would become a great archer and a noble statesman. Giving her blessing to the boy, Ganga once again vanished into the current. Devavrata grew up to be Bhishma, patriarch of the Pandav and Kurav clans, whose story is told in the Mahabharata.

# I
# INQUIRY

RISHIKESH–YAMNOTRI

*Beyond the senses are their objects, and beyond*
*the objects is the mind. Beyond the mind is pure reason,*
*and beyond reason is the Spirit of man.*

KATHA UPANISHAD

# FOOTPATHS AND
# MOTOR ROADS

AT RISHIKESH A NARROW, TWO-LANE HIGHWAY
runs parallel to the western bank of the Ganga, heading into the
mountains of Garhwal. Trucks and buses clog this route, along
with auto-rickshaws, scooters, motorcycles, cars, and Jeeps,
each of them maneuvering for position on the potholed strip of
asphalt that twists its way through lines of open-fronted shops.
Diesel and petrol fumes spew from the exhaust pipes of decrepit
vehicles, their engines straining even before the road begins to
climb. The impatient shriek of horns and the grinding thunder
of internal combustion—metal chafing against metal, gears
clenching and unclenching—blend together in a mechanized
groan of discontentment.

On this side of the river, Rishikesh has very little charm, a
squalid, congested town. At a roadside workshop the cement
walls and unpaved yard are blackened with motor oil and even
the trunk of a nearby pipal tree is coated in grease. Cylinder
blocks and crank cases have been gutted, leaking valves and
burned-out pistons, charred brake shoes and clutch plates scattered about like the dismembered remains of a metallic creature
sacrificed to the demons of the road.

During the monsoon, the streets of Rishikesh are awash in
mud, churned up by the tires of passing vehicles, spattering the
bare legs of cyclists and pedestrians, caking the fur of a pariah

dog that scratches itself with a blackened paw, then dives for cover as a pilgrim bus nearly runs it down.

Rain has been falling since dawn. The buildings are gray with dampness, except for a vivid green smear of algae beneath a dripping air conditioner. Only a red bull, chewing limp corn-stalks as he shuffles down the street, seems unperturbed by the depressing wetness of the morning.

Two footbridges cross the river at Rishikesh, Ram Jhoola and Lakshman Jhoola, named after the heroes of the Ramayana epic. Imposing stone pylons rise up on either side of the Ganga and strung between them are braided metal cables, taut as bow-strings. One can almost imagine an arrow notched into the curve of the bridge and aiming skyward, as if Ram himself had drawn his bow to kill the demon Ravan.

The word *jhoola* means swing and as a constant stream of pil-grims move back and forth across the Ganga, the bridges sway up and down in rhythm with their steps. Most of the year ferry boats cross the river at Rishikesh except when water levels are dangerously high and the current grows too swift. During July and August, at the height of the monsoon, the footbridges are the only link between the western and eastern banks.

Lines of pilgrims move in opposite directions, with just enough space to pass. Some of them are chanting, *"Jai Jai Ram!"* others, *"Bam Bam Bholey!"* as if keeping time to the rocking of the bridge. Their voices are filled with the exuberance of their faith. Crossing the Ganga, I have to hold onto the guard rails to steady myself as Ram Jhoola sways up and down like a trampoline.

Swarg Ashram. Heavenly Abode.

A row of temples and rest houses rise up from the eastern bank of the Ganga. Between the bathing ghats and the ashrams runs a narrow lane. The bazaar that borders this passageway is

made up of tiny shops, most of them selling religious paraphernalia—conch shells and rudraksha beads, cotton scarves and
shawls dyed different shades of saffron, with the names of Ram
and other deities printed in a continuous pattern on the fabric.
Cows roam the congested market, oblivious of the pedestrians
edging past their horns. Money changers sit on the ground with
piles of coins arranged in front of them so that pilgrims can give
alms to the lines of beggars. Also for sale are plastic bottles for
collecting Gangajal, miniature idols of gods and goddesses,
framed lithographs, postcards of riverfront scenes, cassette
tapes of religious hymns. The sacred and profane are both available, with Hindi film music sold alongside devotional songs, or
bhajans. There are even a couple of computer centers, offering
Internet access, where lonely Europeans sit at keyboards, typ-
ing e-mail messages back home.

Tea stalls and restaurants are wedged into the spaces between the shops. The most popular eating spot in Rishikesh is
Chotiwalla's, where a potbellied man in a blue silk dhoti and
fake jewelry sits cross-legged at the entrance. His face, his arms
and torso are painted a pale pink color, his eyes outlined with
black kajal. The choti, from which he gets his name, is a single
lock of hair that is waxed to a point and protrudes from his
shaved scalp like an antenna. Chotiwalla has been here for over
twenty years, seated in the same position with an expression of
impassive calm, ignoring the pilgrims who gawk at him. His
makeup and costume suggest a comic grotesque, face paint
cracking around his lips, bright nail varnish peeling, gilt jewelry
and plastic pearls. Though he affects a posture of divinity,
Chotiwalla is little more than a commercial emblem, a human
novelty who brings in customers off the street. His clownlike
caricature (a registered trademark) is printed on the restaurant's menu.

The gods are everywhere in Rishikesh, a pantheon of

plaster images on the walls of ashrams, painted bright enamel colors—Hanuman, Ganesh, Lakshmi, Saraswati, Durga. Some of them are protected behind wire cages, while others occupy shrines near the bathing ghats. Most of these statues are recent constructions, for Rishikesh is not a town of ancient monuments. Atop an ornate gateway, overlooking the Ganga, stands a life-size diorama of Arjun and Krishn, engaged in the divine discourse of the Bhagavad Gita. Their chariot and horses are reproduced in precise detail, like images in a religious theme park.

The bathing ghats in front of Swarg Ashram are flooded, crumbling cement steps disappearing into the swift current. Only a few of the pilgrims are brave enough to take a dip in the swollen Ganga, clutching at the metal chains and railings to avoid being swept away, the muddy current swirling about their knees. On the wall nearby is a sign: BEWARE OF SHOE THIEVES.

"The worst thing that has happened to Garhwal is the building of motor roads. They take away everything of value from these mountains and bring nothing in return, except for useless commodities."

Sunderlal Bahugana is not a man who keeps his opinions to himself. At seventy-three, he is one of the most outspoken environmental activists in India, a leading figure in the Chipko movement and a controversial personality, who regularly criticizes the government's development schemes.

I had heard that Bahugana was staying at the Paramarth Nature Cure Hospital, near Swarg Ashram in Rishikesh. He was recuperating from a recent hunger strike, protesting the Tehri Dam. When I called on him he looked remarkably healthy for someone who had recently broken a fast. His untrimmed white beard gave him a saintly appearance and he had a gentle, mischievous smile that belied the seriousness of his message.

Bahugana could easily have been mistaken for one of the many mendicants that wander the streets of Rishikesh.

"Development has cursed us with a market economy," he said. "Before the motor roads were built the people of these mountains lived by a system of barter. A man who owned a goat or sheep spun its wool into yarn, which he traded for rice and salt. When I was a boy we seldom used money in Garhwal. Instead we would exchange one measure of ghee for eight measures of salt. Now we have a cash economy and the people suffer as a result. There is no sense of interdependence, no sharing of resources."

When I told Bahugana that I was intending to complete the Char Dham Yatra on foot, he seemed pleased and told me, "Avoid the motor roads wherever you can. That's the only way you'll see nature in its purest state."

During 1981, in an effort to spread the Chipko message, Sunderlal Bahugana walked across the Himalayas, from Kashmir to Kohima. Each day he stopped in a different village and held a public meeting, explaining the importance of planting trees and protecting the environment. Inspired by the principles of Sarvodhaya, a reassertion of Gandhian philosophy, Bahugana lives a simple, ascetic life. He and his wife, Vimla, have an ashram in the village of Silyara, about a hundred kilometers upriver from Rishikesh. They dress in homespun khadi and combine their environmental concerns with social activism, fighting for public health issues, women's rights, and the abolition of caste.

"The greatest burden of a cash economy is borne by the women of Garhwal," said Sunderlal. "With motor roads the men take milk and other produce to the market and then they spend the money that they earn on alcohol and cigarettes, while the women are left to cut fodder, cultivate the fields, and tend their cattle. They see nothing for their labor."

Vimla Bahugana was staying with her husband at the hospital when I visited, though she spends most of her time in Tehri, continuing their campaign against the dam. A thin, deceptively frail looking woman, she could easily have been the one who had been fasting instead of her husband.

"The Himalayas provide the rest of India with water and soil," she said. "If you dam the Ganga, you not only destroy the lives and culture of the people who are displaced but you deprive those who live downstream of the resources they depend on. Once the dam is built their wells will dry up and their fields won't get the silt that makes them fertile."

Both she and Sunderlal admit that they are fighting a losing battle with the Tehri Dam because the government has invested far too much money in the project to back down. When I met them their only hope was that the height of the dam would be lowered, an issue that the government had agreed to consider. This was the concession that allowed Bahugana to end his fast.

Clearly disillusioned by the failure of his campaign against the dam, Bahugana told me that he has turned his attention to other matters.

"If I have anything more to live for, it is to promote tree farming," he said. "Not monoculture like the forestry department but a mixed forest that can be utilized by the people of Garhwal. Five kinds of trees are needed—those that provide food, flowers, fodder, fiber, and fuel."

He counted these on his fingers. Though we spoke in Hindi, "the five F's," as he called them, were named in English. Bahugana has a gift for distilling complex issues into simple concepts. Later on he talked with disdain about chemical fertilizers, how they are nothing but "nasha," an addiction that weakens the soil.

"It is the same with the motor roads," he said, returning to his original refrain. "They have weakened the people of

Garhwal. Earlier a man in these hills would think nothing of walking twenty miles in a day. Now he must ride a bus."

After an hour of conversation, I could tell that Sunderlal was growing tired. Like the sages and mystics, who perform tapasya in order to gain power and authority, Bahugana asserts his quixotic opinions through acts of austerity. While recovering from his hunger strike at the Nature Cure Hospital he combined a regimen of yoga and meditation with a controlled diet, herbal massage, and therapeutic baths.

"They do not give me any drugs here," he said. "It is a healing system based on the four elements in nature: water, wind, earth, and fire."

The Parmarth Hospital is a quiet place, hidden behind the main line of ashrams and temples. There is a private garden for meditation, full of cana lilies and a laboratory where herbal essences and oils are extracted. The complex does not look like a hospital, more like a spiritual retreat.

As I folded my hands and said good-bye, Vimla Bahugana invited me to visit their center in Tehri, on my way up the river. *"Aap ki yatra sukhad rahe,"* she said. May your pilgrimage be full of contentment.

Between Rishikesh and Phool Chatti, where I spent the first night, I counted over a hundred Jeeps. Each of these vehicles was overloaded with pilgrims on their way to Neelkanth, a Shiv temple in the foothills east of Rishikesh. The peacefulness of this walk, which I recalled from earlier visits, has been destroyed by a new motor road, built in the last five years. What used to be an idyllic, secluded path, overshadowed by tropical forests, has been widened and paved so that the vehicles can race back and forth to Neelkanth. The contemplative silence of the walking trail has been replaced by the snarling of Jeep engines and horns blaring at every corner.

Phool Chatti lies about eight kilometers above Rishikesh, at the confluence of the Ganga and the Hemganga, a minor tributary that flows in from the east. There is a large ashram here but the old dharamshala, which once provided shelter for pilgrims, has collapsed into ruins. Fortunately, the new motor road climbs up around the ridge and the riverbank near the confluence remains unspoiled.

The path leading down to the shore was overgrown with lantana and monsoon weeds. With snowmelt and heavy rain, both the Ganga and the Hemganga were overflowing their banks. At places the forest came right down to the water's edge and looking for a place to pitch my tent, I worked my way downstream for several hundred meters until I came to a spit of sand. It was about thirty feet across and mostly level, with two tiny streams on either side. These flowed into the Ganga, which washed up against a line of rocks at the lower end of the beach.

My campsite was completely secluded, hidden from the Jeep road above by a wall of trees. The ashram at Phool Chatti was also out of sight and I knew that nobody would disturb me here. The sand was smooth, without a single footprint, the shrubs and bushes enclosing me in their green embrace. The rain, which had been falling since morning, had finally stopped but the clouds were low and dark, draped between the ridges like a sodden canopy. Unwrapping my tent, I pitched it at the center of the sandspit, about fifteen feet from the water's edge.

Just before nightfall I saw an egret flying low above the river, its white wings in sharp contrast to the gathering darkness. Bats soon took to the air as well, flitting over the shore as they fed on insects. Circling above my head they were virtually invisible against the dark clouds, like fragments of shadows gathering into night.

After I went to bed it began to thunder and I could see lightning further up the valley. Each time it flashed the taut membrane of my tent lit up like a television screen. As I fell asleep I could hear the rain beginning to fall again. Hours later, in the middle of the night, I woke up to the full force of a storm, no longer the gentle sprinkling of drops but a heavy cannonade that shook the tent poles. Though I was dry inside, I felt a sudden sense of panic, thinking that perhaps the Ganga would rise and wash me away. The beach where I was sleeping was only a foot or two above the flooded river and I realized that it was foolish to have camped so close to the shore. Looking out of the zippered flap, I could see nothing in the darkness. The rain blew in upon me and I hurried to seal the tent. All I could do was wait as the storm continued for another hour. The whole time I kept expecting the sand to suddenly give way beneath me and the flood to send me spinning into the depths of the Ganga.

The next morning, when I got up at first light, it was still overcast but calm outside and I could see that almost half of the sandbank had been washed away. Another six inches and it would have reached my tent pegs. Faint streaks of light were coming through the clouds and though the river was higher it looked almost placid in the slate-gray dawn. By now I had become so accustomed to the Ganga's roar I hardly noticed the sound. As the day slowly brightened and I boiled my first cup of tea, I could see movement on the sand between my feet. Hundreds of bugs had come out in the aftermath of the storm, spiders, sand lions, millipedes, and ants, as well as a small, transparent fly that disappeared wherever it landed. By the time I had dismantled and folded my tent, the clouds had cleared and the sun broke through, gilding the layered ridges like the spines of ancient books.

Every five or six kilometers along the pilgrim route are chattis, or rest stops, which mark successive stages of the journey. Some of these are located near villages, others are nothing more than a wayside temple and dharamshala where pilgrims can find shelter for the night. Each one has a name — Phool Chatti, Gular Chatti, Mohan Chatti, Bijni Chatti, Bandar Chatti. Because of the motor roads, many of these rest stops are now deserted. The temples are maintained by villagers or sadhus who take up residence there, but most of the dharamshalas are in disrepair, their roofs leaking, the floors littered with straw, cowdung, charred bits of wood and ash.

The Kali Kambli Trust, a charitable organization based in Rishikesh, still maintains some of the dharamshalas along the Char Dham Yatra route. Following a system that was set up more than a century ago, they issue coupons to pilgrims and mendicants, who can stay in their dharamshalas and receive a measure of flour or rice for their meals. Though the Kali Kambli Trust still exists, its activities are considerably reduced and their dharamshalas have a deserted, derelict appearance, the doors padlocked and the windows barred. At most of the chattis, the only real signs of life are the occasional tea shops, where villagers gather.

For the first few kilometers beyond Phool Chatti, I continued to walk along a motorable road, though most of it was unpaved. At this point, the pilgrim track follows the Hemganga tributary, to avoid a precipitous gorge. The trail eventually cuts over the ridge at a place called Notkhal, descending back down to the Ganga on the other side. The Hemganga is bordered by rice paddies, a patchwork of green, each field fitted neatly into the next. The villages in this valley are surrounded by groves of fruit trees — mango, guava, banana, pomegranate, and papaya.

After an hour and a half of walking I stopped at Mohan Chatti, where three men were sitting on the wooden benches outside a tea stall. They greeted me with surprise and amusement, asking where I was going. When I told them they look bewildered.

"All the way to Yamnotri? On foot?"

I asked how many pilgrims traveled this route and they shook their heads.

"Nobody walks anymore, except for the sadhus and rishis. Why aren't you going by bus?"

The owner of the tea shop was crouched over his hearth. Eyes squinting against the smoke he blew into a twig fire and brought a saucepan of tea to a boil. Pouring it through a plastic strainer he handed me a steaming glass of the sugary brew. When I asked directions there was a long debate over how far I'd be able to walk that day. Notkhal was about ten kilometers ahead but one of the men told me there was a shorter route, where the old walking trail cut up the ridge. It would save me an hour or more. The others warned me that the path was over-grown with weeds and washed away at places.

"It would be better to stay on the motor road. That way you won't get lost."

I should have followed this advice, but a short distance beyond Mohan Chatti, I found where the walking route branched off and headed up the hill. It was a steep climb, a steady zigzag following the profile of the ridge. Bright shafts of sunlight filtered through the leaves and the heat and humidity left me bathed in sweat. For an hour or more I carried on uphill, expecting the trail to level off, but it continued climbing. Soon there was nothing more than a goat path and I could see that nobody had passed this way in weeks. Eventually the trail disappeared completely and I had to scramble through the underbrush. Frustrated and out of breath I reached a cowshed and some terraced fields, from where I could look out across the ridges and get my bearings. After I called out a couple of times a man appeared and looked at me suspiciously. I asked him if there was a path to Notkhal and he shook his head, saying that I had to go back down to the motor road.

Having wasted almost two hours and still exhausted from the climb, I reluctantly retraced my steps. The sun was directly overhead but fortunately there were springs at the side of the road where I could drink and fill my water bottle. By the time I reached the top of the ridge, however, my legs began to cramp and I was ready to collapse. This was only my second day of walking and I was beginning to wonder if I would ever complete my pilgrimage.

Notkhal is a small settlement of six or seven houses, including a Kali Kambli dharamshala. It is situated at a pass, where the motor road crosses the ridge and continues on to Kotdwara. Only one bus goes along this route each day and when I arrived it had just departed. Four people were eating lunch at a "hotel"—an open shed with three wooden tables. The proprietor, Jagmohan Singh, helped me off with my pack and immediately served me a mountain of rice and dal.

A loquacious man with dark, wizened features, Jagmohan Singh was probably fifty, though he looked much older. One of the customers was a woman, who turned out to be a teacher. She was on her way to a government primary school in a village beyond Notkhal. Assigned to work there by the government she didn't seem happy with her posting.

Accompanying the teacher was a man named Bachan Singh, who described himself as a grain dealer. He invited me to visit his village and said that there was Shiv temple in a cave nearby that might interest me. He also explained that there was another shrine for the goddess, known as Bal Kwanri Devi. Every two years the village organized a haryali pooja—literally green worship. This pooja involves the planting of millet in small containers that are kept inside the temple. Over a period of nine days the seeds germinate, while the goddess is worshiped, and at the end of this time the fresh green sprouts are distributed as prasad. Bachan Singh explained that the haryali pooja replaced an earlier tradition of animal sacrifices, which are no longer performed.

After lunch Jagmohan Singh served us each a glass of tea. Handing me my cup he told me that the British had introduced tea to Garhwal as a strategy for weakening the people of this region.

"Before the British came here, everyone used to drink milk, which gives a man energy so he can walk forever. Nowadays, people drink only tea, which hardly gives them any strength, and even if they have to go a short distance they will take a bus."

Bachan Singh nodded his head in agreement. "It's true. If you drink tea it takes away your appetite."

When I mentioned Sunderlal Bahugana's claim that the motor roads had weakened the people of Garhwal, Jagmohan and Bachan Singh reacted with disdain.

"Sunderlal Bahugana doesn't have anything better to do than go on hunger strikes," said Jagmohan, launching into a tirade. It was obvious from what he said that his antipathy was based on caste and regional differences.

"What about the Tehri Dam?" I asked. "Don't you agree with Sunderlal that it shouldn't be built?"

Bachan Singh shook his head.

"That's his problem, not ours. This is Pauri Garhwal. What do we care what happens in Tehri?"

The rivalry between these two regions of Garhwal can be traced back to the Gurkha wars in 1815. In return for defeating the invaders from Nepal, the British took control of all the territory east of the Ganga, while the mountains to the west remained with the Maharajah of Tehri. The Ganga formed a natural boundary, with only a few footbridges in between. After independence these two parts of Garhwal became separate administrative districts within the state of Uttar Pradesh. Traditionally the main pilgrim trail to Badrinath ran along the eastern bank of the Ganga where villages profited from the steady flow of yatris. When the motor road was built, however, it followed a route along the opposite shore. This meant that the people of Tehri had greater access to markets on the plains and the pilgrim traffic through Pauri Garhwal immediately diminished. Despite the construction of new roads and motor bridges in the past few decades, people on the eastern bank of the Ganga still feel a lingering resentment when they look across the river and see trucks and buses on the other side.

By the time I left Notkhal, the clouds had blown in again and it had started to rain. Jagmohan gave me directions and said that I would find the walking trail less than a kilometer ahead. The path dropped straight down from the motor road in an almost vertical descent. Because of the clouds I couldn't see the mountains around me or the Ganga, though I could hear the sound of the river in the valley below. For the first hour I met no one, only a black cow with a brass bell around its throat. I heard it ringing long before I saw the animal appearing through the mist. The slope of the mountain was much too steep for there to be any villages or fields along the path. After I had descended almost a thousand feet, there was a brief lull in the rain. For five or ten minutes the clouds dispersed and I could see the Ganga, flowing through the gorge below, a twisting brown current, slick as wet clay. Looking straight down, I was overcome by a sudden wave of vertigo. The greenery was dizzying and the shifting clouds made it seem as if the mountains were moving. Standing at the edge of the trail I felt exposed and vulnerable.

Farther on, the cliffs gave way to gentler terrain and the valley broadened slightly. The pilgrim trail leveled off, with detours leading to nearby villages. As the rain began to fall more heavily I came to a grove of jamun trees. The ground beneath them was covered with bright purple fruit the size and shape of fresh dates. Picking up a jamun I notice that a bite had been taken out of it. Just then I heard a rustling in the trees ahead and saw three langur monkeys perched in the branches. Their silver coats were dripping with rain and their black faces were turned in my direction, though none of them seemed alarmed by my presence. With careful deliberation they were picking jamuns from the tree, nibbling each one, then tossing them to the ground. As I passed under their tree, the monkeys suddenly leaped aside, crashing through the branches overhead. In their panic, one of them dropped a cluster of jamuns, which I retrieved. These had not been bitten and several of them were ripe, with a fresh, sweet flavor and an astringent aftertaste.

Bandar Chatti gets its name from the troops of monkeys that live on the cliffs nearby, both the silver-haired langurs and the smaller rhesus, which are a reddish brown. My plan had been to spend the night at Bandar Chatti, even though Jagmohan had told me it was deserted. By the time I got there the rain was pouring down and the trail had turned into a muddy stream.

Between the two steep ridges that converge at the foot of the valley, I could see a bend in the river, where it washes against the cliffs. Coming down the path, I had noticed several cement buildings and water tanks, obviously a pumping station. A short distance farther on lay a temple, in front of which were three marble bulls, about two feet high. These represented Nandi, an animal deity associated with Shiv. The bulls were facing a lingam, a smooth oblong rock that symbolizes Shiv's phallic form. Hanging above the entrance to the shrine was a polished brass bell, which worshipers ring to announce their arrival, but the temple door was locked and there was no place for me to take shelter from the rain. On a terrace below lay the ruins of a dharamshala and an abandoned tea shop. Most of the thatch roof had collapsed and the floor was awash with mud and cowdung, certainly no place to spend the night. It was raining too hard for me to set up my tent but as I turned toward the pumping station, I could see a light in one of the windows. A few moments later, a figure appeared in the doorway and beckoned.

Though water was streaming off my pack and my clothes were dripping on the cement floor, Prakash Singh Rawat welcomed me inside. He was a tall, soft-spoken man in his mid-twenties. Without hesitation he insisted that I spend the night. The room itself was spacious but in the center stood two enormous pumps, with pipes and valves as well as an array of fuse boxes and transformers. In one corner, Prakash had a charpai bed and a kerosene pressure stove on which he cooked his meals. He explained that the pumps had not been running for several days because one of the power phases had been shut down. There was only enough electricity for two dim bulbs. Outside the storm was showing no signs of stopping and I was relieved to be under a solid roof. When I thanked Prakash for his hospitality, he laughed.

"What did you expect me to do? Leave you out in the rain?"

After changing into dry clothes, I lit my stove and made some tea. As we drank it, Prakash told me that he had been working at the pumphouse for over a year. Though the pipeline was part of a government development scheme, distributing water to villages on the other side of the ridge, Prakash was employed by a private contractor who paid him only a thousand rupees a month. He said that he was thinking of quitting because it was lonely work and there were no prospects for the future.

"Most of the day I'm here by myself," he said. "There is a village up the hill, where I sometimes spend the night, but it's not an easy life. When the pumps are running they make so much noise, it can drive a man crazy."

After we finished our tea, Prakash suggested that I lie down and rest while he made dinner. Spreading my mat on the floor, I fell asleep almost immediately. About an hour later, I woke up and heard voices. Two men had arrived and were seated on Prakash's bed, talking loudly. Lying on the opposite side of the room, I pretended to be asleep, though I could see that the men had produced a half bottle of whiskey and were pouring themselves a drink. Their manner was surly and they did not offer Prakash a drink, each of them tossing the whiskey down in a single gulp. By the time I sat up, the bottle was empty and both of them were drunk. One of the men interrogated me for several minutes.

"Why are you wasting your time walking, when the motor road is there?" he said.

Later I learned that he came from a village on the other side of the Ganga and worked as a conductor for a bus company that operates between Rishikesh and Badrinath. The two men had crossed over a footbridge several kilometers upriver, and were on their way to a wedding in a village above Bandar Chatti. When the visitors eventually stood up and staggered out into the rain, Prakash seemed relieved to see them go.

"I'm sorry," he said. "People from that side of the river, they don't know how to behave. If you were over there, nobody would have offered you a place to stay."

Half a day's walk beyond Bandar Chatti, I came to a village called Kandi. It was the largest settlement I had seen since leaving Rishikesh and the slate-roofed houses were spread across a broad knoll overlooking the Ganga. The terraced fields on either side appeared well cultivated, with monsoon crops of rice and corn. Orchards of lemon trees covered sections of the ridge and a large stream ran past the village, providing plenty of irrigation. The pilgrim route passed just above the upper houses, which were built close together, each roof almost touching the

next. Even from a distance I could tell that Kandi was a prosperous village.

After crossing a bridge over the stream, I came to a tea shop
where a group of men were sitting and talking among themselves. They welcomed me and inquired about my destination.
Unlike the two men I had met the night before, they seemed to
understand why I was traveling by foot. They said that a few
yatris still passed through Kandi during May and June, though
most now went by motor road. Just beyond the tea shop stood a
Kali Kambli dharamshala, much better maintained than the one
at Notkhal. There was also a government dispensary next door,
staffed by a compounder, who provided medicines and first aid.

"There used to be an eight-bed hospital, built especially for
the pilgrims and a full-time doctor too, but now that so few people walk along this route it has been reduced."

The man who spoke introduced himself as Bhagat Singh.
"We have a Mahadev temple here," he said. "It's not as large and
important as the one at Neelkanth, but if only we could find a
wealthy pilgrim to give a donation—someone from Gujarat,
perhaps—it could become equally famous."

When I mentioned that I was planning to write a book about
my pilgrimage, another man took over the conversation. His
name was Sukhpal Singh Negi and he had recently retired from
the army's education department.

"You must include a description of Kandi in your book,"
Negi told me. "I shouldn't be saying this from my own mouth
but Kandi is the most privileged village in this area. To you that
may not mean much but, *andho key beech may kaana raja*—in a
kingdom of the blind it is a one-eyed monarch."

By now, at least a dozen men had gathered at the tea shop.
Everyone laughed and nodded in agreement. Negi was dressed
in handspun khadi and wore a pair of black-rimmed spectacles

that gave him a professorial air. I learned later that most of the lemon orchards belonged to him.

While everyone listened, he and Bhagat Singh extolled the virtues of Kandi—the dispensary, electricity, a post office, a telephone, and even a polling station.

"These days that is particularly important, with elections every year," joked Negi.

"The water in our stream is very healthy," Bhagat Singh added. "It's excellent for digestion. That's one of the reasons the hospital was built here."

"The other thing that sets us apart," said Negi, "is that whenever two or three men get together in this village, they talk about ways to make Kandi even better. We don't waste our time gossiping like other villagers."

"We have everything," said Bhagat Singh. "Good soil, plenty of water, fruit trees, honest people. The only thing we don't have is a motor road."

"Yes, that's true," said Negi. "Otherwise we could transport our produce much more easily and get a better price. Now we have to use mules or carry it on our backs."

Though he and some of the others admitted that there were disadvantages to being connected to a motor road—"corruption and accidents"—the villagers of Kandi insisted that even though they lived a charmed existence this was the one thing that would improve their lives. After an hour or so, when I got up to leave, the villagers tried to persuade me to stay the night. Only when I promised to return some day would they let me go.

"Good-bye," said Bhagat Singh. "When you come back this way again, we'll have a motor road."

# EXILE IN THE FOREST

BOTH THE MAHABHARATA AND THE RAMAYANA were composed by sages who lived alone in the forest, the former by Vyasa and the latter by Valmiki. These two figures have become a part of their own myths, existing in that ancient, indeterminate past, outside the boundaries of conventional history. Vyasa and Valmiki are usually depicted as white-haired saintly men, wearing ascetic's robes. They lived in simple thatch huts on the riverbank, surrounded by trees. In mystical seclusion, and after long periods of meditation, they were possessed by the forces of myth and scripture, their imaginations overcome by adventures of the gods. To the accompaniment of simple stringed instruments, these sages recited the cycle of stories that make up the two great epics of India, recounting tales of heroism, conflicts between gods and demons, love, sacrifice, duty, and devotion. Their narratives also reflect the intimate presence of nature, the forests, the sacred groves, the flora and fauna of India. It is not surprising that the heroes of both epics spend much of their time exiled in the forest. After gambling away their share of the kingdom the Pandav brothers and Draupadi are banished to the wilderness for thirteen years. Similarly, Ram, Sita, and Lakshman are exiled from their kingdom in Ayodhya and forced to live in the jungle for fourteen years. They survive as hunters and gatherers, while sharing the company of animals and birds.

For the pilgrim who travels on foot through the forests of Uttarakhand the presence of wild creatures reinforces these myths. Probably the most common animals of all are monkeys, both the langur and the rhesus. They live along the pilgrim trail and are often found near towns and temples, where they scavenge for food, displaying little or no fear of humans. These troops of monkeys are protected and seldom harmed for they represent the armies of Hanuman who helped Ram and Lakshman defeat the demon Ravan. One of the most popular figures in the Ramayana, Hanuman is generally conceived as being half man, half ape. He has the powerful physique of a wrestler, with a long tail and simian features. In calendar art or temple friezes, Hanuman is often shown worshiping at the feet of Ram and Sita, whom he rescued from captivity. His greatest attributes are loyalty and subservience, though there are many shrines and temples where he himself is the chief deity.

Hindu mythology and art is full of anthropomorphic images in which the distinctions between human beings and gods and animals are often blurred and fluid. A deity like Vishnu is not only incarnated as the avatars of Ram and Krishn but also as a fish (Matsya), a boar (Varaha), a tortoise (Kurma), or a horse (Kalki). In yet another avatar he takes the form of Narsingh, the ferocious man-lion. Through the power of tapasya, the great sages were able to change themselves into creatures of the forest, just as these animals were often reincarnated in human form. Demons too are capable of assuming the shape of animals, like Mareecha the rakshish, who turns himself into a golden stag. Though stories like this may seem exotic or fanciful today, it is ironic that the modern imagination, with its roots in the rational and scientific traditions of the European Enlightenment, should dismiss the notion of anthropomorphism. After all, the origin of our species has been linked to the earliest ancestors of Hanuman.

JOURNAL ENTRIES:

Clustered blossoms on a lantana bush, bright yellow and pink, as garish as Diwali sweets.

The shadow of a semla leaf—a miniature eclipse of the sun.

A ground orchid in full bloom, white as a starched handkerchief. When I lean down to catch its scent, I find the center of this tubular flower is crawling with ants.

Walking alone, the trail is mine. There is nothing to interrupt my progress, no footsteps but my own, no need to keep pace with a companion or to stop and wait for others to catch up. Having left my wristwatch at home, I rise with the sun and set off whenever I choose. The sky is my clock. I do not carry a map, for the river itself is there to guide me and I can always ask directions from one village to the next.

The forest encloses the path, beneath a colonnade of sal trees with their high, arched branches and leathery leaves. Bauhinia vines clamber up the trunks of wild figs. A delicate mimosa sprig looks like pale green embroidery in the verdant shadows. Even the air takes on the texture of the leaves as it brushes against my skin and sets the forest in motion. When it starts to rain, I can hear a patter in the foliage overhead, long before the drops will ever reach the ground. And when the cloudburst is over the trees continue to shed water for hours.

During the monsoon everything is green—moss-covered rocks, ferns uncoiling out of the bark on a dead branch, the trail ankle-deep in grass. Even when I shut my eyes, there is a persistent green aura and during the night I am haunted by arboreal dreams, the shapes of trees swaying in the darkness.

The pilgrim trail from Phool Chatti to Devprayag, a three-and-a-half-day walk, provides an unspoiled passage through the lower Himalayas. Other than a few scattered villages, much of this region is sparsely inhabited, with sections of heavy jungle on the eastern bank of the Ganga. Though the undergrowth was far too thick for me to see much wildlife, I found the tracks of barking deer and wild boar along the trail, cloven impressions in the mud. Early one morning, as I came around a bend in the path, a kalij pheasant strutted in front of me, its white cockade bobbing up and down. A little farther on a monitor lizard scrambled across the trail. Over three feet long, this prehistoric reptile seemed to hug the ground, all four legs splayed out like one of those jerky dinosaurs in Hollywood films. There were birds everywhere, a verditer flycatcher of powder blue, golden orioles, and green-backed woodpeckers. Passing a line of deserted fields, I was startled by the heavy beating of wings as a peacock blundered out of a nearby tree, then glided into the valley, its long tail streaming behind it like an iridescent comet. At one place, where monsoon weeds encroached on the path, I stepped back abruptly as a graceful dhaman slid out from under my feet. For a second or two I thought it was a cobra, four feet long, metallic green, and fluid as liquid steel. Though I quickly realized it was a harmless snake, the adrenalin in my veins shot through me like a dose of antivenin.

For most of this route the Ganga was only a hundred feet below the path, its constant roar imposing silence on the forest. Through gaps in the trees I could see a perpetual current of muddy water. At places the river was two hundred meters across and other times the channel narrowed to less than half that width. Often the trail climbed up and over the shoulder of a ridge, avoiding gorges and waterfalls. Sections of the path had been carved into vertical rock faces, the limestone hollowed out to a height of five and a half feet, so that I had to stoop down and walk with my knees bent. Water dripped from cracks in the cliffs and the rocks were slick underfoot.

Most of the trail, however, was broad and clearly marked with old stone walls and culverts. At one place I came upon a hoopoe sitting in the middle of the path, its orange, white, and black plumage in contrast to the surrounding green. The bird waited until I was a few feet away, then flew up in front of me and landed a short distance ahead. Hoopoes are comical-looking birds with feathered crests that open out like a paper fan. Their flight is unusual, wings beating a pulsing rhythm, so that they duck and dive through the air. As I approached the hoopoe once again, it waited nervously on the ground, then flew the same distance ahead. This happened at least a dozen times until I began to feel as if the bird was leading me along the path. When the hoopoe finally veered off into the jungle I almost followed.

Light rain had been falling since dawn, turning the forest an opaque green. Ahead of me I saw a skein of smoke, filtering through the trees. At first I thought that grass cutters might have lit a fire to dry themselves. The only person I had met that morning was a woman carrying an enormous load of leaves, which she had cut as fodder.

When I reached the source of the smoke, I saw a man seated inside a shallow cave, on a level with the path. My first impression was that he must be a sadhu, living alone in the sanctuary of the forest. Sitting cross-legged in front of a stone hearth, he was flattening chappatis between his hands with a steady rhythm that made it seem as if he were applauding my arrival. With a flick of his wrist the man tossed the round bread onto a cast-iron tava, positioned over a bundle of burning sticks.

Acknowledging my greeting he gestured for me to have a seat on the ground beside him, then took another pinch of dough and began to roll it between his palms. Something in the way he spoke, the inflection of Punjabi, or perhaps the steel bracelet on his wrist, made me realize he was a Sikh. His long hair was tied up in a topknot and his beard was gray, falling to his chest. He had a gentle face and though he never smiled, his eyes conveyed an expression of childlike wonderment, as if he looked out on the world without complaint.

"My name is Amarjit Singh," he told me, "but people call me 'Saili.' Everyone knows me along this route, all the way from Rishikesh to Badrinath."

He had been living in the cave for over a year and had made himself as comfortable as possible, with strips of burlap on the ground and a thin cotton mattress. There wasn't much space, for the cave was only five or six feet deep. It was more like a fissure in the rocks, which rose above us nearly forty feet. At the top of this cliff grew a banyan tree that had let down its braided tendrils, until they had grown into the soil at the edge of the trail. This matted screen of roots kept out the rain and provided shelter from the wind.

Once he began to speak, Saili continued talking rapid fire for half an hour, allowing me no questions, but telling his story as if it were a recitation. He had been living alone in the mountains for thirteen years, after his wife had died, "leaving me with a daughter, eight days old." Around this time Saili's mother had also died and in his grief, he left the child to be looked after by his elder sister. Distraught and on the point of losing his mind, he started wandering through the Himalayas, walking wherever his heart took him. He depended on charity, though sometimes he worked as a day laborer to earn enough money to buy food. For a while Saili had been a volunteer kar sevak at Hemkund Sahib—a Sikh shrine near Badrinath.

"When I was working there, I once served tea to General Jagjit Singh Arora—the hero of the Bangladesh War," he told me proudly.

Though he had chosen a life of solitude, Saili seemed glad for my company and offered to brew some tea. Not wanting to interrupt his cooking, I refused.

"My brother lives in Delhi. He works for a transport

company. A few years back I went to visit him and I stayed in the city for several weeks, though I wasn't happy there. I felt restless and uneasy in Delhi. Finally my brother bought me a train ticket back to Hardwar, so that I could return to the mountains. On the way, someone robbed me of my cooking pots while I was sleeping at the station. The world has changed a lot," he said, meaning for the worse, though I sensed no bitterness in his voice.

By this time he had finished cooking the chappatis and had placed a small pan of dal on the fire to heat. As I tried to excuse myself he continued talking, telling me about an earthquake six months earlier.

"I was sleeping right here," he said. "And in the middle of the night the whole mountain began to shake. I was afraid the rocks would fall on top of me, so I jumped straight onto the path. The rest of the night I spent shivering with fear, waiting for the sun to come up. I was sure my time had come."

Interrupting him before he could start another story, I stood up and took my leave.

"*Sat Sri Akal,*" he said, using the Sikh phrase of greeting and farewell.

Unlike most sadhus and rishis, who renounce the world and choose a life of wandering and isolation as a means of searching for God, Saili appeared to follow a somewhat different path. He had escaped the tragedies and responsibilities of life, but his quest seemed much more personal, as if the loneliness of the forest were enough to satisfy his longings. He spoke of the mountains and the river with simple familiarity, devoid of myths and deities, as if the surrounding presence of nature had eased his grief and quieted his discontentment.

Sanyas—a Sanskrit word that describes an ascetic's escape from the material world and a loss of identity. Throughout India there are millions of men who have discarded their families, their pos-

sessions, and their past for a life of wandering and contemplation. Some of these rishis or sadhus live along the banks of the
Ganga in caves and simple huts. But most of them have no permanent home, relying on others for charity and shelter. Pilgrims
offer the sadhus food and money in exchange for their spiritual
advice and blessings.

As a child I was afraid of sadhus, their matted hair, long
beards, and saffron robes, bodies smeared with ash. The brass
tridents they carried looked like spears. Sadhus kidnapped
young boys, I was told. They hang you upside down over a fire
and drill a hole in your head to extract the essential oils that are
used for jadoo magic and tantric rituals. The ash on their skin is
collected from cremation grounds and some of the sadhus even
meditate while seated on a corpse, in order to absorb the dead
man's shakti, his inner power and spirit.

These were stories meant to frighten a child.

Yet I have always had an uneasy fascination for sadhus,
their brazen eccentricities and the perpetual loneliness of their
lives, the constant wandering, the chillums of ganja that they
smoke. Some of these mystics have offered to read my palm, or
calculate my horoscope, predicting the future from the hour and
minute of my birth, recalling the stars and constellations that
wheeled in the sky at that precise moment when I escaped the
waters of my mother's womb.

A short distance beyond Saili's cave, I looked across the valley
and saw a cliff that rose three hundred feet straight up from the
river. The angle of the ridge revealed how this huge slab of
limestone had been tilted up by the collision of primordial continents, causing earthquakes much stronger than the one that
frightened Saili. The edge of the cliff formed a straight line,
sharp as an ax blade. Its converging slopes were so steep that
only scattered bushes and tufts of grass grew out of cracks in

the rocks. All along the edge of this cliff it looked as if someone had daubed the surface with chalk, splashes of white against the dark gray stones. Yet it was clear that no human being could have scaled those heights. For several minutes I tried to puzzle through this mystery, until I saw a griffon vulture break free of its perch and glide off down the valley. The white markings were the excrement of these huge birds, which nest on the cliffs.

The vulture Garud is revered as the vahana, or vehicle, of Vishnu and he carries the benevolent god on his wings. At many temples Garud is worshiped as a deity in his own right and often depicted as half man, half bird. He is also known to be the enemy of snakes and fought against the Nag Rajas, a race of mythical cobras with human features that live beneath the earth. Many people believe that Garud protects them from poisonous snakes. Near the village of Pipalkoti, along the final stages of the road to Badrinath, is a tributary known as the Garud Ganga. From this stream pilgrims collect pebbles and take them home to household shrines, where they are kept to ward off snakes.

Garud's sons, Jatayu and Sampati, are important figures in the Ramayana. While Ram and Lakshman went hunting in the forest Jatayu was left to guard Sita. When Ravan came to abduct her in his flying chariot the noble vulture fought with him and tore off many of his arms, though they immediately grew back again and the demon king finally dealt Jatayu a mortal blow. Later in the epic, his brother Sampati flew over the city of Lanka and discovered where Sita was held captive.

Byas Ghat. Confluence of the Nayar River and the Ganga. Descending a series of steep switchbacks, I pass a gang of laborers repairing the path. One section of the hillside has washed away and the men are carrying rocks on their shoulders to build a new retaining wall. A stone mason squats at the edge of the land-slide, measuring the damage with his eyes. It seems a futile effort, shoring up the mountain, which continues crumbling, a scree of shale and mud spilling into the Nayar. Debris obstructs the course of the river, so that the current swells up aggressively, curling over the rocks. For thirty meters there is nothing left of the path, only a series of precarious footholds dug into the col-lapsed ridge. As I make my way across, several rocks break free and tumble down the slope, causing a minor avalanche of mud before splashing into the water a hundred feet below. This process of erosion continues throughout the monsoon, thou-sands of tons of soil and rock plunging into the water and car-ried away downstream.

At the tea shop in Byas Ghat sits an engineer from the Public Works Department (PWD). He is a sullen, disgruntled man, responsible for repairing the pilgrim trail. In a year or two, he tells me, there will be a motor road from Byas Ghat up to Devprayag, connecting with a new bridge that is being built to link Pauri and Tehri Garhwal. Meanwhile, the footpaths must be maintained, though the engineer expresses little enthusiasm for his work. He would much rather ride in a gov-ernment Jeep.

Ramgarh Chatti exudes an atmosphere of decay and neglect. A small temple sits beside the path, its sloping tin roof rusted to a dull ocher. Inside are the images of Ram and Sita, the divine couple, a symbol of Hindu marriage and fidelity. Their statues, carved out of marble, are chipped and tarnished. A moldering coconut and a handful of wilted flowers are the only offerings. Inside the shrine it is dark and smells of mildew. Behind the temple stands a dharamshala, solidly built with a heavy slate roof. Yet its doors and windows are open to the mist and rain. The courtyard surrounding the dharamshala is paved with flagstones. Many of these are cracked while others have been uprooted to patch a water channel that flows across the path. Opposite the temple is a dying pipal tree, most of its branches bare, except for a few paisley leaves. Hundreds of sacred threads have been wrapped around the roots like cobwebs. Beyond the tree is a tea shop, part of its thatch roof caved in and no sign of a fire in the hearth. A white horse is tethered in one corner and a man lies sleeping on a wooden bench.

Lowering my pack and removing my shoes, I sit down to rest on the temple steps. Light rain is falling and the skeletal limbs of the pipal tree drip in the gray light. A few minutes after my arrival an old woman emerges from the doorway of the dharamshala. She is stooped almost double, her uncombed hair wildly tangled and her white cotton sari stained with mud. Shuffling toward me, the woman shakes her head, muttering incoherently. She seems to disapprove of my presence but before I can decipher her words, she turns away and vanishes back inside the dharamshala.

A short while later the tea shop owner begins to stir. When I go across to speak with him, he looks at me with a resigned expression and says he cannot offer me a glass of tea, for he has neither milk nor sugar. Pointing to the roof of his shop he says that it was broken by monkeys who came to raid the mango trees nearby. I ask him about the old woman and he explains that she is a widow and lives alone in the dharamshala. Twenty years ago, she and her husband took sanyas and came to Ramgarh Chatti. Traditionally, this is the final stage of life for Hindus, when all of the responsibilities of home and family have been fulfilled and people can leave the material world behind to prepare themselves for death.

"While her husband was alive they looked after the temple and the dharamshala," said the tea shop owner. "But three years ago the old man died and after that, poor thing, she lost her mind. As you can see, the place has fallen to ruin."

Between Rishikesh and Devprayag, there are three footbridges that span the Ganga, each one a good day's walk from the next. Originally, I had planned to spend a night at Ramgarh Chatti but it was such a depressing place that I carried on for another hour until I came to the last of these bridges. There was no campsite on the eastern bank of the river but on the opposite shore I could see a spring and a level patch of ground. Before crossing over, I also noticed a tiny hut just above the spring, half hidden by the trees and monsoon shrubs. It looked deserted and I assumed it was a seasonal shelter, a shepherd's hut, used only in winter. Though the suspension bridge had recently been repaired its rusty cables swayed precariously as I walked across. In the gorge below, the Ganga was pinched between the rocks, a churning cataract of foam and spray.

As I set down my pack and began to clear a spot to pitch my tent, a movement near the spring made me realize I wasn't alone. Turning my head, I saw a sadhu, all but naked except for a loincloth. He was squatting on a rock, in front of a shallow pool, and pouring water over himself with a brass lota. His long hair and beard were wet and his skin had a yellowish tinge, as if he'd rubbed himself with turmeric. A few minutes later, after the sadhu had finished his bath, I went to fill my water bottle at the spring. Though he returned my greeting with a friendly nod, the sadhu did not speak. He was winding a strip of yellow cloth around his waist and the color matched the jaundiced pallor of his skin. There was a wrinkled scar running down one side of his face from the right eyebrow and across his cheek. When I asked the sadhu how long he'd been living here, he waved his hands, as if to say it didn't matter. After a few more questions were answered in the same manner, I realized that he was either mute or had taken a vow of silence. The sadhu watched me fill my water bottle, then turned away without a word and retreated to the nearby hut.

Later that evening, as I was preparing my supper, I heard a strange sound. Though the rain had stopped, clouds of spray from the Ganga rose up out of the gorge, so that everything— my hair, my clothes, my tent—was beaded with moisture. In the narrow confines of the valley, the noise from the river was as loud as a hurricane. But the sound I heard was higher pitched, a steady moan that lasted for nearly a minute, then tapered off. A few seconds later it was repeated, this time clearer, more musical, like a trombone or a French horn. Only after the third and final call did I realize it was the sadhu blowing on his conch. Looking up, I could just make out his silhouette on the slope above me. As the sound trailed away the night closed in around us.

Om

The sacred syllable that silences all other voices and makes language meaningless. Neither vowel nor consonant but a combination of the two, it serves as an invocation to the gods, and wakens Shiv from his meditation. For the sadhu this was the only sound he uttered, releasing his breath through the inner sanctum of the shell.

Next morning, when I awoke, I heard the sadhu's conch again, a prolonged, melancholy cry that signaled the dawn. As I lay in my tent and listened to that single note, it carried with it a sense of loneliness and purity, one man's lungs emptying in a slow, continuous exhalation that spiraled through the chambers of that hollow shell before escaping into the air.

Just as he had done the night before the sadhu pressed his lips to the narrow opening in the conch and blew away the darkness. Even though I now recognized the source of this sound it remained mysterious, an echo of the Ganga itself, as if the river were reaching out into the depths of the seabed from which this shell had come, that same ocean into which its waters flow.

As the dawn grew brighter I was aware of patterns on the roof of my tent. At first I couldn't tell exactly what they were but as the sky gradually turned from black to gray, I discovered that a multitude of moths had found their way beneath the outer fly of the tent and had settled on the translucent nylon mesh above me. The moths were different sizes and colors, from a dusty brown to white and orange. Their wings were open and motionless, as if pinned against the taut, synthetic membrane. Though there was no regularity to the design, it looked as if the moths had been printed on the fabric, like delicate hand-block images pressed against the light—a lepidopterist's dream.

When I stepped outside the air was full of insects. Blue dragonflies hovered around my head and mosquitoes buzzed my face as I went to the spring to get a drink. An hour later, when I set off across the bridge, I found my path was blocked by dozens of spiderwebs that had been spun during the night. Some of these had insects trapped in them, including moths identical to the ones inside my tent. To reach the other side of the bridge, reluctantly I had to break the webs. Using a stick to brush aside the gauzy filaments, I watched the spiders scramble for safety. Their elaborate nets were strung between the suspension cables and guardrails, almost as if they were part of the bridge itself, like miniature wires and struts. Spray was still rising from the Ganga and these fragile arches were beaded with moisture.

Reaching the far side of the bridge, I glanced back to take a last look at my campsite and was surprised to see the sadhu walking toward me. He was dressed in the same yellow garments but this morning he had wrapped a scarf around his head and there were strings of beads about his neck. In one hand the sadhu held a bamboo staff and in the other a brass begging bowl with a wooden handle. He also carried an empty shoulder bag and I presumed that he was going to get provisions from one of the villages nearby. His stride was purposeful and when he came abreast of me, we nodded to each other. Neither of us spoke as we climbed the path; there was no need for conversation. When we reached the main pilgrim trail, he looked at me and gestured with one hand, as if to ask where I was going. I pointed up the river toward Devprayag and he raised his open palm in a gesture of blessing and farewell. With that, the sadhu turned and headed downriver in the opposite direction.

On the final stage of the trek up to Devprayag, I encountered more people than I had met in the past two days. One man was leading a buffalo and calf, coaxing the animals forward with a gentle tap of his stick. Farther on I passed a train of six mules carrying gravel for the construction of a new footbridge. The mule tier saluted me with a wave of his hand. Another man was carrying a cardboard box on his back, loaded with biscuits and buns. He worked for a baker in Devprayag who supplied tea shops along this route. There were groups of schoolchildren too, dressed in blue uniforms. They called out to me in English phrases they had learned in school. "Good morning." "How are you?" "What is your name?" All the travelers I passed were friendly, except for an irritable old man who was carrying a load of firewood. Without so much as a greeting, he demanded a cigarette from me. When I told him that I didn't smoke he cursed me under his breath.

At the confluence of the Alakananda and Bhagirathi, the waters from Badrinath and Gangotri merge and form a single current.

Downstream from this point the river is simply known as Ganga and its other names are erased. Throughout Garhwal the junctions of rivers and streams are considered sacred but Devprayag is the most significant of these, almost as important as the four main sources themselves.

The town is built on a steep ridge that tapers down to a point where the two tributaries meet. Devprayag is a relatively large town, the houses and dharamshalas built one on top of the other, so that every inch of the slope is covered. From a distance, the older sections of the town look almost like a single structure, an elaborate beehive of windows and doorways built into the side of the mountain. The rooftops, mostly slate or corrugated tin, form a chaotic pattern, like a precariously balanced house of cards. The motor road circles above Devprayag and more recent settlements extend over nearby ridges.

A new motor bridge across the Ganga is being built half a kilometer below Devprayag, though the original footbridge is located just above the confluence, across the Alakananda. It leads directly into the congested bazaars that cater to pilgrims. Once you enter Devprayag it is a labyrinth of lanes and gullies, with rows of shops selling everything from fountain pens and copy books to fruit and bright colored sweets. When it rains the roofs are so close together that the water pours from one to the next and the open gutters and drains become a network of streams. Staircases ascend from one level to the next, branching off in different directions. Most of the doorways open directly onto the steps and in some cases, one house can be entered from three different elevations.

At the center of Devprayag stands the Raghunath Temple, which dates back to the ninth century A.D., though it was recently renovated and painted an industrial gray. The main shrine has a high stone tower, topped by a peaked roof. Vishnu is the main deity worshiped here, the god of sustenance and continuity. In the courtyard surrounding the temple are smaller shrines, one to Hanuman and another to Garud, whose carved image combines the head of a man with the body and wings of a vulture. There is also an image of Shankaracharya, the Hindu reformer who traveled throughout Garhwal in the ninth century and established many of the pilgrim sites, including Devprayag. The priests who officiate at Raghunath Temple make up the bulk of the town's population. Their lucrative monopoly is jealously guarded and cause for a certain amount of bitterness among other residents.

On the eastern bank of the Alakananda, just opposite the confluence, is an extravagant public garden with terraces and pavilions, at the center of which stands an ornate clock tower. Painted a reddish pink, with paths of black and white tiles in a checkerboard pattern, it is an ugly eyesore. I was told that this park was recently built by one of the wealthy merchants in Devprayag as an act of defiance against the brahmins.

As soon as I approached the temple, one of the priests accosted me and insisted on showing me around. He was an elderly man with a white beard, wearing only a wrinkled dhoti and a sacred thread across his chest. Three streaks of sandalwood paste on his forehead converged at the bridge of his nose. Though I didn't really want his company, there was little I could do, and he was pleasant enough. In the end, the panda charged me fifty rupees for his spiritual counsel, which seemed a small price to pay for the absolution of my sins. After we had visited the Raghunath Temple, which was so dark inside the idols were hardly visible, he smeared a vermilion tilak on my forehead, then led me down a series of staircases to where the rivers met. The area near the confluence was surprisingly deserted, with no other pilgrims or pandas about.

The two rivers were at their highest mark and I could see the end of the staircase disappearing into the current. The Alakananda is slightly larger than the Bhagirathi, though both rivers were over seventy-five meters across and they came together in a dramatic churning of water. For most of the year, the confluence is twenty or thirty feet below this point. The priest and I removed our shoes on an upper landing before he led me down to the Ganga. Just at the point where the two rivers met, I was shown a large boulder, partially submerged. A pair of indentations were clearly visible, in the shape of human footprints.

The priest explained that Ram had stood on this rock and performed tapasya, after defeating Ravan in the battle of Lanka. Putting on the robes of an ascetic he came as a pilgrim to the headwaters of the Ganga, where he worshiped and bathed. The panda pointed to another indentation on the rock and told me that this was where Ram had placed his begging bowl. He said that the rock had been discovered less than a hundred years ago, when the staircases were being rebuilt. One of the government engineers who was supervising construction had tried to blast the rock with dynamite, but just as the fuse was being lit, the boulder turned the color of vermilion and Hanuman appeared. After this the footprints were revealed.

From a pouch in the folds of his dhoti the priest took out a handful of flower petals—jasmine, rose, and marigold—placing them in the cupped palms of my hands. Together we waded into the icy current up to our knees and the panda proceeded to recite a Sanskrit prayer, making me repeat each phrase. Though I didn't understand more than a word or two, it was obvious that the prayer was intended to ask for blessing and the cleansing of my sins. Finally, after the prayer was finished, the priest told me to release the flowers into the Ganga. Taking a couple more steps out into the water, I reached a point where the two rivers came together in rippled waves, their separate colors blending as swirls of silt. Standing there I could feel the force of the confluence pulling at my legs as the water coiled around my waist. Lowering my hands into the river, I watched the petals spin free on the crosscurrents and for a moment, I felt as if the Ganga was going to sweep me away.

# THE SONS OF SAGAR

MANY YEARS BEFORE RAM ASCENDED THE THRONE of Ayodhya there was a king named Bhagirath whose story is told in both the Ramayana and the Mahabharata. Bhagirath's great-great-grandfather was King Sagar, who had sixty thousand sons. Toward the end of his reign Sagar decided to perform the royal horse sacrifice, Asvamedha, releasing a white stallion to wander across the land. This horse represented the power and authority of Ayodhya and all of the territories through which it roamed were claimed by Sagar. Anyone who tried to stop the horse or divert its path was immediately challenged to battle by the king's sixty thousand sons, who had formed an invincible army and followed after the horse. Despite their diligence, however, the white steed eventually got lost. A frantic search began and in their desperation the army of Ayodhya uprooted forests and dug deep into the earth, until the gods became concerned that the world would be destroyed. Finally, Sagar's sons came upon a rishi named Kapila, whom they accused of stealing the horse. Furious over this insult Kapila used his supernatural powers to burn all sixty thousand warriors to ash.

Three generations later, King Bhagirath did penance for his ancestors in order to remove Kapila's curse. The only way that the sons of Sagar could be released from eternal suffering was for their ashes to be washed away by the waters of the Ganga. Leaving his kingdom in Ayodhya, Bhagirath journeyed to the Himalayas and meditated at Gangotri. His piety and devotion succeeded in releasing Ganga from the heavens, so that the river fell into the matted hair of Shiv. For this reason the main tributary that flows from Gangotri bears the king's name and is known as the Bhagirathi.

The priest who told me this story was a disreputable-looking panda with two-weeks' beard on his chin and a malicious smile that exposed an uneven line of yellow teeth. He had followed me up and down the narrow lanes of Devprayag until I finally agreed to hear him out. The panda's stories were recounted in a monotonous, singsong tone, like any tour guide who has memorized his lines. Having already heard most of the legends he had to tell I interrupted the panda and asked him directions for the pilgrim trail. At first he did not understand and told me that I could catch a bus to Yamnotri. When I made it clear that I was planning to walk he thought for a moment and told me that there used to be an old footpath that followed the Bhagirathi above Devprayag. Most of it had been destroyed when the motor road was built and now that the Tehri Dam was under construction, he claimed it was impossible to follow this route.

"Thirty years ago, when I was younger," he said, "plenty of pilgrims used to walk the trail, but now it's finished. If you try to go that way, you'll never make it."

I didn't necessarily trust the panda, especially after he insisted that I pay him fifty rupees for his stories and information. He wheedled the money out of me with assurances that I would live a long and prosperous life and that my pilgrimage would release me from the sufferings of this world.

The next morning I set out from Devprayag, after spending a night at the Vijaylaxmi Guest House, where I was able to dry my clothes under a ceiling fan. The rain had stopped an hour or two before sunrise and the sky was brilliantly clear. Though the valley was still in shadow, the tops of the ridges were lit up by the first rays of sunlight. Now that I was over four thousand feet above sea level, the forest had changed. Instead of the dense jungles of broad-leafed trees and creepers, there were open slopes of grass and thorny scrub cover, interspersed with stands of long needle pines. The west bank of the Bhagirathi, above the confluence, is heavily populated, with villages every few kilometers.

Nobody that I spoke with in Devprayag was able to confirm whether it was possible for me to walk all the way to Tehri. In the end I decided to set out along the motor road, hoping I would eventually locate at least the remnants of the pilgrim trail. By this time I had discovered that most people in the villages I passed through were able to give me reliable directions up to a distance of ten or twelve kilometers. Beyond that point their information was less specific and often undependable. As I headed up the Bhagirathi Valley I asked at several roadside settlements but nobody could tell me anything about the pilgrim trail. It was only when I reached Marroragarh, a bus stop twelve kilometers beyond Devprayag, that I learned the walking trail branched off at a village called Tela. This was another three kilometers ahead. Though it still wasn't clear if I could make it from there to Tehri—customers in the tea shop where I stopped debated this point for half an hour—my informants agreed that by nightfall I could probably reach Pindas, a large village with a dharamshala and other facilities for pilgrims.

By now the sun had penetrated the valley and the heat radiated off the asphalt surface of the road. There were only a few trees and I opened my umbrella to get some shade. Over the past few days I had been looking forward to a break in the rain but now I wished that there were clouds overhead and a drizzle to cool me down. When I got to Tela, I had to ask several villagers before someone pointed out the footpath on the ridge below. There seemed to be no direct access from the motor road and I had to walk through freshly plowed fields and scramble over a barricade of thorn bushes. Still uncertain if this was the correct trail, I soon caught up with a farmer who was herding a pair of cows. He nodded when I asked him if this was the path to Tehri. It was a "chey-footia," he said, literally a six-footer, in reference to the width of the path.

"If you keep moving," said the farmer, stopping to let me pass, "you'll get to Tehri in another seven hours."

This surprised me, for I knew it couldn't be that close, and as the day wore on, I became increasingly skeptical of his claim. At no place was the trail even close to six feet wide and most sections were a foot or two. More than once the path disappeared into a tangle of weeds and thornbushes, out of which I had to hack my way with a stick. Progress was slow and each time I rounded a corner of the valley, there was another ridge in front of me. The river was about five hundred feet below and though the opposite slopes were thickly forested, where I was walking there was hardly any shade. It was now the hottest part of the afternoon and I was tired and thirsty.

Eventually I came upon a spring, just below the trail. But as I started down to get a drink the smell of rotting flesh came up to meet me. The stench was overpowering and before I reached the spring I caught sight of a dead buffalo in the ravine, its carcass torn apart by vultures, two of which were sitting on a tree nearby. Swarms of flies filled the air.

Retreating up the hill I headed on until I came to a single mango tree, growing at the side of the path. It was not very large, twenty or thirty feet tall, and there was no fruit on its branches. A stone platform had been built around the roots, a place for travelers to rest. Whoever planted this tree had chosen the ideal spot, for there was a steady breeze coming up the valley. Sitting in the shade, I felt much cooler and could survey the landscape.

There was nobody in sight, though a couple of farmhouses were situated on the ridge below, surrounded by fields of corn and millet. Farther on, I could see a somewhat larger village with terraces of rice paddies descending to the river, like a staircase of velvet green. For some time now I had been hearing the steady rumble of drums and I assumed these were part of a festival or a marriage celebration. After I had been sitting under the mango tree for twenty minutes or so, two women came down the path. Each of them was carrying a bundle of grass that they had cut as fodder. Eyeing me with caution they dropped their loads on the opposite side of the tree and sat down to rest. Both were in their late thirties. They were barefoot, dressed in loose skirts, with cotton blouses and vests that buttoned down the front. These were their working clothes, stained with sweat and mud, torn in places, the sleeves frayed. Each woman had a loose head scarf covering her hair and an iron sickle in her hand.

We exchanged greetings and after they hesitantly questioned me for a while, I asked about the drums.

"The villagers are planting rice," said one of the women, "and the drummers are keeping time for them."

"Is that where you are coming from?"

"No, our fields are on the other side of the river. You can't see them from here but there's a bridge in the valley. Our home is back this way."

The older woman pointed in the direction from where I had come and invited me to visit their house and have a meal. I thanked her but said that I needed to keep moving if I was going to reach Pindas before dark. The two women consulted with each other and estimated it was at least a three-hour walk, though neither of them had been there. I asked if they had ever gone to Devprayag. The two women shook their heads. It was clear that their lives were contained within this valley, rimmed by mountains on every side. Curious about the world beyond their village they asked me questions about America, whether it was colder or warmer there, what crops were grown, how many children I had. Though their home had no electricity or running water, the women explained that these things had been promised for several years. The motor road, which was far above us at this point, had made little difference to their lives, except that their husbands—it turned out that they were married to two brothers—occasionally rode the bus into Devprayag and brought back supplies. The women did not have an easy life and most of their time was spent tending cattle, working in the fields, taking care of children, or doing the cooking. On the day I met them, they had been working since dawn and I could see they were exhausted. The few minutes we spent together beneath the mango tree was probably the only rest that they would get until nightfall.

After talking with the women I began to look at the valley differently. Until now, it was just another section of my route—picturesque but unremarkable terrain. However, once I realized that these women had never been beyond the mountains that we could see, I gained a new appreciation for the landscape and tried to see it through their eyes. In many ways, it was a complete, autonomous world. What lay on the other side of the ridges did not matter. Both the trail and the river passed through this valley but where they came from or where they went was unimportant. Seated beneath the mango tree I could see no more than three kilometers in either direction. Though the valley possessed its own finite beauty, it was not an idyllic world. These two women must have experienced more than their share of tragedy and deprivation. And yet, if this was all of the world that one could see, surely it was more than enough.

Continuing up the trail, I tried to imagine what it must be like to have walked this path every day since childhood, to know each twist and turn. Though I had never been here before, there was a curious sense of familiarity, the recognition of landmarks—an outcropping in the shape of a goat's head, the coppiced branches of a bhimal tree, a monsoon spring leaking through layered moss. When I came to a stream near the fields, I seemed to know exactly where to place my feet, as I leaped from one stone to the next. A few minutes later, the path skirted past rice paddies where lines of women were planting seedlings in unison. Farther on a man was plowing one of the flooded terraces, a brace of oxen wading through the muddy water, which had been churned into a frothy soup. At first I couldn't locate the drummer, then saw him sitting up the hill a ways, under the shade of a dainkan tree. He held the two-sided dhol on his knees and was using a pair of curved sticks to rattle out a steady beat. The village, named Khola, was farther down the ridge, a gray mosaic of slate roofs.

All of this I saw with a renewed sense of the enduring connection between human beings and the land. Each year the villagers planted their fields in the same way, diverting water from the stream to irrigate their crops. Each year the monsoon clouds appeared above the tops of the ridges, bringing rain. Each year the drummer hammered out the same rhythm. The people of this valley measured their lives through cyclical seasons and the mountains seemed to shelter them from the uncertainties and disruptions of the outside world.

Beyond Khola, the Bhagirathi Valley narrowed and the slopes became too steep for habitation. The pilgrim trail continued through patches of scrub jungle and I met no other person for the next two hours. As the sun disappeared to the west, shadows began to slide down the mountains. Approaching a spur of the ridge, I could see where the river took a sharp turn. The path was level at this point and turning the bend, I was confronted by a sight that literally made me stop in my tracks.

The opposite side of the valley, which had been hidden by the spur, was completely stripped of vegetation. A gray expanse of shale and limestone dropped straight down to the river. Near the bottom was a level area where I could see two yellow bulldozers digging their way through a pile of debris. Farther on, a network of unpaved roads had been carved into the mountain, like a series of jagged scars. Earthmoving equipment was parked at different points—more bulldozers, power shovels, and diesel compressors. Beyond these was a large construction site, with enormous tin sheds and long metal chutes running up the face of the ridge. It was a scene of total devastation, a man-made disaster zone.

Though the main dam at Tehri is situated about twenty-five kilometers upstream, a smaller dam is being built at Pindas, part of a giant hydroelectric project that has been under construction for over twenty years. Estimates for a completion date range from five to ten more years. The village of Pindas and a number of other settlements along the Bhagirathi will eventually be inundated, along with the town of Tehri.

Approaching Pindas, the trail descending toward the river, I had a feeling of foreboding. After half a mile or so, I came to a ruined dharamshala. It was a complex of five or six buildings, which at one time could have housed several hundred pilgrims, though now it was deserted. The doors and windows had been removed and nettles grew between the empty walls. A spreading banyan tree stood at the far end of the dharamshala, its roots covered by a circular platform. As I got closer, I could see a man lying beneath the tree, his body wrapped in a white cotton sheet. At first I thought it was a corpse but then I saw the figure stir, though he did not open his eyes or look at me.

Expecting the village to be just ahead I kept going along the path but it came to an abrupt end, where a section of the hill had sheared off. Below me was a stream. A gang of laborers were breaking rocks at the water's edge. One of the men beckoned to me, pointing out another trail that snaked its way around the landslide. When I reached the streambed, however, the same man told me that I was forbidden to go any farther and pointed me back up the trail. He was obviously a supervisor, for he sat on a boulder at the side of the stream while the rest of the laborers were pounding rocks. Unfriendly and clearly drunk, he demanded to know my purpose, while waving a finger to indicate that I must turn back.

The supervisor finally told me that the village of Pindas was situated on the hill above. Retracing my steps, I passed the dharamshala and banyan tree again, where the shrouded man was still asleep. The climb to the village was short but steep and I arrived there out of breath. Immediately I was attacked by two dogs, a pair of scruffy mastiffs. One was black, the other a reddish brown. They lunged at me, teeth bared, and I had to use my umbrella to fend them off. Two men who were seated outside a house did nothing to stop them, watching me with sullen stares. Eventually, the owner of a tea shop came to my rescue, chasing the dogs away by throwing rocks. After all of the hospitality and goodwill that I had encountered up to this point, it was a shock to arrive in a place where I was clearly unwelcome.

To make matters worse, however, I discovered that it was impossible to walk from Pindas to Tehri. The pilgrim trail had long since been destroyed and the motor road took a circuitous detour. Even if I had wanted to continue on foot, I was warned that nobody but the construction crews was allowed in the vicinity of the dam. I had no choice but to spend the night in Pindas and catch a bus to Tehri the next morning.

With the dogs still lurking about I ended up pitching my tent on the flat roof of one of the deserted buildings. That night I hardly slept, for the construction continued long past midnight, under a blaze of arc lamps that lit up the valley like a constellation of electric moons. The sound of the river itself was muted by the deafening roar of gravel and rocks poured down the metal chutes. This noise was like a crash of thunder, or more likely the final death rattle of the mountains. The air was full of dust and without a breeze. I soon discovered that the cement roof had absorbed the sun's heat during the day and remained uncomfortably warm all night. As I lay awake, exhausted but unable to sleep, I kept thinking of the valley I had left behind, the rice fields at Khola, the mango tree at the side of the trail, and the friendly voices of the two grass cutters.

There was only one bus a day between Pindas and Tehri, and it left at 7:30 in the morning. I was able to get a front seat beside the driver, who had a shrine on the dashboard. Before we set off, he lit a handful of incense sticks, which he placed beside a plastic bust of Shiv. The shrine also contained a coconut and two chrome images of Nandi the bull.

After we had driven a mile or two I understood why our driver felt a need to propitiate the lord of destruction. Most of the route was unpaved, a temporary road that had been built for construction vehicles. At many places there was a drop of five hundred feet or more to the river. The surface of the road was badly rutted and sections were nothing but channels of mud. Hardly wide enough for the bus itself, there was little or no room for other vehicles to pass. Each time we came around a corner I expected to collide with a truck or Jeep. Several times the driver had to brake suddenly and swerve into the hillside.

Along the way we passed a number of temporary camps where gangs of laborers were housed in corrugated tin sheds or sagging canvas tents. The bus was soon filled with passengers, who stood in the aisles and climbed upon the roof.

With grinding gears and shuddering under the weight of so many people the bus began to climb out of the valley, circling around a series of hairpin bends. The river was now far below us. After we had gained about a thousand feet in altitude, I was able to see the Tehri Dam for the first time. Once again I was struck by the monumental scale of destruction. The entire face of the mountain had been torn apart with dynamite and crowbars, bulldozers and jackhammers, a wasteland of mud and rubble.

Jawaharlal Nehru once called these dams "temples of the future." The hydroelectric project at Tehri will harness the Ganga's power and provide electricity throughout northern India but it has been hampered by controversy. Many conservationists have expressed concerns about the environmental impact of the dam and a grassroots movement in Garhwal has been protesting construction from the day it began. Others see the Tehri Dam as a form of sacrilege, modern technology obstructing the inexorable current of a holy river that symbolizes the cosmos. For the pilgrim who seeks peace in the continuity of nature, this temple of the future offers no solace. Instead, the dam interrupts his journey and leaves the mountains desecrated and despoiled.

Millions of tons of dirt and gravel have been excavated from the riverbed to obstruct the path of the river. The height of the dam is over five hundred feet and it is more than half a kilometer in length. Through the windshield of the bus, I could see an endless convoy of dump trucks carrying dirt to the top, while a line of eight or ten graders, moving in unison, leveled the surface and packed it down. The scale of the Tehri Dam is of epic proportions, representing an ongoing battle between man and nature. Seeing the gangs of laborers in their hard hats and uniforms, I couldn't help but think of the sixty thousand sons of King Sagar reincarnated as an army of construction workers—a relentless, unstoppable force digging up the earth in search of a white horse, the symbol of power.

My bus took an hour and a half to reach the top of the ridge, two thousand feet above the river. Here the government has built New Tehri, to replace the old capital of Garhwal, which will soon disappear beneath the waters of the dam. Residents of Tehri have been given property and homes, built at government expense, to compensate for what they will eventually lose. The new settlement is constructed mostly of cement, with rows of boxlike buildings regimented across the ridge. It is a modern, organized town unlike the decaying, chaotic structures in the valley. Eventually, the residents of New Tehri will look out across a reservoir, stretching twenty-five kilometers upstream.

After depositing some of the passengers at the top of the ridge, the bus crossed over and headed down to the old city. Because of the dam, we had to circle around and approach from the north. Here too the devastation was complete. Upstream from Tehri the Bhagirathi valley opens out into a sizable plain, three or four kilometers in width. Much of this area used to be fields and farmland but all of the topsoil has been scraped away to be used as fill for the dam. Vast mounds of sifted earth were piled at the sides of the road, waiting to be carted away in dump trucks. Even though it was the middle of the monsoon, there was no greenery at all, only mud and rocks.

In the end, I was forced to walk the last kilometer into Tehri because the bridge across the river was blocked by a group of protesters. Most of them were schoolgirls, wearing green and white uniforms, their hair done up in braids and ribbons. They were sitting in a circle at the center of the bridge, blocking the lines of vehicles that were trying to get across. Accompanying the students were two young men with drums and there was a disarmingly cheerful mood to the protest. They were singing songs and clapping, almost as if it were a school picnic rather than a demonstration. Hanging from the steel girders of the bridge was a banner that proclaimed their demands.

This protest centered around the opening of schools in New Tehri, which the students were required to attend. Most residents of the old city still occupied their original homes and the government was trying to get them to vacate these properties. By shifting all of the schools to the new settlement at the top of the ridge, the authorities were attempting to force people to abandon the old city. I was told that the dam would be tested in November and water was going to rise up to the level of the bridge. Until now, the people of Tehri had been playing a waiting game, holding onto their properties while pressing for more compensation. By moving the schools the government was forcing their hand, and the protest was clearly more than just a spontaneous student uprising. The girls who blocked the bridge had been chosen to represent the townspeople, because it was unlikely that the authorities would harass them. They were demanding that buses be provided to carry them up to New Tehri and back down again each day, a proposal that had been rejected by the government.

Though motor vehicles were not allowed across the bridge, the protesters permitted pedestrians to go back and forth. As I walked by, the schoolgirls waved and laughed. On the opposite side of the river stood a contingent of ten or twelve policemen, leaning against a Jeep. They had rifles on their shoulders and bamboo staves in their hands but the morose expressions on their faces showed that there was little they could do.

Unlike Rishikesh and Devprayag, Tehri is not a town of great religious significance. It lies at the confluence of the Bhilang Ganga and the Bhagirathi but its temples are not particularly famous. Most of the town has a dusty, fly-bitten appearance, with a noisy bus stand and cluttered bazaar. As the former capital of the princely state of Tehri Garhwal, it has a number of palatial buildings, though most of these have crumbled into disrepair. The main landmark is a clock tower that overlooks a dusty parade ground in the center of the town. As a concession to the sentiments of the townspeople, a replica of this tower has been constructed in New Tehri. Walking through the streets of the old city one cannot help but feel that Tehri is about to be destroyed. Though the markets are busy and the traders animated, a mood of desperation hangs in the air, as if everyone is trying to make as much money as they can before the water begins to rise.

Despite its name, the River View Hotel, where I got a room, did not overlook the Bhagirathi. Instead it faced onto a cemented street with open drains that attracted mosquitoes and flies. Beyond the rooftops of the town, I could see the upper rim of the dam, with clouds of dust rising above it like smoke from a volcano. The hotel was overpriced and advertised itself "for national and international tourists." My room was dark and smelled of urine. The bathroom had a hole in the floor for a toilet and at that hour of the day there was no running water or lights because of a power outage in the town. Despite the magnitude and vast expense of the hydroelectric project, here in Tehri there was not enough water or electricity to go around. Even with the windows wide open, my hotel room was hot and dingy. I was already depressed by the sight of the dam and the ruination of the valley. This was not where I had imagined my pilgrimage would lead and I kept wishing that I could return to the forested trails I had left behind. The whitewashed walls were streaked with stains and the aluminum table in one corner was missing a leg. It seemed as if all evidence of the natural beauty of the Himalayas had been destroyed, the forests decimated, and the legends of kings Sagar and Bhagirath all but forgotten. Just as I was about to lie down on the bed, however, I noticed that it was covered with a printed cotton spread. In the center was the stylized image of a white horse.

After some searching I found the corrugated tin shed that serves as Vimla and Sunderlal Bahuguna's headquarters in Tehri. It is located next to the ruined pylons of an old footbridge across the Bhagirathi. To one side is a small temple with two plaster idols of the goddess, one of which is an image of Ganga, carrying a water vessel on her shoulder. The main structure of the dam rises directly in front of the shed, a massive wall of earth that stretches from one side of the gorge to the other. Less than fifty meters away the river is diverted into concrete tunnels and the sound of rushing water is deafening.

Vimla Bahuguna seemed oblivious to the noise, though we had to raise our voices in order to carry on a conversation. She said that Sunderlal was still in Rishikesh but introduced me to two other activists, both men in their sixties. The main room in the shed was sparsely furnished, with books and papers piled along one wall. Pamphlets and environmental publications were hanging from a string like prayer flags, beneath paintings of the Dalai Lama and Jayaprakash Narayan, a leader of the Sarvodhaya movement. We sat on the floor and talked about the dam. From their comments, it was clear that the activists had conceded defeat, though Vimla Bahuguna seemed the most defiant of the three.

"Once this dam is finished," she said, "the power and shakti of the Ganga will be drained away. It's not only an environmental disaster but the destruction of our spiritual and cultural heritage as well."

One of the men added bitterly, "Who is this dam for? Not the people of Garhwal. We have sacrificed our homes, our farms, our fields, just so the government can make electricity to run more air conditioners in Delhi."

While the two men seemed content to sit and talk, Vimla kept herself busy rolling incense between her fingers, forming the black paste into tapered cones. From time to time she would look up and add her comments to the discussion. As soon as she finished with the incense, Vimla brought out a pen and paper and began to write a letter, which she asked me to carry to the Sarvodhaya ashram in Uttarkashi, explaining that she had been trying to contact them for several days but the telephone lines were down. Unlike the other activists she refused to sit idle, even for a few minutes at a time, and in everything she did there was a sense of purpose, reflecting her commitment to social and environmental causes.

Born in the village of Malideval, not far from Tehri, Vimla Bahugana was educated at a school started by Sarla Behn, one of Gandhi's disciples. At the age of twenty-one she joined the Bhoodan movement under Vinoba Bhave and has been a Gandhian activist all her life. Though her husband, Sunderlal, is a much more prominent figure in the Chipko movement and the agitation against the Tehri Dam, Vimla Bahugana is equally involved in these struggles. Despite her quiet, unassuming manner, she exemplifies Gandhi's ideals of self-sufficiency, social equality, and passive resistance.

# LAKE OF THE GODS

THE BHAGIRATHI VALLEY, BETWEEN TEHRI AND Uttarkashi, lies in a rain shadow. Even during the monsoon this area is much drier than most of the valley downstream, with sparse vegetation and no forests at all. Cacti and thorn bushes grow on the slopes along either side of the river and only where there is irrigation are there any fields. Though the altitude is four to five thousand feet above sea level, temperatures are almost as hot as the plains. No trace of the old yatra trail remains, for the motor road has usurped this route and a steady stream of buses and taxis carry pilgrims back and forth to Yamnotri and Gangotri.

Traditionally the route of the Char Dham Yatra cuts over the ridges above the town of Darasu but there are several alternate trails leading from the Bhagirathi into the Yamuna Valley. To avoid the motor roads I decided to cross over at higher altitudes, by way of a lake called Dodi Tal.

The hotel where I spent the night in Uttarkashi was right next to the bus stand and well before dawn the drivers of pilgrim coaches began blasting their horns to signal departure. One or two of them kept up a steady honking until there was nothing I could do but climb out of bed and start on my way. For the first five kilometers I walked in darkness through the town and along the main motor road. The headlights of buses were blinding as they roared past, sending me stumbling into the hillside. There was no rain but the humidity made the air feel heavy as if the diesel fumes had congealed around me. Gradually the sky grew brighter though the sun was hidden by clouds and the valley was a bleak gray, the landscape bereft of color.

As soon as I turned off the main road, however, I found myself in a magnificent pine forest. Propagated by the forestry department, chir pines (*Pinus longifolia*) have a controversial history in Garhwal. Growing forty to fifty feet in height, with shaggy crowns and reticulated bark, they are imposing trees. The problem with chir forests, however, is that little else survives because of the matted carpet of needles they shed on the ground. Added to this, the pines catch fire easily during the dry months of May and June. Only a few weeks before I started my pilgrimage, large areas of Garhwal had been burned in forest fires, ahead of the monsoon's arrival. The forestry department has planted huge tracts of chir throughout the Himalayas, because it is easy to grow and has commercial value, both as timber and for the resin that is tapped from the pines. This practice of monoculture has been criticized by many environmentalists and the chir pine has gained a dubious reputation over the years.

Yet there is an undeniable beauty about these graceful stands of conifers that cover the mountain slopes. In the monsoon a few hardy plants and shrubs push their way up through the carpet of needles and the reddish brown color of the pines turns a fresh green. Moisture darkens the trunks of the trees so that the patterns in the bark are clearly defined, like ornate columns. Walking beneath the pines one cannot help but feel a sense of sanctuary, particularly when the mist spills down the ridges and encloses the forest in an opaque cloud.

———

Ahead of me I see an old man walking by himself. Though his stride and bearing are still youthful, he carries a cane. When I catch up to him he greets me with a look of surprise and amusement, raising his right hand in a friendly salute. He wears a wool cap on his head and his features are creased and weathered, the dignified striations of age. Like most of the men in Garhwal he has a mustache, neatly trimmed and stained yellow by tobacco smoke. His eyes are rheumy but alert, and the first thing he tells me is that he is deaf.

"My ears don't work anymore," he says, with a confiding laugh.

We walk together for a ways and each time I ask him questions he looks at me and nods as if he understands, then launches into a subject all his own. The old man is an army pensioner, retired from one of the Garhwal regiments. He talks about the places he has seen—postings in Rajasthan, Kashmir, Assam. When we come to a stream that crosses the road, the old man waits patiently as I stop to remove my boots. He himself is wearing a pair of rubber chappals and splashes across, while steadying himself with his cane.

Soon afterward he asks abruptly, "What news of the war?"

For a moment I'm not sure what he means, then realize he is talking about the recent border conflict in Ladakh. Raising my voice, I tell him that the fighting seems to have subsided, though I haven't seen a newspaper for over a week.

"Eighteen men from my village are in the army," he says. "The Pakistanis should never have done this. Here in the hills we say that if a man's land is divided between two brothers, then one cannot encroach on the other's fields. For this reason there is bound to be trouble."

During the summer of 1999, hundreds of soldiers were killed in Ladakh, fighting over barren land at twelve to eighteen thousand feet. Many of the Indian troops came from Garhwal.

In Uttarkashi I saw a poster announcing a memorial gathering, commemorating the martyrdom of a soldier from the region. On the poster was a picture of the dead man, probably taken from his identity card. The young Garhwali was in uniform, a beret on his head and a look of proud bewilderment in his eyes.

Eventually the old man turns off in the direction of his village, which lies on the opposite side of the valley, across a wooden bridge. As we say good-bye he salutes me once again. I wonder what it must be like to live in perpetual silence, unable to hear the sound of rushing water or the wind in the pines.

One of the landmarks along the route to Dodi Tal is a fish hatchery, where brown trout were first introduced in Garhwal around a hundred years ago. Though this imported species has been able to flourish in a few isolated lakes, the trout have not survived in streams and rivers, perhaps because of the temperature and chemistry of the water or the presence of other predatory fish like the mahseer.

The trout hatchery appeared deserted, a cluster of broken-down buildings and rectangular tanks, some of them full of water, others empty. As I walked past the complex it looked as if the place had been abandoned years ago, the whole area overgrown with monsoon weeds, the walls and fences falling down. Later I was assured that the hatchery was still functioning and that the forestry department had a caretaker posted there year-round, though I saw no evidence of this.

About a kilometer beyond the trout hatchery I came to a tea stall next to a bridge. A group of four men were playing cards in one corner, so engrossed in their game of rummy that they hardly noticed my arrival. As I lowered my pack and sat down, the owner of the shop added sticks to his fire and put a pan of water on to boil. When I asked directions he pointed out a trail on the near side of the stream but warned me that there was a landslide up ahead, part of which I could see from where I sat. He explained that it was passable but dangerous and suggested that I take a detour that circled above the landslide, though this would add another hour to my walk.

Fortified by a cup of tea and Gluco biscuits, I decided to try and cross the landslide. When I got closer, it looked much larger and less promising, the trail disappearing beneath an avalanche of rubble and dirt. Glancing up I could see where a whole section of the mountain, nearly two hundred meters across, had sloughed off into the valley. The surface of the landslide looked unstable with water seeping out between the stones and flowing through a slurry of mud, the consistency of cold porridge. Huge boulders and tree trunks were strewn across the slope, the wreckage of a forest that had collapsed under the onslaught of monsoon rains. According to the tea shop owner, the landslide started four years ago and with each successive monsoon it had grown worse. Footprints in the mud indicated the route that others had taken but these soon vanished as I scrambled over the first pile of boulders. My pack made me top-heavy and clumsy as I edged forward. About a third of the way across I came to a place where a good-sized spring was spilling out from beneath an uprooted oak. Wherever I tried to place my boots the mud and gravel began to give way. I was about to turn around but rocks had started falling down the slope behind me and it was equally dangerous to go back. Just then, I saw a man coming from the opposite direction. He shouted and beckoned to me, saying that I should cross lower down, though his route seemed no better. With the mud giving way beneath my feet, I braced myself as best I could, then leaped across the spring and grabbed one of the branches of the fallen oak. Though I knocked several rocks loose, the spot where I landed was relatively stable, and from here I was able to crawl across the rest of the landslide, moving crablike over the loose debris. During the course of my trek, I crossed a number of landslides but this one was the most frightening because it was still moving, like a glacier of shale and mud.

A short distance farther on I came to Sangam Chatti, from where the trail began to climb toward Dodi Tal. The path was paved with flat pieces of slate, laid side by side, like upended cobblestones. These made it difficult to walk, though without them the surface would have been slick with wet clay. Fortunately it wasn't raining, though as I climbed up the valley I could see a black shoal of clouds coming in behind me. Six kilometers above Sangam Chatti is the village of Agora, where I hoped to spend the night. When I finally arrived at the edge of the terraced fields, a young boy raced down and met me, asking if I wanted to stay in his guest house. My plan had been to camp above the village but with the storm approaching, I agreed to take a look at the accommodations he had to offer.

As we climbed through fields of cholai and corn, the boy told me that his name was Rajesh and he was ten years old. At the side of the trail grew pumpkin vines with broad green leaves and sweet karela, which had spread like weeds. Agora consists of about thirty slate-roofed houses. A few women and children were about but no men that I could see. One group of women were shelling walnuts in the courtyard of a house and farther on we passed a pit loom, dug into the ground, with a thatch roof over the top. An unfinished shawl lay at the center of the loom with a warp of woolen threads stretched taut, as if it were a stringed instrument, a rustic harp, half buried in the earth.

One of Rajesh's friends joined us as he led me up to a low cement building with a veranda and four rooms. By this time the clouds were sweeping across the valley, a dark curtain of rain moving steadily in our direction. Having no desire to pitch my tent in a storm, I agreed to take a room for the night. Despite his young age, Rajesh was confident and self-possessed as he unlocked the door and told me what the charges were. He said that his mother would prepare a meal for me if I wanted. When I asked him where his father was, however, he shrank away and fell silent. In a subdued voice his friend explained that Rajesh's father had been killed four years ago; a stone had fallen on him while he was crossing the landslide below Sangam Chatti. Since then, Rajesh and his mother ran the guest house by themselves.

In recent years Dodi Tal has become a popular destination for trekkers. The villagers of Agora and several nearby settlements have taken advantage of the lake's growing popularity. No one can deny that these people, who have struggled to farm the mountains for generations, deserve to reap the benefits of tourism. At the same time there is a risk that Dodi Tal will soon go the route of other destinations in the Himalayas, where the mountains are swarming with herds of sunburned trekkers sweating their way up the trail.

The remote beauty of the mountains is often destroyed by those who seek to find it. At least for now, most of the route to Dodi Tal remains unspoiled and only during the months of May and June is it overcrowded. One cannot begrudge the villagers of Agora the opportunity to make a few rupees by opening guest houses and tea shops along the path, but the real danger is that outsiders will follow and construct larger and uglier hotels, or set up "nature resorts" and "adventure camps" that will attract droves of would-be mountaineers. After this, some ingenious bureaucrat, assigned the task of promoting tourism in Garhwal, will decide that the motor road should be extended all the way to Dodi Tal in order to share the beauty of the lake with those who prefer to sit behind the wheel of a Jeep rather than exert themselves. Contractors will immediately seize the opportunity to dynamite their way up the mountain and reap a fortune out of public funds. Instead of a two-day trek, the journey from

Uttarkashi to Dodi Tal will become a two-hour drive, and the lake will be surrounded by a ring of cement cottages and food stalls. Having seen so many other places ruined I cannot help but be a pessimist, though I hope that I am wrong.

In Agora there were two guest houses, including the one in which I stayed, and a third in the settlement of Bhebara, two kilometers farther up the trail. The next morning, as I set off for Dodi Tal, I met a Scandinavian couple who had spent the night in Bhebara, along with a research party from the Botanical Survey in Dehradun. Their team of six scientists was headed up to collect specimens of rare plants and herbs from the high-altitude meadows above the lake.

While speaking with them, I noticed a poster on the wall of the guest house in Bhebara. It was written in both English and Hindi with photographs of two French tourists who had disappeared in May. Jean-Philippe Tavaud and Virginie Durif were last seen trekking in the Hanuman Ganga Valley beyond Dodi Tal. The poster, printed by the French Embassy in New Delhi, offered a reward for any information. When I asked the guest house owner about the French couple, he shook his head despairingly.

"Last month they found the woman's body, but not the man. Nobody knows what happened," the owner said. "Her hands were tied behind her back and her throat was cut."

None of the villagers I spoke with could say for sure who was responsible but everyone I met was disturbed by the murder. Some blamed it on the Frenchman, speculating that he must have killed his companion and escaped into the mountains. Others said that the murderers had to be Nepalis, who illegally dig for rare herbs in the mountains. Later I was told other stories about foreigners who had been killed and robbed but these were recounted in a furtive, inconclusive manner that made it difficult to differentiate between truth and rumor.

In fact, Garhwal is probably one of the safest places in India and crimes like this are rare. Yet it is foolish to assume that nothing will happen. There will always be desperate, ruthless people, and the Himalayas are not without other dangers too. Whether it be a landslide, a falling rock, or a swollen river, one needs to approach the mountains with caution.

Though many people in Garhwal live within the forest and much of their livelihood depends on trees and wild plants, most villagers have an innate fear of the jungle, whether it be the threat of leopards and bears or the invisible spirits that haunt these slopes. The folklore of Garhwal is full of stories about ghosts—bhoots and prets or malicious devtas that transform themselves into ferocious beasts. Nightfall brings with it a universal human fear of the unknown, those shadowy threats that lie hidden in the darkness. After the sun has set very few villagers venture outside their homes, and I was often asked why I chose to travel alone and spend the night in my tent. At the same time most Garhwalis are fearless when it comes to the more obvious dangers in these mountains.

The path from Agora to Dodi Tal crosses several cliffs that drop away five hundred feet into the valley. Glancing down from the edge of the trail I was surprised to see a woman standing on a narrow ledge above a vertical rock face. She was cutting grass with a small sickle, leaning over the precipice as if it wasn't there. Just looking at her made me dizzy. If she had slipped and fallen there would be nothing to stop her until she reached the stream. The grass was still wet from last night's rain and as the woman moved forward, her sickle slicing rhythmically, I couldn't help but hold my breath. Like an acrobat without a net she moved casually across the cliff, stooping forward to gather and bundle the fresh green fodder into sheaves.

A quarter of a mile farther on I entered a dense forest of

moru and kharsu oaks, huge trees that closed off the sky. Their trunks and branches were draped with moss and ferns, as if each tree was a forest unto itself. Unlike the steep slopes of grass that made me feel exposed and vulnerable, here the path was a sheltered passageway through a tunnel of leaves. Growing beside the trail stood an ancient moru oak, nearly twenty feet in girth, its roots forming a staircase and its branches spreading out like heavy beams in a baronial hall. As I climbed past the tree, reaching out to steady myself against its wet bark, I noticed that someone had strung a chain of monsoon flowers around the oak. They seemed to have been freshly picked that morning—a garland of peacock orchids, pink and yellow balsam, white petals of wild ginger, and purple strobilanthes. These had been threaded on a cotton string and tied around the trunk so that the bark and green moss was girdled with a ring of floral colors.

Though it was impossible to know exactly who had tied the garland of flowers around the tree, I imagined it must have been the women who were cutting grass. An hour later my assumption was confirmed when I reached Manji, a set of chaans, or seasonal shelters, where the dairy farmers of Agora keep their buffaloes in the summer. These animals are tethered inside the chaans and fed a diet of grass and oak leaves, collected by the grass cutters. Manji is a good-sized settlement with about a dozen chaans. The ripe smell of wet buffalo dung and wood smoke filled the air. Children were running about, one of whom was brandishing a makeshift cricket bat, carved from a sliver of pine. Stopping to rest at one of the chaans, I was immediately offered a bowl of kheer—rice pudding boiled in milk and cream. Served with a knob of fresh butter, it was so rich I had trouble finishing the bowl. When I asked the owner of the chaan about the string of flowers, I was told that these were an offering to Vijar Devta, a forest spirit who protects the grass cutters when they go out into the jungle.

From as long ago as I can remember I have heard stories about Dodi Tal. Though I was never able to visit this lake as a boy, I have always carried a clear picture of it in my mind, from old Kodachrome slides that my father projected on the white-washed walls of our home. These transparent images, their chemical colors fading with time, have been fixed forever in my memory. A pool of still water, tall trees encircling its shoreline — cedar, fir, and oak. The lake is full of brown trout, so plentiful that you can catch them on a safety pin baited with a pinch of dough. An old forest bungalow stands on a meadow near the water's edge and on the opposite shore is a wooden temple with a sloping roof. All of this I envisioned from my parents' slides and stories.

For years I had wanted to hike to Dodi Tal but during the 1960s and early '70s, when I was growing up, this region of the Himalayas — including the sources of the Ganga — was inaccessible to foreigners. Because of the border war with China in 1962, the government of India established what was known as the "Inner Line," which marked off a restricted zone, or "sensitive area," we were forbidden to enter. Later, when the Inner Line was finally retracted in the late seventies and I was able to hike back into the mountains, I kept putting off the opportunity to visit Dodi Tal. Though eager to see the place, I couldn't help but feel a curious uncertainty, as if by going to the lake I would destroy those idyllic images preserved in my imagination.

In a way Dodi Tal became my own personal Walden, a secluded place of boyhood myths, a natural sanctuary in which I dreamed of living off the land — catching trout to feed myself, building a cabin out of cedar planks, homesteading in the heart of the Himalayas. Even though I had never been there, I felt strangely possessive about Dodi Tal and grew resentful when others told me that they had trekked to this lake. At the same time, for years I couldn't bring myself to go there, as if the Inner Line was still holding me back.

Climbing up the zigzag path, I felt a growing sense of excitement at the thought of finally reaching the place that I had always dreamed of visiting. About two hundred meters before Dodi Tal the trail levels off and runs parallel to a shallow stream that spills from the lower end of the lake. As I hurried forward in anticipation, a spark of orange caught my eye, so dazzling it made me stop. At first I thought that someone had left a handful of marigolds at the side of the path, another offering to the devta, but as I looked closer I found a cluster of tiny mushrooms growing on a decayed stump. Their fiery brilliance reminded me of the colors in a coral reef, phosphorescent beads of light.

Six or seven tea shops stand near the head of the trail at Dodi Tal, though all but one was empty when I reached the lake. These crude thatch huts intrude on the final approach, yet I hardly noticed them as I walked to the water's edge. The clouds lay overhead, no more than thirty feet above the surface of the lake, a woolly, gray ceiling that obscured the ridges on either side. The water was a dark green color, reflecting the foliage along its banks. Dodi Tal is roughly circular and less than a hundred meters across. The trees surrounding it are mostly moru oaks and rhododendrons, with a few firs and pines. To my right, across a wooden bridge was the old forest bungalow and nearby a newer rest house, under construction. Above me, on the left, stood the temple—not made of wood as I had imagined but constructed of stone and plaster, with painted images on the outer walls.

My preconceptions of Dodi Tal were not that different from what I saw, though in a strange way it was like a double vision of two similar but separate lakes, the one in front of me and the other that still existed in my mind. Everything was slightly out of place, as in a stereoscope, the ridgelines and contours of the lake not matching perfectly, though close enough to make it seem as if these were two images in one.

As I pitched my tent on a grassy terrace below the bungalow, I knew that rain was about to fall. The clouds were growing darker and the air was suddenly agitated. By the time I'd pushed the last stake into the ground, heavy drops were coming down and I scrambled under cover. On purpose I had positioned my tent so it faced the lake and I left the door unzipped, allowing me to sit and look out across the water. The nylon fly of the tent protected me from the rain and framed the scene so that all I could see was the lake and the trees. It was as if I were observing Dodi Tal in its purest state hundreds of years ago, before anything had been built along its shore. The different shades of green were speckled by the monsoon shower, the surface dimpled with concentric rings.

Dodi Tal is said to be the birthplace of Ganesh, the elephant-headed god, though this seems to be a recent interpretation of the myth. His mother was Parvati, consort of Shiv. When Ganesh was still a young boy, Parvati was bathing in the lake and told him to stand guard. Shortly thereafter Shiv arrived and Ganesh, who did not recognize his father, blocked his way. Incensed by the lack of respect that he was shown, the god of destruction immediately opened his third eye and burned the boy's head off his neck. When Parvati came running and saw what had happened she threw herself weeping on the ground next to her son's decapitated body. In an attempt to console his wife, Shiv promised that he would bring Ganesh back to life by giving him the head of the first creature that passed by. At that moment, an elephant wandered out of the forest and Ganesh's head was replaced by a long, sensuous trunk, short tusks, flapping ears, and baleful eyes.

Looking at the lake one can easily imagine a goddess bathing in its waters, while a nervous young boy stands guard, his back discreetly turned. All at once, Shiv comes striding up the trail, carrying a trident in one hand. Even Freud could not have imagined a more volatile family confrontation, but unlike the myths of Greece and Europe which usually end in tragedy, Hinduism resolves the conflict with a poignant and fanciful turn of events. If only Oedipus had been turned into a sphinx, what riddles would he have asked?

Revered as a god who removes all obstacles, Ganesh (or Ganapati, as he is also known) has become one of the most popular deities in modern India, a particular favorite of the middle class. He is usually depicted with a round potbelly, eating sweets with his trunk. The image of Ganesh, enshrined in a house, an office, or a shop, is believed to bring good luck. Most Shiv temples in Uttarakhand include a shrine to Ganesh, where he is worshiped separately. His vehicle and companion is the mouse.

Ganesh is also recognized as the scribe of the Mahabharata. When the sage Vyasa requested him to take dictation of the epic, Ganesh agreed on one condition. He insisted that Vyasa sing the Mahabharata "without pause or hesitation," so that his pen would never stop writing. The sage replied that he was willing to follow these instructions but only if Ganesh understood the meaning of every word he copied down. As they proceeded with the transcription, Ganesh kept stopping from time to time to fully comprehend the story, allowing Vyasa to catch his breath and compose the next few lines. Through this process the lyrical complexities of the oral epic were transformed into a written text.

The present temple at Dodi Tal is built of stone masonry, the outside walls whitewashed and the roof made of tin. Two wooden pillars and the plaster images beside the entrance are painted bright colors, a bas-relief of Hanuman carrying a mace, Shiv in the form of a mendicant, and Krishn with his flute. Above the doorway is an image of Ganesh, seated cross-legged in his customary pose. At his feet is a tiny mouse and hanging from the rafters two dried brahmkamal flowers with papery white petals. Inside the shrine is a stone idol of Ganesh, along with other gods and goddesses. Most Hindu temples, though they are dedicated to a particular deity, contain several different images, somewhat like a joint family household in which two or three generations live together under the same roof. Before entering the temple I rang a heavy brass bell that hung from the door. There were skylights in the roof and a wooden floor but the temple was musty and damp. The unpleasant odors of stale incense smoke and mildew made me soon retreat outside. On leaving the temple, I saw a small rodent, about the size of guinea pig with dusty gray fur. The tiny creature ran across my path and disappeared under a pile of stones. It was a mouse hare, relatively common at this altitude in the Himalayas. Except for the fact that it didn't have a tail, it looked exactly like the mouse that crouches by Ganesh's feet.

Just above the temple is a one-room hut occupied by a sadhu who looks after the shrine. The villagers refer to him as Maharaj-ji and having taken sanyas, he has no other name. When I peered in at his open door, the sadhu was sitting on the ground. He had an aluminum tray on his lap and was cleaning rice. His bearded face was calm and gentle. With a welcoming gesture he pulled out the skin of a barking deer from the shadows behind him and placed it near the fire for me to sit upon. When I asked him where he'd got the skin, he said that some hunter had given it to him.

"Are there a lot of animals here?" I asked.

"Yes," he said. "But you don't see many of them this time of year. In winter they come to the lake to drink—kakad, ghoral, serow, thar, and bharal, as well as bear and leopard."

"Do you stay here all winter?"

He nodded and explained that he had been living at Dodi Tal for the past seven years. Though the sadhu was talkative, his voice remained a low whisper, as if he were speaking to himself.

I mentioned the mouse hare that I had seen a few minutes earlier and he laughed, then told me the story of Ganesh.

"This is his birthplace. Everything is written in the Puranas and even Dodi Tal is mentioned, though in Sanskrit it has a different name."

I asked about Vijar Devta and the garland of flowers tied around the oak. The sadhu smiled and waved his hand dismissively.

"There are so many spirits in the forest, people find a way to worship all of them." When Maharaj-ji spoke about God he used the name Prabhu and said that he was everywhere, hiding in the jungle, or in a cave high up in the mountains. If Prabhu wanted to reveal himself, he would, otherwise he kept out of sight. At that moment a figure appeared at the door, one of the men from the Botanical Survey, who had brought a container of rice and a handful of dehydrated soya protein as an offering.

"You see how Prabhu feeds me," said the sadhu, taking the container and setting it aside. He invited me to eat dinner with him that evening, though I had already made arrangements with the owner of the tea shop. Later on, I met a Belgian who was staying with the sadhu, an earnest young man who had constructed a large arrow out of ringal bamboo. It was about twelve feet long and lashed together with vines, like a flimsy raft. The Belgian explained that he was an art student in Brussels and arrows were his chosen motif. Wherever he went he took photographs of arrows, and when he returned to Belgium he planned to "make an exhibition" of his work.

Just before dusk the sadhu and I went down to the lakeshore to watch the Belgian launch his arrow. Maharaj-ji laughed and said the man was crazy. "He has spent two days working on this arrow. It makes no sense."

By this time the rain had stopped and the lake was perfectly still. A fine mist drifted above the water like incense smoke. We watched the mad Belgian carry his arrow down to the shore and slide it into the water, so that it glided away like a leafy barge that wrinkled the surface of the lake. Using a pocket camera he snapped a roll of film from different angles, while the sadhu and I watched in silence. The farther out the arrow sailed the harder it was to see, its flat shape blending into the green water. Trout were rising on all sides, dimpling the meniscus of the lake, as if curious to inspect this strange device.

# YAMUNA DEVI

DESCRIPTIONS I HAD READ OF THE ROUTE ACROSS the ridges above Dodi Tal and into the Yamuna Valley suggested that it was an easy place to get lost, particularly during the monsoon when paths are overgrown with weeds and the mist obliterates all landmarks. As a precaution I hired a young man from Agora to guide me over this stretch of the pilgrimage. His name was Jagmohan and he owned one of the tea shops at Dodi Tal. Business was slow this time of year and it didn't take him more than half an hour to lock up his supplies in an old tin trunk, extinguish the fire in the clay hearth, and barricade the front of the tea shop with rough planks of wood.

Our trail led us up the valley above Dodi Tal, along a stream that flows into the lake. It wasn't raining but there was a heavy dew that morning. We had to wade through a waist-deep sea of grass and cross the stream half a dozen times. Before long my clothes and boots were soaked. Two thousand feet above us lay the crest of the ridge. The sky was clear when we started out and I was looking forward to the views of Bandar Punch and other snow peaks from the pass above Dodi Tal. Until now I had been walking at lower altitudes, unable to see the high Himalayas, and I was eager to reach the top of the ridge and catch sight of these mountains before the clouds closed in.

The trail proved heavy going, twisting upward in a relentless climb. We soon crossed the tree line and left the forest below, ascending a steep slope that was cloaked in fields of yellow and pink balsam. Stunted rhododendrons and junipers grew among the rocks and boulders. I could feel the altitude weighing me down, a dull ache in my lungs and a leaden feeling in my legs. Jagmohan, who was twenty years younger than me and carrying only a light knapsack, waited impatiently as I dragged myself up the path, pausing at each corner to catch my breath.

Soon I could see the first clouds above us, loose strands of white against the blue. Looking back, I spotted the lake but the mist was rapidly coming up the valley and within ten minutes there was nothing below us but an ocean of white. Here and there a few ridges rose above the clouds, green islands that were soon submerged. By this time the pass was only a hundred feet above me and I could see where the trail crossed through a narrow cut in the ridge. Though all I wanted to do was sit down and rest, I knew I had to keep going if there was any chance of seeing the snows. Step by step I pulled myself up the final climb, panting in the thin air and wishing that I could free myself from the weight of the pack.

Jagmohan was three or four switchbacks above me and I saw him stop just short of the pass, beckoning for me to hurry. Already I knew it was too late. The sky was more white than blue and suddenly, over the ridge I saw the mist come pouring down, like milk boiling over the lip of a pan. Ten minutes later I reached the top, unable to see more than a few feet ahead of me. The only way I knew that I had crossed the ridge was the gust of cold air blowing past me, carrying with it a blanket of moisture. Throwing off my pack in disappointment I lay down in the wet grass, gasping from the exertion of the climb. For twenty minutes or more, Jagmohan and I waited, hoping that the mist would clear and give us a view of Bandar Punch, but there was nothing to see except the swirling interior of the clouds. A few hours later, as we traversed the ridge, there was a momentary break in the mist, and I saw a fragment of the snows, a single white peak that appeared for just an instant, as if to tease my imagination and prove that the mountains were actually there.

Bugiyals are alpine meadows that stretch from the tree line to the upper limits of rock and snow. During the monsoon these verdant slopes are carpeted in wildflowers—white anemone, blue spiderwort, mauve geraniums, pink begonias, purple gentians, red goosefoot, and scarlet potentilla. Even the mist cannot obscure their colors, and walking across the bugiyals above Dodi Tal was like being in a psychedelic dream, the moist, opaque clouds, wet green grass, and bright blossoms underfoot. The fragrances that rise from these natural flowerbeds are as varied as the different hues: the tang of wild caraway, the sour, grassy scent of sorrel, and the subtle sweetness of thyme.

The Botanical Survey team, who were camped at Dodi Tal, had chosen this time of year to collect rare flowers and herbs because the bugiyals are in full bloom. They planned to count and catalog the different species as a part of their scientific research. But there were others too in search of these flowers who had less honorable motives. Many Himalayan plants are extremely valuable and used as herbal medicines. Though the forestry department restricts the harvesting of wild herbs, it does not have the resources to patrol the higher elevations of Garhwal and the illegal gathering of roots and flowers goes on unabated. As Jagmohan and I crossed the meadows we came upon two separate parties of herb poachers. The first group, made up of six Garhwalis, was sitting by the side of the trail with their digging tools in hand. They were unfriendly, eyeing us with suspicion as we passed. The second party consisted of Nepalis and though they stopped and chatted for a while, none of them was willing to say anything about the plants they gathered. Jagmohan explained that one kind of root, a species of aconite or monkshood, can fetch as much as six hundred rupees a kilo.

The poachers carry the herbs down to towns and villages along the motor road, where contractors buy the contraband and smuggle it out of the mountains to medicinal factories on the plains. Though the forestry department maintains checkpoints along the main roads, corruption is rampant and the contractors bribe their way through any barriers that are set up. In certain parts of Garhwal the government has made efforts to cultivate wild herbs, but compared to the organized activities of the poachers, these projects generate only a small proportion of the plants that are turned into medicines. The poachers make no efforts to preserve or sustain the species they harvest. Already many of these plants are facing extinction and within a few years they will be rooted out altogether, unless serious and concerted efforts are made to stop the destruction.

As Juan Mascaro has written in the introduction to his translation of the Upanishads, "A flower can be an object of trade: something to buy and sell for money. This is its lowest value. It can also be an object of intellectual interest, but then it becomes an abstraction and from a purely intellectual point of view a nettle may sometimes be more interesting than a flower. But to the soul the flower is an object of joy, and to the poet it can be a thing of beauty and truth; a window from which we may look in wonder into the Beauty and Truth of the universe, and the Truth and Beauty in our own souls."

One of the most popular stories from the Ramayana involves the medicinal properties of Himalayan herbs. During the battle of Lanka, the warriors of the animal kingdom joined forces with Ram and Lakshman to fight against the demon Ravan.

Hanuman the monkey god was always by their side, ever loyal and resourceful. In the course of this battle Lakshman was mortally wounded by a demon's arrow. Hanuman immediately flew off to the Himalayas to find sanjivini booti, a plant that gives eternal life. When he arrived on the mountaintop he saw the meadows of wildflowers and herbs but couldn't distinguish sanjivini booti from the rest of the plants. In his impatience, Hanuman uprooted the entire mountain and carried it back on his shoulders.

The image of a muscular Hanuman flying through the air with a snow peak on his shoulders is a familiar part of calendar art in India. Walking through the bugiyals one can easily imagine the difficulty he faced, unable to differentiate between hundreds of species of flowering plants, not knowing which of these were poisonous and which had healing properties. This knowledge has been cataloged over centuries and refined through traditional ayurvedic systems of medicine. Though none of the plants can provide eternal life, the value of these herbs is undeniable. Unscrupulous traders and poachers are, in essence, uprooting the mountains and destroying the source of these healing herbs.

Bugiyals are perhaps the most fragile part of the Himalayan ecosystem. Even as I walked across the meadows, I felt as if my boots were leaving indelible prints in the wet earth. The soil is rich but easily eroded and at many places we passed the scars of a recent landslide, where the lush green carpet had slipped away to reveal an ugly gash of rock and exposed earth. Seasonal streams cut through the bugiyals, ripping away the plush surfaces and carving new ravines and valleys into the face of the mountain. All of this is part of a natural cycle for it is the monsoon rain that allows these plants to flourish, but human beings add to the destruction.

Not only are the meadows a source of rare herbs, they are also pastures, where shepherds graze their cattle and goats. The abundance of green fodder has attracted migrant dairymen for years. Muslim gujjars have camped on the bugiyals over many generations, herding their buffaloes up to the mountains during late April or early May and remaining here until September and October. They travel on foot several hundred kilometers each year, accompanying their animals to these high pastures, following traditional routes from their winter camps in the Siwalik Hills.

Crossing the bugiyals, Jagmohan and I passed a cluster of gujjar huts—high, domed structures made of thatch that looked like giant hayricks in the mist. Sections of the meadow near these huts had been dug up by the hooves of buffalo, leaving a mire of mud and dung. The fragrance of the plants was replaced by the sour odors of cattle and wood smoke. A little farther on we came upon a herd of buffalo, tended by four or five children who waved as we walked past. Earlier we had met two of the gujjar men carrying jerry cans of milk down the mountain to Sangam Chatti. Each container must have weighed at least forty kilos and the gujjars relayed it down the mountain, walking over thirty kilometers every day.

The buffaloes watched us pass with suspicion, swinging their curved horns from side to side and flaring their nostrils belligerently. With their black hide and angular bone structure they looked prehistoric. It is hard to believe that beasts as large and ungainly as these can negotiate the steep trails but buffaloes are prized in the Himalayas, for they produce much more milk than cows. The gujjars are acknowledged to have the best breed of buffaloes and as they travel through the mountains their cattle are often traded or sold to the villagers of Garhwal. In the herd we passed there must have been more than a dozen calves, some of them only a few days old. Circling below the animals, I saw a lone albino calf. Standing by itself on a grassy knoll, it was the same color as the mist, a pale, ghostly creature surrounded by a tide of green.

For three hours we carried on across the bugiyals, staying as high as we could to avoid the cliffs below. The mist was so dense that it was easy to lose one's sense of direction and I was relieved that Jagmohan was there to show me the way. Eventually we began descending and as the mist parted I saw a goatherd's hut below us. It was a makeshift shelter, constructed of stones and thatch, with strips of plastic sheeting covering part of the roof. Outside the hut lay an enormous red dog, a bhootia, or Tibetan mastiff. The goats and sheep, a flock of about a hundred, were huddled together on a ridge above the hut. Though their eyes followed us as we passed, the animals remained completely still, like a woolen shawl draped over the shoulder of the ridge. Approaching the hut, Jagmohan called out several times, afraid that the dog would attack, though it ignored us and remained asleep.

After a couple of minutes one of the goatherds came out of the hut. The area near their camp was covered in black mud and round pellets of dung the size of buckshot. The smell of goats was overpowering, and leaning against one wall I could see a wooden churn and beside it a large puddle of discarded buttermilk. A second shepherd emerged from the cavelike entrance of the hut, then a third and a fourth. They were all Garhwalis, rough-looking men, with gray hair and gnarled hands. Their clothes were made of homespun wool, a coarse tweed that was heavily patched. Though they seemed unfriendly at first, one of them offered Jagmohan a hookah to smoke. As we talked the conversation turned to the French couple who had disappeared and the goatherds seemed defensive, as if they thought that I had come to investigate the crime.

At that point the clouds lifted briefly and the valley below was visible, where the Hanuman Ganga flowed from the foot of Bandar Punch into the Yamuna River. Unlike the broad meadows we had crossed, the opposite slope of the valley was lined with rugged cliffs and rocky moraine.

"That's where the woman's body was found," said one of the goatherds, pointing across the Hanuman Ganga and shaking his head. "They must have been trying to cross the river but there isn't a path on that side of the valley."

Like others I had spoken with, the goatherds were clearly upset by the recent murder and the suspicions it had raised. They themselves had been questioned by a police party a few weeks earlier and proclaimed their innocence, blaming the herb gatherers. "It must have been the Nepalis. Only they could have done such a terrible thing."

After taking leave of the goatherds, we hadn't gone more than a hundred yards when I saw a pair of ravens fly up in front of us, making a loud croaking noise. In a ravine to the side of the path lay a dead cow and next to it three bhootia dogs. These mastiffs had shaggy black fur and looked like bears. Part of the cow's stomach had been torn open and the entrails were hanging out, where the bhootias had been feeding on the carcass. None of them barked but they watched us threateningly, like wary predators on a kill.

The trail from the goatherd's hut was the worst that I encountered on this trek. It was hardly a path at all, more like a rocky channel that plunged straight down the ridge. Rain began to fall and the trail was soon flowing ankle-deep in mud. At places I felt as if we were sliding down a waterfall. Even when we came to the tree line, passing through stands of birch and rhododendron, the trail continued to follow the shortest route into the valley, which often meant negotiating drops of ten to fifteen feet.

Later I learned there was another trail that provided a more gradual descent but Jagmohan kept insisting this was the only way. I have never accepted the claim that going downhill is harder than climbing up but this time it was true and after the first few hundred meters, my knees ached and my legs were trembling from the exertion of trying to stay upright. Several times I lost my footing and was lucky to make it down the ridge without a serious fall.

After an hour or so we entered a thick forest of maples and moru oaks. Here the trail leveled off just enough so that I could admire these trees. Their trunks were so tall and their limbs so high that no grass cutters could reach their leaves. Draped with bearded moss, layered ferns, and polypods, the dripping forest had a primeval quality, a surrounding eeriness of gray-green light.

By this time we were looking for a place to camp and eventually came to a clearing. At the lower end were terraced potato fields, surrounded by a crude stone wall. A broken-down hut, with half its roof caved in, stood on the near side of the fields. It looked as if no one was living in the ruined chaan but as we got closer, a man came dashing out and started shouting and throwing rocks. Fortunately these weren't directed at us but instead at a troop of langurs in the fields. The monkeys slowly ambled out of range and took their seats on the stone wall. Several of them were holding uprooted potato plants in their hands. They displayed a casual arrogance, like insolent trespassers who refused to be driven out of the fields. Running after them the man kept shouting and hurling stones until the langurs finally retreated to the forest.

When we reached the chaan the man was coming back toward us. He was a Nepali, short and stocky, with Tibetan features. The gray sweater he wore was covered in burrs. His name was Bim Bahadur and he invited us into the chaan. Though one part of the hut lay in ruins and the floor was covered in mud, there was a square wooden platform about three feet off the ground, where we could sit. Bim Bahadur quickly lit a fire and put water on to boil for tea. It was dark inside and the only light came through a crack in the roof, where a wooden shingle had been slid aside to let out the smoke. This also allowed the rain to enter, and the fire hissed every time a drop of water fell on the flames. The rest of the platform was dry enough and it felt as if we were sitting in an attic, with the roof sloping down just above my head. Bim Bahadur was a friendly, talkative man and seemed pleased to have our company. He told us that he had been hired by the owner of the potato farm to guard the crop. All kinds of animals came into the fields, including porcupines and wild boar, but langurs were the most destructive.

"They pull up the potatoes by the roots, then take one bite and throw the rest of the plant away. In a couple of hours they can destroy a whole field."

Despite his complaints and the obvious discomforts of the chaan, Bim Bahadur had an easygoing laugh. He said that he came from a village in the western part of Nepal and had migrated to India five years ago in search of work. Originally he had come to Garhwal to work as a porter, carrying pilgrims up to Yamnotri. Nepalis often shoulder the dandies, or sedan chairs, that are used to ferry elderly Hindus up to the source of the Yamuna. Bim Bahadur admitted that in comparison, guarding the potato fields was an easy job.

That night we stayed at the chaan and I pitched my tent on a patch of grass outside. Over the smoky fire, Jagmohan cooked our meal of rice and dal. He flavored the simple dinner with sprigs of a green herb that he had picked on the bugiyals, a kind of wild oregano that had a sharp, aromatic taste.

It was still raining heavily the next morning when we set out for Hanuman Chatti. The langurs had spent the night in the trees at the edge of the clearing. There were about twenty of them, a bedraggled-looking group. Their silver fur was wet and their black faces were morose as they huddled together on the branches of a moru oak. Each of their long tails hung straight down behind them, dripping with the rain.

The Hanuman Ganga, which flows from the glaciers of Bandar Punch, is a short, swift stream that races down the valley before joining the Yamuna. Bandar Punch literally means the monkey's tail, and this snow peak gets its name from another episode in the Ramayana. During the final battle of Lanka, when the monkey army formed a bridge across the ocean and attacked the demon's fortress, Hanuman led the charge. After his tail caught fire, he jumped from roof to roof, setting the entire city of Lanka aflame. When the conflagration was complete, Hanuman flew back to the Himalayas and plunged his burning tail into the snowfields of Bandar Punch to extinguish the fire. In this process the ice began to melt and the river was formed, which now bears his name.

As we descended into the valley the sound of rushing water grew louder and louder. With all of the rain, the Hanuman Ganga was the color of brewed tea, roaring through the gorge as if a dam had burst. We reached Hanuman Chatti around midmorning and took shelter in one of the tea shops above the confluence. It is an unattractive, crowded settlement, with rows of tiny shops and cheap rest houses. Situated in a narrow gorge the town has a claustrophobic feeling. Though the height of the pilgrimage season is May and June, even in August there were plenty of yatris. After coming down from the forests and bugiyals, I couldn't help but feel depressed by the squalor of human habitation. From the tea shop owner we learned that a section of the motor road three kilometers below Hanuman Chatti had washed away in a landslide and buses were only coming that far. A couple of Jeeps were stuck on this side and these were ferrying pilgrims back and forth. Jagmohan was eager to leave but instead of returning home by the route we'd taken, he was hoping to catch a bus to Uttarkashi.

I headed in the opposite direction, crossing the bridge at Hanuman Chatti and following the pilgrim trail to Yamnotri. Leaving the confluence behind, I found the valley much more interesting. There were spectacular cliffs on the west bank of the Yamuna, towering rock faces, green slopes of grass, and groves of Himalayan elm and broad-leafed dogwoods. I passed a number of pilgrims going in both directions. Many of them were draped in pink or blue sheets of plastic to protect them from the rain. Others rode on ponies and mules, sitting uncomfortably in the saddle and holding umbrellas over their heads. Every three or four kilometers there was a rest stop. At each of these places stood a cluster of tea shops and dharamshalas. The trail became a soup of black mud and mule dung, littered with scraps of bright plastic and paper—toffee wrappers, discarded cigarette packets, and bottle caps. About five kilometers beyond Hanuman Chatti a gang of men with pickaxes and crowbars were cutting away a section of white limestone cliffs to extend the motor road. Eventually this road will go all the way to Janki Chatti, which is only six kilometers below Yamnotri. Once again, I felt despondent at the steady ingress of these motor roads. Parked nearby was an old diesel compressor that was leaking oil. It looked like the relic of a doomed expedition that had dragged this machine as far as it could go.

Yamuna Devi, the river goddess worshiped at Yamnotri, is the twin sister of Yama, god of the dead and lord of the underworld. Their father is Surya, the solar deity, and their mother is Sanjana, whose name means conscience. Yama lives beneath the earth and judges the dead. He is often depicted in a morbid green color with a gangrenous leg, from which a rooster pecks worms and maggots. Yama rides a buffalo and is accompanied by two ferocious dogs that guard the entrance to the underworld. Pilgrims who bathe at Yamnotri believe that their ritual ablutions at the river's source will spare them from a violent death. Once the least developed and most remote of the four main sources of the Ganga, Yamnotri is now easily accessible and the temples and pilgrim facilities have been expanded to accommodate thousands of yatris a day. Unlike the other three tributaries, which flow together within the mountains of Garhwal, the Yamuna follows a more circuitous route. Though its source is only forty kilometers away from Gangotri, as the crow flies, the river leaves the Himalayas at Kalsi, to the west of Rishikesh and Hardwar. Flowing for several hundred kilometers, across the plains of northern India, the Yamuna finally joins the Ganga at the sangam in Allahabad.

One of the myths about this river explains its meandering course. It is said that Balaram, the elder brother of Krishn and the eighth avatar of Vishnu, got drunk one day and demanded that the river come to him so that he could bathe. When Yamuna Devi ignored his command, Balaram—renowned for his physical strength and capable of pummeling demons to death with his bare fists—picked up his plowshare and plunged it angrily into the river. Dragging the plow behind him, Balaram wandered through the mountains in an angry stupor, diverting the river's course until Yamuna was finally forced to plead for his forgiveness. Anyone who has seen how this river twists and turns, forming elaborate oxbows between the ridges, can appreciate the origins of this story.

Pilgrims travel from all over India to bathe at Yamnotri and as I walked up to the source, I met Hindus from as far away as Kerala and Tamil Nadu. Most of them were undertaking the Char Dham Yatra and many had already been to Badrinath,

Kedarnath, and Gangotri. Though the traditional sequence is to first visit Yamnotri and then move eastward, today the tour companies often take pilgrims in the reverse order because it is more convenient.

One group of four young men had come from Rajasthan and this was the first time they had seen the Himalayas. Dressed in cotton dhotis and bright orange turbans, they looked as out of place as I did with my backpack. These men spoke enough Hindi so that we could converse but their dialect was difficult to follow. We walked together for a couple of kilometers and they kept exclaiming on the steepness of the terrain, telling me that their home was in the desert near Jodhpur, where the highest hills rose less than a hundred feet. Everything they saw seemed to pique their curiosity, from the tiny oxen plowing terraced fields to the monsoon greenery of the forests. Though they talked enthusiastically about the temples they had seen on their pilgrimage, what seemed to intrigue them most of all was the stinging nettle growing along the path.

"Whoever heard of a plant that bites?" said one, with a bewildered laugh.

Many of the pilgrims were elderly men and women. Though some of them rode on mules or were transported in dandies, carried by Nepali porters, quite a few of these aged pilgrims were walking. One woman who must have been over eighty was coming down the trail, supported by her middle-aged son. Dressed in a plain white sari that was damp from the rain, she was barefoot, stepping cautiously through the mud. Farther on I passed an old man who seemed hardly able to stand. Leaning on a bamboo staff, he was taking one step at a time and stared straight ahead with a look of exhausted determination. At the pace he was going it must have taken him three days to cover the distance from Hanuman Chatti to Yamnotri. Many of the yatris believe that if they die along the trail, they will be released from the sufferings of a future life.

Among the pilgrims there was a general mood of spiritual camaraderie and we greeted each other with cries of *"Jai Yamuna Devi!"* Signs painted on the rocks exhorted yatris to help each other and to share the hardships and rewards of the pilgrimage. Most yatris were traveling in groups of families or friends who were making the journey together. As I passed one man he fell in step with me and introduced himself as Sanjay, telling me that he was a lawyer from the town of Bijnor, just east of Hardwar. About a year ago he claimed to have suffered a near-death experience, and in his unconscious state he had a vision of Shiv and Saraswati, who instructed him to undertake the Char Dham Yatra. At the same time they taught him the secrets of precious stones and gave him the ability to read palms. "After I came back to life, I started wearing a yellow sapphire on my index finger and it changed my whole view of the world. I became very spiritual and took up yoga."

When we stopped at a tea shop, Sanjay asked me to show him my palm. Reluctantly I opened my hand, telling him that I didn't believe in palmistry. Many years ago, friends in Delhi insisted that I have my fortune told and the man who read my palm—a well-known astrologer—studied the lines for several seconds, then suddenly closed my fingers into a fist and refused to tell me what he saw. Whether he had seen a terrible fate or sensed my skepticism, I've never been sure. This time Sanjay squinted at my palm for five or six minutes, flattening it out, then pressing my fingers together to accentuate the lines. With an uneasy sigh he finally shook his head then looked away, telling me that perhaps it was better if I didn't know what lay ahead. Though I still refuse to give any credence to palm reading, it spooked me for a while and I was glad to part company with Sanjay soon afterward. Before we said good-bye, he produced a camera and insisted that we have our picture taken together. "For memory's sake," he said.

I could have gone all the way up to Yamnotri in one day but decided to spend the night at Janki Chatti, where I stayed in a dharamshala. Stringing up clotheslines from all four corners of the room, I hung my tent and clothes to dry. The rain had not let up since the day before and continued to fall throughout the night, rattling against the tin roof.

When I woke up next morning at dawn the clouds were still draped across the mountains and there was a light drizzle. Without my pack, I found myself racing up the five kilometers to the source, even though sections of the trail were as steep as a staircase. At that hour I met only a few pilgrims, though later in the morning when I returned to Janki Chatti there was a steady procession of yatris on their way to Yamnotri.

Here the valley narrows to a point where the opposite slope is hardly fifty feet away. Some of the oaks on either side lean out across this gorge, their branches almost touching. At places the trail is carved into the cliffs. Sections of the path have been paved with cement, which actually makes walking more treacherous in the monsoon, when algae turns the surface slick.

The temples at Yamnotri remain hidden from view until the final bend in the path. To the right the mountains open out into a broad gallery of cliffs where I counted six waterfalls dropping out of the clouds. To the left and ahead about a hundred meters is an untidy cluster of fifteen or twenty buildings squeezed into the upper end of the valley. The main temple itself was built only ten years ago. Earlier it was a temporary structure that had to be renovated each spring after the winter snow and ice had melted. Many of the newer buildings at Yamnotri are made of cement—flat, ugly walls that appear characterless against the granite cliffs.

I stopped to have a cup of tea at one of the stalls below the temple, and while I was sitting there two priests arrived and offered to guide me around. They were friendly young men, dressed in nylon jackets and jeans, with bright vermilion tilaks on their foreheads. At the tea shop I could purchase a pooja thali, or tray, containing all of the necessary items for worshiping the goddess, including a coconut and a plastic bottle for collecting water from the source. But as I told the priests, I wasn't interested in performing the full pooja and only wanted darshan of the goddess.

Rain was still falling as I crossed over a bridge above the river. At this point the Yamuna was hardly five feet in width, its source divided between dozens of tiny streams and waterfalls that descend into this valley. A few yards from the temple is a hot spring that flows out of a crack in the mountain, spurting jets of steam and leaving a gray rime of minerals on the rocks. The priests take cloth sachets of rice and dip these into the boiling water. The rice cooks in minutes and is fed to the pilgrims as prasad, in exchange for donations.

As I removed my shoes and approached the temple, two elderly priests stood up from where they had been keeping dry under a tin awning. The door of the temple was closed, since it was still early in the morning, but the priests quickly unlocked it and allowed me to pay my respects to the goddess. The light was poor but I could just make out the image of Yamuna Devi, draped in yards of embroidered cloth. Only her face was visible, an impassive expression carved out of dark stone. The priest pointed to a smaller idol, off to one side. Made of white marble, this was "Gauri Ganga," he told me. The contrast between the two river goddesses was striking—one pale, the other dark. Like her brother Yama, god of the dead, Yamuna Devi has a brooding, shadowy demeanor. She seems to belong to that sulfurous underworld from which the hot spring boils to the surface, the innermost sanctum of darkness and mystery. After I had completed my darshan of the goddess, the priests poured water into my palm with a silver spoon. I drank this water, then received a yellow tilak on my forehead and a pinch of suji halwa as prasad. Directly in front of the temple was a wooden box for offerings but after I put a few rupees inside, the priests made it clear that they expected to be tipped as well.

There are two tanks for pilgrims to bathe in at Yamnotri, where the flow from the hot spring is mixed with water from the river. The upper tank is reserved for men and the lower one, which drains from above, is only for women. I had arrived early enough in the morning to bathe alone, though later in the day it was so crowded that pilgrims had to stand in line before taking a dip. Stripping down to my shorts I stood in the rain for a minute, feeling the cold moisture all around me. The surface of the tank was steaming and the water was a murky green color so that I couldn't see the bottom. Recalling that pilgrims who perform ablutions at Yamnotri are spared a violent death, I couldn't help but wonder if the French woman who was murdered two months earlier had bathed in the hot spring.

Setting these thoughts aside, however, I stepped down into the tank. At first it felt so hot that I hesitated before going in any further. A series of steps, each about a foot high, descended into the tank and when I reached the bottom the water was above my waist. Exposed to the rain my head and shoulders were still cold despite the feathers of steam rising all around me. Folding my hands together I ducked beneath the surface of the tank. The immediate sensation of fluid warmth was comforting, and I stayed down as long as I could, eyes closed, my body hunched into a fetal position. Coming up for air a minute later, I let the water stream down my face before quickly plunging under again, eager to feel the soothing heat against my skin. Three weeks of walking were immediately forgotten and the aches in my joints and muscles were washed away. The questions and doubts that worried me at the beginning of this pilgrimage quickly dissolved in the enveloping warmth of the tank. Once more I stood up to breathe, then took a third and final dip, immersing myself in the source.

# II

# EXPERIENCE

## YAMNOTRI–GANGOTRI

*The waters of the sky or those that flow,
those that are dug out or those that arise by themselves,
those pure and clear waters that seek the ocean
as their goal—let the waters, who are
goddesses, help me here and now.*

RIG VEDA

# DECEMBER

FOUR MONTHS LATER, WHEN I RETURN IN WINTER, the green slopes of the Yamuna Valley have faded to brown. It hasn't rained for weeks. There are no clouds, no monsoon mists. The wildflowers and herbs on the bugiyals have withered into the soil. Seasonal springs are dry and the miles of mud that I walked through have turned to dust, a chalky tan that powders my boots.

Bandar Punch stands out against the sky, a sharp white silhouette, its twin summits connected by the serrated profile of an intervening ridge. I find it hard to believe that I never saw this mountain when I was here in August. It is huge, dominating the valley and rising above the lower ranges like a whitecapped tidal wave. On the lower slopes of Bandar Punch much of the snow has melted and black rocks show through—bleak cliffs and fractured troughs of stone.

The cold air has a brittle texture. Though the afternoon sun is warm, as it angles in between the pines, each breath I take seems to crystallize when it enters my lungs. I inhale the crisp odor of dry needles and the resinous scent of pine sap, which has formed thick scabs on the bark of trees along the trail. I can also smell a trace of wood smoke on the wind, the charred fragrance of burning twigs.

All of the chattis along the yatra route are closed. At this time of year there are no pilgrims going up to Yamnotri and the only people I pass are villagers on their way home. Several of the men are spinning wool as they walk along, using a drop spindle that twirls in their hands like a child's toy. Two teenage boys are leading a gray mule loaded down with bags of rice — provisions for the winter. A group of women are collecting decayed leaves in gunnysacks to fertilize their fields. Work continues on the extension of the motor road though progress has been slow, hardly a hundred meters since I was here in summer. Where the limestone cliffs are being cut away to widen the trail, a gang of laborers huddle around a fire. At first they look surprised as I walk by, then laugh uproariously.

The Yamuna itself has changed, no longer a flooded torrent but a ribbon of clear water that curls between margins of exposed rocks. Above the confluence at Hanuman Chatti the river is hardly ten or fifteen feet across and though there are waterfalls and rapids, at many places one could easily wade to the opposite shore. Earlier in the day, driving up the motor road, I saw where the Yamuna writhed between the ridges, following the drunken course that Balaram plowed. But in winter the current is calm, as if the river goddess has been placated. There are long pools where the water hardly seems to move at all, turning color from rusty green to turquoise blue as sandbars swell beneath the surface. Even where the Yamuna washes up against a line of cliffs it slides quietly past the rocks with only the slightest disturbance — a placid, sinuous stream. The sound of the river has also changed, the deafening roar of its floodwaters softened to a muted whisper, like distant voices on the wind.

Janki Chatti is deserted, tea stalls and restaurants boarded up. The dharamshalas and hotels are closed from November to

April and padlocks on the doors have been sewn up in cloth covers, stamped with sealing wax to discourage intruders. By now the sun has gone behind the ridge and only the high snow peaks are lit, a brassy color that quickly fades to sooty white. A pair of choughs, black as crows but with red beaks, flap from rock to rock, calling to each other with whistling cries. The valley is in shadow and the temperature has dropped below freezing. A leaking tapstand near the side of the trail is caked with ice.

As I reach the upper end of Janki Chatti, I see a figure coming toward me, an elderly man bundled up in a wool coat with a tattered balaclava on his head. We greet each other and he asks where I am going. When I tell him my plan to camp on the fields above, he shakes his head discouragingly.

"It's much too cold," he says. "I can give you a room."

The old man explains that he is the caretaker for one of the rest houses. Though most of the doors are locked and sealed, he has access to one room, which he is willing to rent. For him it is a chance to make a little extra money and for me an opportunity to avoid pitching my tent in the dark.

The rest house is directly above the trail but we must climb over a stone wall because the gate is chained and locked. The main building is a low cement structure with fifteen or twenty doorways opening onto a rectangular courtyard. Hari Shankar, the caretaker, leads me to the far end of the rest house where he shows me my quarters. As soon as we step inside, I regret taking him up on his offer. My flashlight casts a yellow beam over the piles of mattresses, quilts, and dented pillows that have been stacked from floor to ceiling. All of the bedding from other rooms has been collected here and the air is musty with the smell of unwashed linen. Next to the door is a single wooden bed, buried beneath layers of blankets and sheets. Hari Shankar shifts these aside and says encouragingly, "In here you won't feel cold."

He himself lives in a tin shack beside the rest house. A brahmin, Hari Shankar comes from the village of Kharsali, across the river. Later that evening, sitting by his fire, he tells me that he often hears leopards calling at night. They make a rough sawing noise, like the purring of a cat, but much louder and more menacing. During the pilgrim season the leopards keep their distance, retreating deep into the forest, but in winter they grow bolder and prowl about the empty buildings, feeding on stray dogs. Squinting in the smoky firelight, Hari Shankar imitates the call of a leopard, a hoarse, asthmatic sound that ends in a cough.

Returning to my room, I climb into my sleeping bag instead of using the piles of bedding. With the door closed, the smell of soiled sheets and quilts is stronger, the stale-sour stench of pilgrims who have long since departed. I fumble with the bolt on the window to get some air. A dog is barking on the far side of the valley, an anxious, hysterical yelping, as if it were lost. Other than this the night is silent. As I try to fall asleep, I listen for leopards and imagine them moving like liquid shadows through the deserted lanes of Janki Chatti, leaping from one rooftop to the next. A glimmer of starlight comes through the open window and I can just make out the mountains of cotton quilts that surround me in the darkness.

Once again I have left my wristwatch at home but I know that sunrise comes just after seven o'clock. As soon as the first light of dawn enters the window, I get up and make a cup of tea on my petrol stove, shivering as I wait for the water to boil. Leaving my pack in the room I start out along the trail to Yamnotri.

The sky is cloudless and the jagged snow peaks are gilded with streaks of yellow light. In the valley it is still gray and cold. My breath condenses as I start to climb, making my way up the twisting trail. The cliffs that dripped with water during the monsoon are now decorated with huge icicles hanging above my head and though there isn't any snow the ground is frozen. The waterfalls that I saw tumbling through the mist in August are mostly dry but some are draped with white incrustations that spill down the ravines like veins of milky ore. Though the moss and ferns have dried on the branches of the oaks, the dark green foliage remains throughout the winter. Most Himalayan trees do not lose their leaves in autumn but cast them off in spring and summer, as new foliage emerges. For this reason their limbs are never bare, even in the dead of winter.

At this hour of the morning there is no breeze at all and the forest is completely still. I stop to cast my eyes over the opposite ridge, hoping to catch sight of wild animals or birds, but there isn't the slightest movement. The landscape seems frozen, like a photograph in which nothing will ever change—this moment preserved in time. Even the stands of ringal bamboo with their brittle yellow leaves that rustle in the faintest breath of air remain motionless. I find myself transfixed as well. Staring at the cliffs across from me, I wait for a signal to release me from this spell, the twitching of a mountain goat's ear, or the flutter of a thrush's wing. But there is no sign of life. I can hear the sound of water in the gorge below but the river is hidden from view. Then all at once I see two birds come wheeling into sight, gliding across the tops of the ridges, a pair of griffon vultures. They seem to defy the stillness of the morning, the motionless air.

In certain Garhwali myths it is the vultures who created the earth. Tara Dutt Gairola recounts one version of the story in his book *Himalayan Folklore:*

In the beginning there was neither earth, nor sky, nor water. Nirankar, the Guru, alone existed. The Guru rubbed his right side and from the sweat thereof a female vulture was born. The Guru rubbed his left side and from the sweat thereof a male vulture was produced. Thus the female vulture was placed over the male. The name of the female vulture was Soni Garuri, and of the male, Brahma Garur. The Guru was surprised that while he wished to create human beings who would serve him, vultures were produced instead. The male vulture flew to the east and then to the north. He then came to marry Soni Garuri. Soni Garuri said, "O dear, you and I have been created by the same Guru and are brother and sister. How can we marry each other?" She then made taunting remarks about his ugly shape, which caused Brahma Garur to weep. Then Soni repented and picked up the tear-drops which had fallen from the Garur's eyes. The tears penetrated into her womb and she became pregnant. She flew to the abode of Brahma Garur and begged him to build a nest for her to lay eggs in. The Garur retorted, "You are an unchaste woman. How did you become pregnant? You are also very ugly. I cannot accept you as my wife." Soni began to weep. Brahma, who was moved by her helplessness, said, "There is neither earth nor water. Where can I build a nest for thee? Come, and lay eggs on my wings." Soni replied: "You are the vehicle of Vishnu and would be polluted by my laying eggs on your body."

The egg dropped down and was divided into two halves. The lower half became the earth and the upper half the sky. The fluids inside the egg became the sea and the fleshy substance the land.

Thus did Nirankar create the world.

Hari Shankar had told me that several sadhus lived at Yamnotri throughout the winter. As I reached the top of the final climb, where the switchbacks end and the trail levels off, I saw the temple and other buildings, still in shadow. I could also hear the sound of ringing bells echoing between the ridges. Passing the empty tea shops and crossing the bridge, I climbed the steps to the tank where I had bathed in August. The hot spring let off clouds of steam in the cold morning air. As I approached the Hanuman temple I could hear voices singing inside. The morning aarti was under way and when I peered through the door one of the figures inside beckoned for me to enter. Four sadhus and two other men stood with their hands folded in front of the image of Hanuman. The statue was three feet high and painted a bright vermilion. Hanuman's garments were made of embroidered silk and on the wall behind him was a pink satin backdrop. In one hand he held a mace. Next to the image of Hanuman was a smaller idol of Yamuna Devi. The sadhus were singing Sanskrit hymns and their voices harmonized in a tenor chorus far more inspirational than the recorded kirtan that blares over loudspeakers during the pilgrim season. Though I could understand none of the words, it was a moving experience to simply stand there and listen to their singing. After a quarter of an hour the aarti ended and the sadhus clapped their hands in unison, then prostrated themselves in front of the deity, kissing the cold stone floor.

The Hanuman temple at Yamnotri is actually a cave that has been enclosed with a wall in front. The interior is painted yellow, with some of the stones highlighted in red and green. The oldest sadhu sleeps next to the deities, on a low bed tucked into a shelf of the cave. There was a fire burning in a square grate, which was covered immediately after the prayers were finished. This fire is only used for worship and cooking is done in an adjacent room, where the rest of the sadhus live.

Following the aarti each of us was given a sip of Yamuna water by one of the younger sadhus, who poured it into the cupped palms of our hands. He also distributed puffed rice and roasted channa as prasad. I could tell there was an established hierarchy within the group, for the two younger sadhus attended to the ceremony while their elders gave instructions. In addition to the four ascetics there was a young brahmin from Kharsali and a Nepali boy, who seemed to be an acolyte.

The eldest sadhu must have been over seventy, and he had a benevolent smile and gentle eyes. His long white hair was wrapped around his head in matted strands like coils of rope. He wore an unstitched strip of cotton cloth that was tied about his chest and fell below his knees. His only other garment was a woolen shawl that he draped about himself when he sat down. The baba told me that he had been living at Yamnotri since 1967. He had seen the dham change from a couple of simple shrines to the present complex of rest houses and tea stalls. Complaining that the government didn't do enough to protect the sanctity of the source, he said that many of the rest houses were only there to make money instead of serving pilgrims. He also blamed the forestry department for doing little to protect the plants and wildlife in the valley. "All kinds of animals used to come here in winter—bharal, thar, ghoral, leopards, and bear, but I haven't seen them for years. People are digging up the wild herbs everywhere and burning all of the trees for firewood." In the thirty-three years that he had lived there the baba had never gone down the valley, not even as far as Janki Chatti. "I live here thirteen months of the year," he said with a laugh.

When I asked about the trail to Saptrishi Kund, a lake in the mountains above Yamnotri, the sadhu said it was another twelve kilometers farther on but warned me not to go there at this time of year. "It gets so cold you cannot breathe. Come in summer, when the flowers bloom. Their perfume will make you dizzy." At this point one of the younger sadhus told me that he had accompanied the baba to Saptrishi Kund many years ago. When they reached the lake the baba had blown his conch so loudly that it caused an avalanche. After we had talked for half an hour or more the sadhus served breakfast, pieces of toasted bread soaked in honey and butter. They also offered me a glass of tea made with cloves, cinnamon, and ginger. "This will give you warmth," they said.

Though these sadhus seemed to live a relatively comfortable life at Yamnotri it was obvious that once the snow fell in early January, the valley would be cut off completely from the rest of the world. In addition to their isolation the sadhus faced other threats at this time of year. During severe winters the snow and ice often damaged the temple buildings, collapsing roofs and walls. The baba told me that twelve years ago an avalanche came down the valley and destroyed the Yamuna Devi temple and swept away the bridge. That year the snow was piled so high that the entrance to the Hanuman temple was completely buried and the sadhus had to tunnel their way out of the cave.

Even the goddess forsakes Yamnotri during winter. Each November, after the festival of Diwali, the priests remove the image of Yamuna Devi from her temple. She is carried down the valley to Kharsali, which is her winter home. The deity is transported in an ornate palanquin on the shoulders of the priests. Drummers and dancers accompany the procession, which marks the end of the pilgrimage season.

Many of the shrines throughout Garhwal are closed during winter and the gods and goddesses are put away in seclusion for several months, observing a ritual hiatus. The timing of these ceremonies varies from temple to temple. Driving up to Hanuman Chatti the day before, I had passed several processions of villagers carrying their deities down to the riverbank to immerse them in the waters of the Yamuna, in preparation for closing the shrines. Above the town of Barkot I passed a procession of forty men and women carrying a local goddess to the river. Her palanquin, a portable shrine made of wood and silver, was festooned with scarves of red and pink and yellow. The deity inside was hidden from view, as if she were a veiled bride. Hanging like tassels from the corners of the shrine were whisks of black hair that looked like yak's tails. There were two drummers, one who carried a large double-sided dhol and the other a tambourine-like drum, known as damaun. When I passed them they were beating a desultory rhythm and the whole procession looked forlorn, with all of the devotees bundled up against the cold. The only member of the group who seemed at all animated was an older man carrying a ceremonial sword, which he waved above his head as if he were defending the goddess. Later on I saw another similar group gathered on the banks of the Yamuna. Some of them were bathing in the river, even though the temperature was close to freezing.

Kharsali lies directly across the river from Janki Chatti. It is home to the brahmin priests who preside at the Yamnotri temples. By tradition they control much of the pilgrim traffic up and down this valley. Unlike the sadhus who live an ascetic existence, forswearing material possessions and depending on the charity of pilgrims, the brahmins jealously guard their spiritual domain and enjoy the wealth that it provides. Most of the property in Janki Chatti belongs to the brahmins and they earn rent from many of the rest houses and food stalls along this section of the pilgrim route.

Situated on a broad plateau just above the river, Kharsali is a large settlement of about two hundred houses. A generous expanse of terraced fields surrounds the village. Most of the houses are traditional Garhwali homes, two-story structures made of stone and wood, with carved balconies overlooking a narrow courtyard where buffaloes, cows, and goats are tethered. The cattle are usually stabled on the ground floor while members of the household live above. Roofs in the village are made of slate and the homes are built close together, with narrow lanes between. In winter the roofs and courtyards are often used for drying pumpkins and squashes, as well as nuts, herbs, and spices. Many of the houses in Kharsali have storerooms that stand apart from the main building. These are sturdily built to keep out insects, rats, and other vermin, the wooden doors tightly sealed. One of the storerooms that I looked inside had a lower chamber for keeping potatoes and above this were separate compartments for rice, wheat, and other grain. The doors and lintels were ornately carved with floral patterns, which decorate most of the woodwork in Garhwali homes.

There were several small shops in Kharsali, selling dry goods, cooking oil, packaged biscuits, and cigarettes. One of these also served as a post office, and when I asked the proprietor how often the mail was delivered, he said, "Every day until the snow falls. After that it depends if the postman can walk up from Hanuman Chatti."

When I visited Kharsali on my way back down from Yamnotri, I had a feeling that the whole village was preparing for the winter storms that would come in January. Though Kharsali is far more accessible than Yamnotri and fifteen hundred feet lower in altitude, the village can be snowed in for weeks at a time. Each of the houses had stacks of dry wood that had been gathered for fuel, as well as piles of leaves and grass for fodder.

In the midday sun, a group of fifteen or twenty men were gathered in a courtyard near the center of the village. Soaking in the warmth of the day, they were smoking and talking among themselves. With the pilgrims gone and the crops harvested there wasn't much to occupy their time. Yamuna Devi was safely locked away in her winter quarters, a surprisingly modern building on the outskirts of the village. Her shrine was made of cement and looked more like a middle-class bungalow than a sanctuary for the river goddess. The building was painted a dull ocher and the only decorations were a few strings of tinsel above the main door and an old election poster pasted on one wall promoting a candidate from the Bharatiya Janata Party.

Though the brahmin priests of Kharsali attend to the worship of Yamuna Devi, the largest temple in their village is dedicated to Shani Devta, god of the planet Saturn. He is known throughout India as a dark and unpredictable deity. Astrologers warn that if a man is born under the inauspicious sign of Saturn he will endure continuous suffering and misfortune. For this reason Shani is worshiped more out of fear than devotion.

The temple of Shani Devta stands in the center of Kharsali, facing an open courtyard paved with flagstones. It is an unusual structure, about sixty feet high, made of wooden beams and rough-hewn blocks of stone. Though the walls of the temple form a rectangular tower, none of the lines is straight, and the building has a precarious appearance, as if it were about to fall down. All of the villagers I spoke with remarked on the antiquity of this shrine and said that it had stood there longer than anyone could remember. There is no written record of its construction and several of the villagers told me that Shani Devta's temple was much older than any of the other shrines in the Yamnotri Valley. One of the young men in the village, who appointed himself my guide, showed me a faint inscription carved into a stone staircase leading up to the entrance. He said that it was written in a language nobody could decipher.

The only doorway to the temple is about fifteen feet above the ground, a narrow opening in the wall through which you have to stoop to enter. Inside there is darkness, no lamps or candles. Having removed my boots I could feel the wooden boards underfoot that creaked with our weight. There was a stale smell inside the temple, like a closet that is seldom opened. As my eyes adjusted slowly to the darkness I was able to make out the shape of a ladder. It was actually the trunk of a deodar tree that had been sawed in half and notched at intervals. The wood was polished smooth from years of use and crawling upward I felt as if I was inside a hollow tree. Reaching up, my hand brushed against the edge of the ceiling, which opened onto another floor. A few chinks of light came through the walls on the second level, just enough for me to see that the interior was bare, like a dusty, disused attic. I felt uneasy, as if we were burglars breaking into a vacant house. The structure didn't feel like a temple at all, more like a sanctuary for ghosts. Another ladder took us up to the third floor, which was divided into several smaller rooms.

One of these was occupied by the shrine of Shani Devta. Most of the space was empty, except for a wooden altar against one wall. The idol itself was wrapped in silk and cotton scarves, with only the face visible, a silver mask with androgynous features—wide eyes and broad lips that bore no trace of emotion, a humorless god who seemed to ignore our presence. My guide had lit a match for me to view the deity and in that brief flash of light the room seemed suddenly smaller, the stone walls closing in around us. In front of the deity was a tray for worship, which contained several small bowls. The young man picked up the tray and putting his thumb into one of the bowls, he smeared a vermilion tilak on my forehead. He also offered me some suji halwa as prasad but I declined because it looked as if it had been there for weeks. After that, my guide lit another match and showed me two large clay pots that lay on a shelf above our heads. They looked like giant eggs, each of them two feet in diameter. He explained that nobody knew what these contained. The pots had never been opened in anyone's memory but every year they were repositioned—the one on the left was moved to the right and the one on the right was moved to the left. This was one of the ceremonies conducted in honor of Shani Devta during a festival in early April. Though I questioned the young man and others in the village about the significance of the clay pots, nobody could give me an answer. They shrugged their shoulders in response, an unexplained mystery handed down from the past.

Before leaving Shani Devta's temple, I was shown another room on the third floor. Again, it was mostly empty but had a square window that the young man opened. A narrow wooden balcony, hardly wide enough for one person to kneel upon, overlooked the slate rooftops of Kharsali. The window faced toward Yamnotri and crouching on the balcony I could see the snow peaks at the head of the valley.

Directly across from the temple of Shani Devta stood another shrine. This one was made almost entirely of deodar wood and intricately carved, so that not a single surface was without some form of decoration. The roof was peaked and all along the eaves hung a fringe of wooden tassels, many of which were missing or broken. Each of the columns supporting the roof and all of the walls had floral designs chiseled into the wood, as well as images of animals, birds, and mythological beasts. Inside the shrine, however, it looked abandoned. There was no resident deity or idol that I could see and when I asked about this temple the villagers of Kharsali said that it was hardly ever used, except during the annual festivals for Shani Devta. Some of the woodwork was cracked and weathered but most of the temple's exterior was in relatively good condition, the deodar wood aged a rich brown color. Jammed into the cracks or nailed into the wooden beams and pillars were hundreds of coins, including old silver rupees bearing the image of Queen Victoria or George V, along with other more recent offerings.

The most intriguing aspect of this temple, however, was the image of a tiger that stood atop its roof. About three feet long and made of bronze, it had a curving tail and stripes etched into the tarnished metal. The mouth was open in a snarl and from its position on the peak of the temple roof the tiger seemed to be surveying the mountains with a predatory eye. The villagers identified the statue as a "bagh," which is the term most commonly used for leopards, though it can also refer to tigers. In Garhwal there is often confusion between the two, for tigers are extremely rare in the mountains, while leopards are more common, though seldom seen. Hindu iconography uses the tiger in many different ways, most commonly as the vahana, or vehicle, of the goddess Durga. When I inquired about the significance of the tiger at Kharsali, a few of the villagers said it was the vehicle of Shani Devta. Others contradicted this and claimed that Shani actually took the form of a bagh when he roamed through the jungle and those who worshiped him would never be attacked.

The bronze image was not very old and I was informed that it had been cast in the town of Dehradun, at the foot of the Himalayas, and brought up to Kharsali ten or fifteen years earlier. Crouched beneath the eaves of this temple, however, I discovered a much older tiger, which had been carved out of wood. It was badly weathered and worn with age but far more beautiful than the metal image. The Garhwali craftsman who created this beast had given it a stylized form. The tail curved up and over its back, the eyes were alert, and the mouth was open in a threatening grimace. Its body was not as sleek as the metal tiger's but nevertheless it conveyed a sense of feline grace and power. Though the wood was so badly damaged it was impossible to tell if there were stripes or not, this ancient image of the bagh was covered with silver coins nailed into its shoulders and flanks, giving it the appearance of a leopard.

The morning after I visited Kharsali, I was setting out along the pilgrim trail, when I saw a man come running down the hill. He did not call out but waved his hand anxiously for me to stop. I had never seen this man before and was puzzled by his sudden appearance and the urgency he conveyed. Even though he was rushing down the path above me, it took several minutes before he arrived at the point where I was standing. Out of breath and looking anxiously about he spoke in a nervous whisper.

"Do you want to buy a tiger skin?"

Startled, I looked at him in disbelief. He was a thin, wiry man with a gray mustache, and his clothes were ragged and patched. He blew into his cupped hands for warmth and was shivering, whether from cold or anxiety, it was hard to tell. The word he'd used for tiger was "sher" and I asked him if he really meant a tiger or was it the skin of a leopard that he was trying to sell?

The man nodded reluctantly and confirmed it was a leopard.

"Did you shoot it?" I asked.

Glancing over his shoulder once again, as if the forest guards were tailing him, he shook his head.

"No. It was shot by someone else. But I can get the skin for you."

"What am I going to do with it?" I said.

Sensing the tone of disapproval in my voice he stepped back and hesitated.

"Do you want to buy the skin or not?" he asked.

"No," I said.

Eyeing me suspiciously, he turned without another word and disappeared back up the trail. It was obvious that he was a poacher from one of the villages nearby. Seeing an outsider walking alone, he must have thought that I would be interested in buying a leopard skin, even though it is illegal. Perhaps others like myself had come before and willingly bought from him. This strange, abrupt encounter left me feeling unsettled and depressed. For the rest of the day I kept thinking of the leopard skin, the intricate pattern of its spots, black rosettes on a field of gold.

Like the rare flowers and herbs that are dug up from the bugiyals and sold for medicine, tigers and leopards have become a commodity, their teeth, claws, and bones ground up to provide cures for human frailties. In this way their value is lessened and we lose touch with the elemental quality of nature. There can be no comparison between the dry skin of a leopard and the experience of walking through a forest knowing that feline predators still inhabit the Himalayas, even if they remain invisible. We do not need to see these great cats to feel their presence but once they are gone forever, the forests will be diminished by their absence.

# LOST TRAILS

FOR YEARS THE YAMUNA VALLEY WAS CONSIDERED
one of the most isolated and undeveloped regions of Garhwal,
compared to the more prosperous and populous valleys of the
Bhagirathi and Alakananda. To the west lay the rugged ranges
of Jaunsar, which form a natural barrier between Garhwal and
the hill districts of Himachal Pradesh. Being the most remote
territory of the former kingdom of Tehri Garhwal, this section
of the mountains suffered neglect from both the maharajah and
the British. Even after independence the Yamuna Valley was
largely ignored and only recently have the people of this region
been able to assert political demands and get a share of government resources. With the extension of motor roads the watershed of the Yamuna is gradually opening up, and towns like
Barkot and Nainbagh have grown considerably in the past ten
years. Nevertheless, there are many villages that remain isolated
and at higher elevations the mountains are sparsely populated
and covered in forests of virgin oak and pine.

Jaunsar district, along the western bank of the river, is associated with many of the myths and legends from the Mahabharata. The village of Lakhamandal, for instance, is named after
a palace of wax in which the heroic Pandavs nearly lost their
lives when it was set on fire. Not only are these stories part of
Jaunsar's mythological history, they are also a way of life. Some

of the villagers in this part of the Himalayas practice polyandry, with several husbands sharing a single wife, though the custom is fast disappearing. This tradition can be traced back to Draupadi, who was married to all five of the Pandav brothers. In this way the people and culture of Jaunsar are inextricably linked to the symbolic heritage of their religious past. As with many popular Hindu traditions, however, there is also a reversal of these myths. In a number of temples near the headwaters of the Yamuna there are shrines dedicated to the Kuravs, who are generally considered villains in the Mahabharata. During certain festivals in parts of Jaunsar the exploits of the Kuravs are celebrated, as if they were the heroes of the epic rather than their Pandav cousins.

I had originally planned to walk down the Yamuna Valley to a village called Gangani, where the main branch of the pilgrim route cuts across to Uttarkashi. However, this would have meant following the motor road for several days, which didn't appeal to me. At a tea shop in Syana Chatti, where I spent one night, I got into a conversation with three dairy farmers. They advised me to take an alternate route, climbing up to the village of Kupra, then crossing over to Kapola and from there to Uprikot and Uttarkashi. These men assured me that this was a much shorter way to go, though none of them was sure exactly how long it would take. The most optimistic estimate was that I could reach Uttarkashi in a day.

"It all depends on your stride," said one of the men. "If you walk steadily, you'll get there in a few hours. If you go slowly and keep stopping, it could take a week."

Having learned from past experience that distances in the mountains are difficult to predict, I was skeptical of their pronouncements on the relative shortness of this route. What interested me most of all, however, was that I would be crossing two forested ranges far above any motor roads. The farmers explained that for most of the route there was a clearly marked trail and only at a few places would I need to "find my way through the jungle," as they put it.

Though I didn't have a map with me I wasn't concerned about getting lost, for the weather was clear and even in the most isolated regions there are usually chaans or villages along the way where one can ask directions. At the very worst I would have to camp along the trail for a night or two. I had my tent and enough supplies to keep me fed for several days.

Just above Syana Chatti a new bridge was being built, the first stage of a motor road to Kupra village. After scrambling over a landslide caused by this construction, I found myself on an old chey-footia trail that circled up the ridge through a forest of ash and dogwood trees. Even though it was a steep climb, the walk was pleasant and I covered the first five kilometers in under an hour. Kupra is situated about fifteen hundred feet above the Yamuna and from that height there is a spectacular view of Bandar Punch. The village is fairly large, about a hundred houses clustered together on the northwest face of the ridge, which broadens into a series of gently rolling slopes. Most of the area around Kupra is heavily cultivated and terraced fields corrugate the mountain.

In the center of the village stands a wooden temple similar to the one I saw in Kharsali, except that instead of a tiger on the roof of this shrine there is a monal pheasant. The beams and pillars are carved with images of buffaloes and goats as well as the horned heads of serow and ghoral, two species of goat-antelope found in these mountains. There were also a number of snakes depicted on the wooden pillars and one of the men I spoke with told me that this was a nag mandir, where the cobra is worshiped as the primary deity. Unfortunately, the temple was closed for winter, a brass padlock on the door. In a shed to one side I saw a stack of enormous iron cooking vessels, which the villagers use to prepare feasts during festivals.

The monal pheasant on the roof was carved out of wood and painted yellow, green, and purple, with a prominent crest. From its perch atop the temple, the bird seemed as if it were about to give a shrill warning call and fly away into the valley. Also known as the impeyan pheasant, monal are one of the most flamboyant birds in the Himalayas and relatively common at higher altitudes. In fact, only a short distance beyond Kupra I flushed a covey of monal, one of which was a large male with iridescent plumage who exploded out of the bushes with a chuckling scream and rocketed down the hill, followed by three dusty brown females. There is nothing more startling than the sudden flurry of wings when a pheasant takes to the air.

Even though it was winter there were plenty of birds to be found. Aside from the monal, I came across two other kinds of pheasant, kalij and koklas, as well as a pair of gray partridges at the edge of a millet field. Lower down, along the riverbank, I had seen white-capped redstarts and spotted forktails. In the bushes beside the trail were dozens of streaked laughing thrushes that scooted about in the dry leaves like feathered rats. I also kept hearing the whistling call of scimitar babblers, hiding in the undergrowth. Red-billed blue magpies and black-capped jays interrupted the silence of the forest with their raucous chatter. Just above Kupra, I saw flashes of yellow at the edge of the forest and spotted a party of ten or fifteen grosbeaks, feeding on dry berries and nuts.

Few things in nature can capture our imagination as vividly as birds, with their effortless flight, the color of their feathers, their musical cries. They can soar, glide, flap, and flutter through the air, perch on trees, rooftops, and rocky crags, peck and scratch about in the soil, even swim and dive underwater. Unlike human beings and most mammals they are not confined by the force of gravity, at least not to the same degree, and experience the world in all three dimensions. How many of us have wished, at one time or another, that we could be a bird? Their presence in a forest brings the trees to life and unlike insects, who may claim the greatest diversity of species, birds seem to have a mind of their own. They flock together but also scatter. Inherently eccentric, birds never seem to travel in a straight line, despite the saying, "as the crow flies." Anyone who has watched a crow sculpting the wind with its wings will understand that there is no curve or spiral, no circle or parabola, that these artists of the air cannot describe. Even the most diminutive birds have a rare quality that continually fascinates us.

Resting under the shade of a rhododendron tree, I watched as a feeding party of tiny birds passed through the branches overhead. Altogether there must have been five or six different species in the group. White-eyes and red-headed tits were the first to arrive, flitting nervously through the leaves. These were followed by leaf warblers, green-backed tits, and velvet-fronted nuthatches, picking at the dry moss and bark in search of seeds, worms, or insects. Their movements were quick and agitated, each bird intent on gleaning hidden morsels from the tree. Though they communicated among themselves through chirps and whistles, the birds seemed independent of each other, like flighty gourmets sampling delicacies at a movable feast.

Rounding the crest of the ridge above Kupra I immediately smelled smoke. During winter, after the villagers finish cutting fodder, they often set these slopes on fire to burn away dead grass and promote new growth. At this time of year there is seldom any danger of these fires spreading out of control, but if it is particularly dry the forests are occasionally threatened. This system of burning grass in Garhwal is controversial. Most environmentalists claim it is a shortsighted practice that marginally increases the fodder yield, while destroying many plants and saplings. Others believe that burning off the grass in winter protects the forests against more serious fires that break out during May and June. There may be some truth in this but nothing is more destructive than a fire, even one that is deliberately lit, for it burns everything in its path and drives away birds and animals.

The trail I was following cut straight across a line of cliffs on the southern face of the mountain. The cliffs dropped away five hundred feet or more, and ascended an equal distance above the path. Most of the fires were burning slowly upward, ruffled plumes of smoke unfurling on the breeze. At a few places the flames had already crossed the trail and the ridge was blackened, a charred expanse of soot and ash. Not knowing how far the fires extended I was hesitant to keep going but there was clearly no other way around the cliffs. At points the smoke was so thick I had to hold a handkerchief over my mouth and nose though as soon as the wind changed direction, I was able to breathe again.

The grass fires had spread up to a point where the main ridge curved in on itself like a shallow bowl and the cliffs gave way to trees. By the time I entered the forest my eyes were burning and my throat felt raw from the smoke. The destruction caused by the fire may not have been that great, but I felt as if I had just passed through a smoldering wasteland, the near-vertical face of the mountain scorched bare of life.

During the monsoon I had found plenty of seasonal springs; but now most of the ravines were dry and even the larger streams were reduced to a slow trickle between the rocks. In the forest, however, there was a distinct feeling of dampness. The branches of the oaks were so thick overhead that hardly any sunlight reached the forest floor. At places there was frost on the ground, turning the carpet of dead leaves a ghostly white. Eventually I came to a rivulet flowing through a mossy channel. Throwing down my pack I splashed water on my face to clear my eyes from the smoke. Cupping one hand I drank as much as I could from the spring, tasting a pleasant bitterness in the water that came from minerals in the soil.

I had been sitting by this spring for about five minutes when I heard footsteps. A short while later two men appeared through the trees, one of them carrying a muzzle-loading shotgun. Both of them were in their sixties, thin and slightly built with weathered faces and stubble on their chins. They seemed almost as surprised to find me there as I was to see them. The two hunters raised their hands in a cautious salute.

After drinking at the spring, they sat down and each smoked a bidi. When I asked them what they were hunting for, they claimed that the gun was only for protection, in case they were attacked by bears or leopards. It was a rusty weapon with a single, twelve-gauge barrel. The ramrod was made of brass and the wooden stock was pitted and scratched. The gun must have been as old as the hunters themselves for it had a hammer mechanism for firing, which was uncocked.

"What animals live in this forest?" I asked.

"Ghoral and barking deer," said one of the men.

"What about musk deer?"

Both eyed me nervously, with the same furtive expression as the poacher who had tried to sell me the leopard skin.

"Yes, there are probably a few in this forest," said one, "but we haven't seen any."

I tried to ask more questions though the men were clearly uneasy. They quickly changed the subject, inquiring if I had any medicine for a toothache. One of the hunters held his hand gingerly against his jaw. From my first aid kit I gave him two painkillers, which he swallowed immediately. After that, they headed off in the direction of Kupra.

Poaching is a serious problem in Garhwal and the musk deer is one of the most endangered species in the Himalayas. Scent glands from this timid creature can fetch thousands of rupees and are used for manufacturing perfume and medicine. Though synthetic equivalents are now readily available, there is still a thriving black market in musk, one of the most obscene trades in the world today. A rare and harmless creature is slaughtered for a tiny gland that weighs no more than six ounces. Illegal hunting for the musk deer is highly organized, with a network of poachers and middlemen stretching all the way from Nepal, through India and Pakistan. Earlier, in August, I had met a Nepali laborer near Hanuman Chatti who told me that he had recently accompanied a professional poacher and they had shot a total of seven musk deer in these forests. Though the penalties for trading in musk are high, the forestry department is poorly equipped to deal with poachers and they are seldom arrested. Compared to the commercial hunters who use high-powered rifles, the two men I met, with their battered muzzle loader and rotting molars, hardly seemed a threat to the musk deer. At the same time, however, they would certainly have killed one if it had crossed their path.

The hunters had given me directions to Kapola and for the next mile and a half the trail was clearly marked, as it rounded the north face of the ridge. At places there were patches of snow but it was easy walking and eventually I came out of the woods and onto sloping pastures. Ahead of me I could see a ruined chaan and next to it a pond of water about thirty feet across and a hundred feet in length. It was a dirty green color and the frozen mud along the shore had been trampled into craters by the hooves of buffaloes that had wallowed here in summer. During winter the cattle are herded to lower elevations and the surface of the water hole was covered with a brittle skin of ice.

Beyond the frozen pond the trail dispersed in a maze of goat paths and there was no way to tell which of these I should follow. Casting about, I discovered several more chaans, all of them abandoned for the winter. Near one of these was a troop of rhesus monkeys that were quarreling with each other, their nasal screams and snarling strangely out of place in the silence of the mountains. I couldn't tell what they were fighting over but the larger monkeys kept charging at each other with their teeth bared. They were so caught up in their battle that none of them noticed as I walked by.

My instincts told me that I should continue on a level but after following several indistinct trails, I kept coming to the edge of an impassable cliff. It was as if the mountain had been cut in half by a cleaver, a straight wall of rock dropping away into the valley. Eventually, in frustration, I began to climb the ridge, hoping that somewhere higher up I'd find a path to take me across the cliffs. Entering the forest once again I scrambled through the underbrush, keeping as close to the edge of the rock face as I dared. From the trees above me I could hear the plaintive, pulsing cry of Himalayan barbets. These birds make a wailing sound—*piao...piao...piao*. In the folklore of Garhwal barbets are said to be the spirits of destitute farmers complaining about the burden of unpaid debts. Green, clumsy-looking birds with broad beaks and purple heads, Himalayan barbets are about the size of a small crow and they often sit atop the highest trees. Their melancholy cries can go on for hours, with more than a dozen birds calling at once in a despondent chorus.

After climbing five or six hundred feet I came to an open meadow, bordered on the one side by cliffs and on the other by moru oaks. Where the ridge leveled off I could see the snow

peaks of Bandar Punch. The wind was blowing from the north
and it was strong enough to make me feel uneasy while walking
near the cliff, as if a sudden gust might sweep me off my feet. At
the highest point on the meadow stood a cairn of rocks with a
leafless branch stuck in the middle like a flagstaff.

By this time I was exhausted from the climb and shrugging
off my pack I lay down in the grass next to the cairn. After a few
minutes I noticed that the twigs on the branch were decorated
with glass and plastic bangles of different colors, which must
have been left as offerings by women cutting grass. There were
also a number of coins, ten, twenty-five, and fifty paisa pieces,
which had been pressed into cracks in the bark. It was a
makeshift shrine, with no visible deity or permanent structure.
Yet the crude shape of the cairn surmounted by the twisted
branch conveyed an eloquent simplicity. Seen against the dramatic backdrop of the high snow mountains, it affected me as
much as the temples at Yamnotri or Kharsali, with their elaborate decorations. Whoever had built the cairn, perhaps several
different people over several years, must have recognized a spiritual presence in this place. The dead branch trembled in the
wind and as I lay there in the dry grass, still breathing heavily
from my climb, I could feel the emptiness beyond the cliffs, a
sense of negative space. If I were to have rolled off the edge I
imagined that it would take forever to fall into the valley. Looking in the other direction I saw the snow mountains arranged
against the sky like an artificial backdrop. Though several kilometers away they seemed almost close enough to touch.

The barbets were still calling mournfully and after a few
minutes two lammergeiers came racing overhead. Their wings
made a loud humming noise as the pair shot out over the cliffs
and disappeared into the sun. The name lammergeier means
"lamb vulture" in German and these birds have an undeserved
reputation for killing sheep, especially in Europe, where they

have been hunted to the brink of extinction. Salim Ali, India's greatest ornithologist, defends the lammergeiers in his classic book *Indian Hill Birds*. "In spite of frequent allegations, it has never been known to attack live animals," he writes. With a wingspan of up to nine feet, the lammergeier is sometimes called the bearded vulture because of a tuft of black feathers that protrudes beneath its chin. Though it does not have an ugly bald head and neck like most vultures, the lammergeier is a scavenger. These birds have a peculiar habit of carrying bones high into the air then dropping them on the rocks below. When the bones shatter the lammergeier swoops down and feeds on the marrow.

From the top of the ridge I could see where several valleys converged and beyond these lay a series of ranges to the south; but at that moment I felt as if I were sitting on the edge of the world. I probably would have rested there for several hours, content to lie in the grass and meditate upon the scene, but a few minutes after the lammergeiers soared past I heard the sound of a breaking branch. It came from the direction I had climbed, about fifty meters down the ridge. Rolling over I looked back, puzzled by the noise. Almost immediately there was another cracking sound and I noticed a movement in one of the oaks. At first I thought it must be a villager cutting firewood or fodder, then I heard a gruff, mumbling sound and realized it was a black bear. Sitting in the branches of the oak, it was feeding on the few remaining acorns that hadn't fallen to the ground. Lying perfectly still, I watched the bear reach up and twist a clump of leaves with one paw. Though the animal was too far away for me to observe its face, I could clearly see the white chevron on its chest.

Of all the creatures in the Himalayas, bears have the worst reputation for being ill-tempered and dangerous. Their eyesight is poor and they rely mostly on their sense of smell. With the wind blowing in the opposite direction, I probably walked right under this bear, neither of us noticing the other's presence. Lying next to the cairn I realized that the wisest thing for me to do would be to circle around the upper end of the meadow and slip back into the forest. There was obviously no way that I could descend directly into the valley and I certainly didn't want to get trapped between the bear and the cliffs. Rising cautiously, I shouldered my pack. The bear grunted several more times but these were sounds of contented feeding rather than aggression and it took no notice of my hurried escape.

Though there wasn't a path where I entered the forest, I knew that if I kept going down the north side of the ridge, eventually I would rejoin the trail. The moru oaks rose above me like massive columns supporting matted domes of leaves. After the bright sunlight on the ridge and the strong wind, the forest was dark and still. I could see where one or two of the oaks had been felled by shepherds for timber but the forest was mostly unspoiled. Every few feet I stopped to make sure the bear wasn't following but there was total silence. Even the barbets could not be heard. Finally, after half an hour, I found myself back at the spring where I had met the two hunters earlier that day. It was discouraging to have gone in a circle and wasted so much time, but the experience of being on the ridge was more than adequate compensation.

By now it was late in the afternoon and as I reached the frozen pond, the sun was starting to go down over the ridges to the west. The rhesus monkeys seemed to have resolved their dispute and were foraging in a clump of barberry bushes near the empty chaans. Once again I was faced with the dilemma of finding a path across the cliffs and after several wrong turns I eventually discovered a faint trail that led me down to a parallel ridge from where I could see the village of Kapola. It was over a thousand feet below, right at the bottom of the valley, a group of fifteen houses encircled by fields.

As the light was fading I began to hurry down the ridge. The path was slippery with gravel and pine needles. Having walked most of the day I was tired; and the steep descent made my knees ache. It seemed to take forever to reach the stream, and by the time I staggered into Kapola, it was almost dark.

A couple of dogs began to bark but there was a group of men standing near the edge of the village who shooed them away and welcomed me. One of them was a young man named Chander Singh, whose father turned out to be the pradhan, or headman, of Kapola. He immediately invited me into his house for a cup of tea and offered to let me stay the night.

Much smaller than Kharsali or Kupra, Kapola did not seem as prosperous a village, though the houses were solidly built and well maintained. Being winter most of the fields lay fallow. Cattle were tied indoors on the ground floor of Chander's house. Above this were two stories with open balconies. In the courtyard outside a couple of women were grinding grain, using heavy wooden pestles in mortars carved from stone. Each of the rooms in the house had low ceilings, no more than six feet high, and the beams were made of oak. There was no chimney and the house was filled with smoke from the cooking fires. As we drank our tea, Chander explained that the nearest motor road was about fifteen kilometers down in the valley, where the stream from their village joined the Yamuna. When he learned that I was on my way to Uttarkashi, Chander said that he had some business there and offered to accompany me the next day. In the fading twilight, he pointed out a high ridge on the other side of the village that we would have to cross.

Though I suggested that I pitch my tent in the fields nearby, Chander was adamant that I should sleep in his house. "What would it look like if I let you stay outdoors?" he said, shaking his head. This spontaneous hospitality was something I found wherever I went in Garhwal, particularly in villages cut off from motor roads. Later that evening a group of six men gathered in Chander's house. Most of them were from Kapola though one man told me that his home was in Bhebara, near Dodi Tal. He was visiting his daughter, who was married to a man in Kapola.

We sat around the indoor hearth and after a few minutes one of the men produced a bottle from the pocket of his coat. It contained a homebrewed liquor called kacchi, which literally means "raw stuff," and is made from unprocessed cane sugar. A clear drink, not quite as strong as vodka, kacchi is virtually flavorless with a slightly bitter aftertaste. Though I have drunk kacchi in the past, this time I declined when offered a glass, explaining that I was on a pilgrimage. The men accepted this excuse and did not press me to have a drink. Pouring an inch or two in their glasses and tossing it back in a single swallow, they emptied the bottle quickly. Soon afterward a second bottle appeared from the folds of another man's coat and the conversation grew livelier. The visitor from Bhebara was particularly talkative. He claimed to have accompanied the police party that went to search for the French couple who were murdered in May. Through him I learned that the Frenchman's body had finally been discovered and that several goatherds had been arrested for the crime. In gruesome detail, the man from Bhebara described how they had found the woman's body with her hands tied behind her back and her head cut off. He said that the goatherds had confessed to robbing and killing the French couple, after the police found them in possession of their belongings.

"You should never walk alone in the mountains," he said. "It isn't safe."

When I told him about the bear I'd seen that day he nodded emphatically. "You see. What would you have done if it had attacked you? Tomorrow, you must take Chander Singh with you. He will show you the way to Uttarkashi."

Meanwhile, Chander had helped himself to the dregs from the second bottle and was staring into the fire with a contented look on his face. While the others grew more voluble the kacchi seemed to make him silent and withdrawn.

Since I was not drinking, a plate of rice and dal was brought for me by one of the women in the household. At the same time a third bottle had appeared and the men's speech was getting slurred. Abruptly two of them began arguing though the others calmed them down, and most of their conversation was friendly banter. After finishing my meal I excused myself and went into an adjoining room to sleep.

Lying in bed I could hear a rattling noise on the floor boards above me, as if a child were playing with a top. It took me awhile to figure out that someone on the upper floor was spinning wool into yarn; this sound was the spindle twirling across the wooden floor. While the men in the household were drinking in the other room the women and children were upstairs. I could hear their muted voices over the sound of drunken laughter.

The next morning Chander Singh was suffering from a hangover and he seemed relieved when I suggested that I carry on alone. After a cup of tea I headed up the valley in the direction Chander had indicated. About two thousand feet above Kapola lay the ridge that I would have to cross over into the watershed of the Bhagirathi. On the other side of this mountain was the village of Uprikot and from there I could continue on to Uttarkashi. Once again the distances were vague and I was told that it could take anywhere from a few hours to a couple of days. Chander's only other instructions were that when I came to a landslide about a kilometer beyond Kapola, I should cross the stream and go up a side valley to the right. Under no circumstances was I to turn left, for even though there was a larger trail in that direction it ended near some chaans, beyond which there was nothing but cliffs.

This all seemed simple enough, for the path was four feet wide and easy to follow until I reached the landslide. A treacherous-looking detour circled up and around the top. I made my way carefully across, dislodging a couple of rocks but safely reaching the other side. Here I began to search for the route that Chander had described. There was a smaller valley cutting up to the right but no obvious trail. The stream itself was only eight feet across and I found a spot where I could jump from rock to rock without getting my feet wet. On either bank was a broad expanse of boulders and dead trees that had been washed down by monsoon floods. Clambering over the debris, I searched for traces of a path but there was nothing to be found.

After half an hour I was ready to give up and go back to Kapola to ask for help, when I heard a jingling sound. Coming up the streambed was a woodcutter leading two mules, each wearing a garland of brass bells. Tucked into a scarf around the woodcutter's waist was a huge daranthi, a kind of machete with a curved blade. His mustache was twisted into two points and with his wool hat cocked to one side, the man looked something like a pirate at a costume party.

He was friendly enough, however, and helped me find the trail that I'd been searching for; it was hidden under weeds and brambles. The woodcutter confirmed that this would lead me to the top of the ridge, though he himself was headed in a different direction to gather dead branches for fuel. As it turned out, he was the last person I saw for the next eight hours.

The side valley was much narrower and thickly wooded on either slope. The trail kept cutting back and forth across a shallow stream bordered by moss-covered rocks and under-growth. The top of the ridge was hidden from view and though

I continued climbing steadily it was hard to tell how much progress I was making. This valley felt several degrees colder and it seemed as if the sun never reached below the tops of the highest trees. A pale carpet of frost lay on the ground, and when I stopped to drink at the stream the water was so cold it made my jaws ache.

After a while the path threaded its way through a grove of horse chestnut trees. Their branches were linked together like muscular arms and the ground was littered with polished black chestnuts and dry green hulls. Ahead of me I saw four langur monkeys feeding on the nuts and as I approached more and more langurs appeared, bounding through the undergrowth and diving from tree to tree like acrobats. Altogether there must have been over fifty, the largest troop I've ever seen, many of them gangly infants, clutching at their mothers with worried expressions. Three big males stood their ground, watching me with somber black faces like a council of elders sitting in judgment by the side of the trail. They were no more than ten feet away as I walked past. With silver hair and long, curled tails they looked much more dignified than the scruffy gang of rhesus monkeys I'd seen the day before.

A short distance beyond the chestnut grove was another landslide that blocked my path. Once again I had to crawl up the side of the hill, through a dense stand of ringal bamboo. Growing to a height of six or seven feet the ringal had stems no bigger around than my index finger. The leaves were a dry, yellow color and rustled loudly as I pushed them aside. When I eventually regained the trail it descended immediately to the stream where I found myself at the junction of three ravines that came together in a jumble of boulders. The path disappeared completely and there was no indication which way I should go. One of the ravines ended in a waterfall about fifty feet high and the other two looked barely passable. In the end I chose the middle one, because it seemed to lead more directly to the top of the ridge.

An hour later I was still scrambling over rockfalls and wading through bamboo thickets. By now I was completely lost but figured that I would eventually make it to the top of the ridge and find my way from there. Several hundred feet above me I could see where the oak forest gave way to fir trees and through their latticed branches, patches of blue sky were visible. Encouraged by the thought that this might be the pass, I worked my way out of the ravine. As soon as I reached the firs there was less undergrowth and I was able to make better progress.

To my dismay, however, the hillside did not open onto the pass. Instead it turned out to be a spur of the main ridge, which was still another eight hundred feet above me. I did discover the abandoned remains of a temporary shelter where shepherds camp in summer. Though I was sure the main trail could not be far away, the two or three indistinct paths I found seemed to lead in the wrong direction and petered out after a few hundred feet. My only option was to continue straight up the ridge, which grew steeper and steeper as I ascended. In the end I found myself climbing a vertical slope, grabbing at roots and branches to pull myself up. Wherever I could find a place to rest I'd stop, usually against the trunk of a yew or rhododendron tree.

By this time it must have been well past noon and I hadn't eaten anything since the night before. My pack felt like an immovable weight on my shoulders and made it difficult to climb, catching on shrubs and bushes. Though the air was still cold, my clothes were drenched in sweat and I was covered with dirt and leaves. Hauling myself up a few feet at a time, I had lost all interest in the surrounding forest and my only concern was to reach the pass. At one point I heard a barking deer begin to call. It must have been alarmed by the noise I was making and kept crying for twenty minutes or more, each bark a single note repeated every fifteen seconds. Farther down the valley another kakad began to call, answering the first, but they were hidden by the trees and I was too exhausted to try and catch sight of them.

For a while I wasn't sure that I would make it to the top because I kept coming to cliffs or other obstructions and each time I had to divert my route. Though I was carrying plenty of food, I was too tired to eat. Besides, the ridge was so precipitous, if I had tried to remove my pack, I might have slid straight down the hill. Once I started to fall it would have been impossible to stop myself. The distance to the top was difficult to gauge since the trees blocked off the view but eventually sunlight began to penetrate the leaves and I knew that I was close. Using my knees, elbows, hands, and feet, I made a last effort to hoist myself up, when suddenly there in front of me was a broad path, coming in from the left.

After catching my breath I followed this trail up to the pass. Almost immediately the ridge leveled off and I came to an amphitheater surrounded by oaks. One section of this glade was covered with snow in which I found the tracks of a barking deer, probably the one I'd heard calling earlier.

Each step I took was an effort, even though the walking was much easier now. Just beyond the amphitheater I came to a saddle in the ridge, where I collapsed beneath a moru oak. Unlike the ridge between Kupra and Kapola, which I had crossed the day before, this one was forested on either side and there were no dramatic views. In fact, the pass itself was completely sheltered, with only a scattering of dappled sunlight on the ground. For ten or fifteen minutes I lay there with my eyes closed and if anyone had come upon me they would have thought that I was dead.

When I eventually opened my eyes, I felt sure that I had breathed my last and gone straight to heaven. Two rays of sunlight were streaming through the branches of the oaks and falling directly on a smaller tree that stood twenty feet away. Though it had no leaves this tree was covered in flowers that seemed to glow in the shafts of light.

Lying there against the roots of the massive oak, my first impression was that I must be hallucinating, for the vision of this flowering tree and the sunlit glade was magical. I dared not move for fear of disturbing the perfection of that scene. The amphitheater lay just beyond the tree and the surrounding forest gave me a comforting sense of enclosure, particularly the overarching branches of the oaks. There was no spectacular view of snow peaks or dramatic cliffs, no lammergeiers soaring overhead, not even the slightest breeze. But in the stillness of that glade I was acutely aware of something much greater than myself. Awe is the only word that might describe the experience. I had walked right past the flowering tree but in my exhaustion I hadn't noticed the blossoms and only now was I aware of its transcendent beauty. The catharsis that it evoked was so powerful that I felt weightless, as if the ground had dropped away beneath me. Lying there I found myself in tears, emotions welling up inside of my chest, as if the roots of that tree had penetrated deep into my soul.

I'm not sure how long I lay there staring at the flowers but after a while I saw a movement at the edge of the glade. Two yellow-throated pine martins appeared, ambling down the slope with fluid grace. About the size of otters, they seemed like creatures in a dream with winter coats and flowing tails. The pine martins didn't make a sound, leaving the silence of the clearing undisturbed. Neither of them saw me as they passed beneath the flowering tree, pausing and lifting their heads, as if to sniff its fragrance. Within five minutes they were gone, disappearing across the white crescent of snow, on the far side of the amphitheater.

When I finally got to my feet I knew that I had experienced something profoundly spiritual. But at the same time I could not help but question my response, trying to rationalize what I had observed. Walking over to the tree I tried to discern what species it was, amazed that anything would bloom in winter. The flowers were different shades of pink, with florets of ten to twelve buds bunched together. They had a delicate fragrance, hardly noticeable but with a lingering sweetness like a faint perfume. Later I identified the tree as *Daphne bholua*, a species not commonly found in Garhwal.

Already I had begun to doubt the significance of what I had seen. The image of this flowering tree bathed in sunlight was undeniably powerful but my exhaustion could have exaggerated the beauty of the scene. Those sensations of release and weightlessness may well have come from discarding my pack. Was I weeping from awe or was it simply relief at finally finding the pass? I began to wonder if the experience meant anything at all. However, when I turned my gaze away from the sunlit flowers and returned to where I'd left my pack, I looked up at the trunk of the moru oak. In its bark I saw a glint of metal that made me realize I was not imagining things. Pressed into the crevices and dry moss were coins that others had left in recognition of the sanctity of this place. Though completely alone, I was aware that the experience I had just gone through was shared with others who had passed this way before. Their offerings reconfirmed the mystery of the glade.

# WINTER SOLSTICE

SURYA. VEDIC DEITY OF THE SUN. OLDEST OF GODS.
He rides across the sky each day in a glowing chariot with a single wheel, pulled by seven horses. (There are those who say it is one horse with seven heads.) His fiery brilliance blinds us so that he is perceived in many forms. Sometimes his skin is gold, sometimes brass, sometimes copper. At daybreak Surya's twin sons, the two Ashwins, lead his procession, riding in their own chariot to chase away the night. They are followed by Usha, goddess of the dawn, first bride of Surya, unblemished daughter of the sky. She illuminates the heavens with her innocence and prepares the earth for her husband's arrival.

Surya has many names: Dinakar, maker of the day; Bhaskar, creator of light; Vivaswat, radiant one; Brahapati, lord of the stars; Karmasakshi, witness of men's works; Loka-chakshu, eye of the world.

He also has many consorts and a multitude of offspring. In the *Puranas* there is a story about his wife, Sanjana, whose name means conscience. She bore him three children—Manu, Yama, and Yamuna Devi the river goddess. But Sanjana could not tolerate the oppressive brightness of Surya's presence, nor his inflamed passions, so she finally ran away from him. In her place she left Chhaya, a handmaiden whose name means shade. For many years Surya did not notice the difference and he fathered three more children with Chhaya, one of whom is Shani—the planet Saturn. Eventually, Sanjana's son Yama grew jealous because Chhaya favored her own children. When Yama tried to kick his stepmother she cursed him and his leg was infected with sores. Immediately Surya became suspicious, since a mother's curse can never affect her own child.

Realizing that he had been deceived and overcome with desire for his wife, Surya went in search of Sanjana, who had retreated into the forest for a life of chaste contemplation. Attempting to hide from her husband, she transformed herself into a mare. But Surya quickly saw through her disguise and changed himself into a stallion so that he could mate with her. Eventually the couple assumed their original forms and Sanjana reluctantly returned home. Her father, Vishwakarma (architect of the universe), then offered a solution to Surya's overwhelming radiance. Taking his son-in-law and grinding him upon a stone, Vishwakarma reduced the sun's brightness by one-eighth, so that Sanjana could bear her husband's presence.

The fragments of light that were cast off in this process became weapons of the gods—the discus of Vishnu, the lance of Kartikeya, and the trident of Shiv.

In the town of Uttarkashi stands a huge trident made of brass, copper, and iron that marks the site of a Shiv temple destroyed in 1803 by an earthquake. The trident is almost twenty feet tall and fixed to a circular pedestal. A cement shrine has been built around it, though for many years it stood in the open. Even though the earthquake left the original temple in ruins the trident remained upright and is said to have withstood any efforts to knock it down. The exact history of this emblem is unclear. Some claim that it was forged by Nepali craftsmen during the Gurkha occupation of Garhwal. These invaders are credited with building the main temple at Gangotri, and many shrines in

Garhwal exhibit Nepali influences. Others believe that the origins of the trident at Uttarkashi go back much farther to a time when the Bhagirathi Valley was ruled by people from Tibet.

The famous Chinese traveler and pilgrim Hsuan Tsang is believed to have visited Garhwal in 634 A.D. His journals contain descriptions of a town called Brahmapura, which some historians have identified as Uttarkashi. According to Hsuan Tsang, Buddhists and Hindus lived together in this region and there was regular trade across the passes into Tibet. Most scholars agree that the Buddhist population was driven out of Garhwal by the Hindu reformer Shankaracharya, in the ninth century A.D. Another name for Uttarkashi was Barahat and until the end of the nineteenth century this was the last permanent settlement on the pilgrim route to Gangotri, which lay a seven-days' journey upriver. Though the town has suffered a series of major earthquakes, two of them in the last ten years, it remains the district headquarters for western Garhwal and a busy commercial center. What was once described by a British traveler as "a most wretched place, consisting of not more than five or six poor houses surrounded with filth and buried in a jungle of nettles, thorns and the like," Uttarkashi is now a sprawling town that occupies a broad valley on both banks of the Bhagirathi.

It continues to serve as a staging point for the Char Dham Yatra, with connecting motor roads between Yamnotri and Gangotri. During the pilgrimage season the main bus stop is choked with vehicles and even in winter it is a major hub of transport for the region. Uttarkashi has also become a center for ashrams and other spiritual retreats, where Hindus from all over India come to escape the discontentment of modern life and absorb themselves in religious contemplation. The Bhagirathi flows through the center of the town and there are numerous temples and bathing ghats along its banks.

In the complex genealogy of Hinduism there are two races, one that is descended from the sun, the other from the moon. This primal lineage, with its two parallel branches, can be traced back to the gods of the Vedas. Out of their immortal promiscuity these divine beings produced generations of lesser deities and demigods, who in turn created inferior offspring through their successive coupling. The end result of this adulteration was man.

The solar race, or Surya-vansa, is ostensibly descended from Surya, though the true progenitor is believed to be Ikshwaku, the son of Manu. He was born from his father's nostril, when Manu sneezed, an ignoble beginning for a noble dynasty. Ikshwaku was the first ruler of Ayodhya and from his line arose the legendary kings Sagar and Bhagirath. The god Ram, an incarnation of Vishnu, also was born into this solar race, taking the form of a human king in order to fight against evil demons who threatened the earth.

Max Müller, the German scholar who played a major role in translating Sanskrit texts for a western audience, adds an interesting footnote to the story of Ikshwaku. He writes: "I take it, not as the name of a king, but as the name of a people, probably the people who inhabited Bhajeratha, the country washed by the northern Ganga or Bhagirathi."

It is difficult and perhaps futile to try and establish a coherent link between historical facts and mythological events. At the same time, Hindu scriptures and oral traditions contain innumerable hints about India's ancestral past. There are those who would argue that the Ramayana and Mahabharata epics can be interpreted as the chronicles of two great dynasties. The Ramayana contains the stories of Ram and the solar race, while the Mahabharata records the legends of the Pandavs and Kuravs, descendants of the lunar race, or Chandra-vansa.

Even in winter the sun bakes down on the Uttarkashi Valley, burning away the mist at dawn and warming the air, so that by noon it is dry and hot. As I headed up to Gangotri I had no choice but to walk along the motor road. The ribbon of asphalt ran parallel to the river, following its twisting course. Since this was not the pilgrimage season there was little traffic, the occasional bus overloaded with passengers and luggage, a few motorcycles, government vehicles, and Jeep taxis that ply between the towns and villages along the Bhagirathi. With the temples closed in winter, buses and Jeeps go only as far as Dharali, a small settlement twenty kilometers short of Gangotri.

The paved surface of the motor road felt hard and unyielding underfoot. Though it was easier walking than the trek from Yamnotri to Uttarkashi—no scrambling up hillsides or steep descents—it was difficult in other ways. The sun's warmth was absorbed by the black surface of the road and I could feel the heat radiating back up at me. There was a measured monotony to the kilometer posts I passed and each time I came to a bend in the road, I saw another bend ahead of me, almost identical to the last. Though the chances of getting lost were slim there was also little to be discovered. After a while my shins began to ache and I tried to walk on the unpaved margins of the road. By the time I reached the town of Bhatwari, twenty-seven kilometers beyond Uttarkashi, I was suffering from a mild case of sunstroke, made worse by a greasy breakfast I'd eaten along the way. My head was throbbing and I would vomit several times later during the night, only able to keep down a sip or two of water at a time. Fortunately by the next morning I felt better and was able to continue.

At places the highway was being resurfaced and I passed several gangs of laborers, breaking stones or shoveling away the rubble of a landslide. Barrels of tar were being heated over open fires, the oily black smoke billowing up in poisonous clouds. The laborers carried buckets of melted pitch and poured it onto the road, their hands and feet wrapped in rags to protect them from the heat. They looked unhappy and exploited, condemned to this miserable roadside existence. Both men and women were working, while their children played in the dust nearby.

There was something medieval about the bubbling black cauldrons of pitch and these stooped figures carrying dripping buckets of smoking tar. It was the most primitive and hellish method of paving a highway. Even the ancient road roller, with its huge metal wheels and rusting engine, looked like a demonic mechanism designed to crush the laborers beneath its weight. As I stopped to watch the roadwork, I couldn't help but wince at the grotesque absurdity of this scene. Here in the final days of the twentieth century, in the heart of the Himalayas, I was presented with a vision of gothic horror. The only thing missing was a slave driver with a whip, though in his place sat a PWD contractor, smoking a cigarette and picking burrs out of his nylon socks.

Farther on, near a spring that crossed the road, I found a woman scraping at the surface of the highway with a stick. By this time it was late afternoon and the tar had softened in the sun. The woman, who must have been from one of the villages nearby, had collected a ball of pitch about the size of a walnut. As I stopped to drink at the spring, I saw that she was using the tar to patch a hole in her bucket.

Though the Bhagirathi itself was beautiful, a clear river flowing between polished rocks, there were no dramatic views along this section of the road. The mountains rose two or three thousand feet on either side of me and occasionally I caught a glimpse of snow peaks, but nothing like the panoramas that I encountered near Yamnotri. There was little to elevate the soul and walking became nothing more than drudgery.

The motor road follows the same alignment as the old walking trail, which has long since disappeared. Scattered along this route are numerous chattis, where footsore pilgrims once halted for the night. But the road has obviously changed the character of the valley and each of the towns and villages it passes through exhibit a depressingly modern facade, with billboards advertising soft drinks, cigarettes, televisions, and different brands of tires. The slate roofs have been replaced with tin, the stone walls with reinforced concrete, and the ground is littered with plastic bags and refuse. Paved roads have brought one form of progress to the region and obviously there is the convenience of traveling by bus or Jeep, but the changes wrought by this development can only be weighed against the ugliness and squalor, the intrusive elements of the outside world, and the abject misery of those laborers hauling tar.

At a number of places above Uttarkashi I came upon signs for NATURE RESORTS. From what I could see most of these were enclaves of cement cottages or tented camps and all of them were closed for the winter. Like the ashrams in Uttarkashi, they provide a sanctuary for pilgrims who want to escape the pressures of urban life and meditate upon the spiritual ethos of the mountains. The irony, however, is that most of these resorts are located only a few hundred feet from the motor road and though they overlook the river it is hardly the sort of place where one can escape into nature. There are barbed-wire fences and gates, rocks splashed with whitewash to mark the parking areas, empty flowerbeds, and lines of latrines. The majority of these resorts seem designed to keep the natural world at bay.

Garhwal Mandal Vikas Nigam. Roughly translated the name means Garhwal Regional Development Agency, a state government undertaking responsible for promoting development and tourism in Uttarakhand. There are numerous GMVN rest houses throughout the watershed of the Ganga, most of them along the motor roads leading up to Yamnotri, Gangotri, Kedarnath, and Badrinath. The concept behind this agency is that by providing accommodation and other facilities for tourists and pilgrims the region will attract more and more visitors. This will generate jobs and commercial opportunities for the people of Garhwal. In essence it seems a logical idea but like most visions of development, it is inherently flawed.

Tourism the world over has a pernicious way of destroying exactly those things that make it attractive. The beauty of the Himalayas lies in their unspoiled grandeur. But the increasing number of pilgrims and tourists, ushered in by the building of motor roads and rest houses, destroys that beauty even as it seeks to make these mountains accessible to everyone. There is no way to reconcile the two and for this reason I find a disturbing contradiction in the term eco-tourism, which is currently in vogue.

There are many places in Garhwal that could be offered up as examples of the destructive legacy of tourism, but one of the most glaring sites is the hot spring at Gangnani, a two-days' walk above Uttarkashi. It is possibly the most disheartening place in the Himalayas, a mineral spring that bubbles out of the cliffs overlooking the Bhagirathi. Garhwal Mandal Vikas Nigam advertises its rest house at Gangnani on signboards along the highway. Reading these one imagines an attractive complex of mineral baths in which a weary pilgrim can soak his sore muscles. Instead one finds a filthy slum of tea shops and cheap hotels built into the face of the cliff. The hot spring overflows with dripping sewage from each of these establishments and the incrustations of minerals are caked with garbage. The scene at Gangnani proves how the transient presence of thousands of human beings can desecrate what must have been, not long ago, a dramatic phenomenon of nature. Today it is little more than a steaming, fetid drain.

Even in its most benign projects Garhwal Mandal Vikas Nigam tends to exploit the natural resources of this region. A few miles above Uttarkashi is a bottling plant for mineral water. GMVN sells this water in one-liter plastic bottles under the brand name Bhagirathi. The label reads, "Pure Ganga Jal Derived From High Himalayan Herb Zones." Though the bottles themselves are often recycled, they are a source of pollution and it would seem the agency might better serve the people of Garhwal if it provided clean drinking water to isolated villages, rather than selling bottles of purified Gangajal to thirsty pilgrims.

Near Gangnani the Bhagirathi passes through the main thrust of the Himalayas. Unlike the other tributaries of the Ganga, which flow from the southern face of the mountains, the Bhagirathi cuts directly through the highest range of snow peaks and has its source on their northern slopes. This suggests that the river predates the mountains and as the Himalayas rose up with the impact of colliding continents, the Bhagirathi carved its narrow passage through the rocks, defying those geological forces that pushed up the highest mountain range on earth. In geological terms alone, the origin of the Ganga is a remarkable phenomenon that no myth or legend can adequately describe. Here is the relentless force of water seeking its own path to the sea, cleaving a channel through impenetrable walls of stone.

Ascending this valley one can see the scars of erosion on the cliffs and feel the weight of the mountains thrusting upward. The rocks themselves bear evidence of the powerful forces of nature, granites formed out of magma from the earth's core, speckled with mica and other crystals, slabs of shale, round boulders in the riverbed and shelves of sand. This process has been evolving over millions of years, but even in recent times the Bhagirathi has demonstrated the unstoppable fury of its current. In 1978, during the monsoon, a huge landslide blocked the gorge above Gangnani, forming a natural dam. For several days the water backed up behind this wall of mud and stone but eventually the Bhagirathi broke through and swept downstream in a flash flood, killing hundreds of people along the riverbank. The effects of this flood were felt beyond Garhwal as a sudden wave of water spewed out into the plains. Fields and villages were washed away along with sections of the motor road. Even today the remains of this landslide are visible near the village of Sukhi, where a section of the mountain, several kilometers in breadth, has collapsed into the valley.

Harsil means the stone of God and according to a plaque at a roadside temple this is the place where Shiv cut off the head of King Jasodha, a legendary warrior who challenged the authority of the gods. Jasodha's wife had prayed to Vishnu, asking that her husband be given the power to conquer every land in the universe. Impressed by her devotion and purity, Vishnu granted her this boon on the condition that she remained faithful to her husband. In a short span of time King Jasodha took over the world with his invincible army. Having conquered every territory on earth he turned his attention to the land of the gods. At this point the pantheon of Hindu deities became concerned and Shiv was sent to challenge him. They fought a battle that lasted for many days but even the most powerful of gods, with all of his celestial weapons, could not defeat Jasodha. In desperation Vishnu contrived a deceitful plan. Changing himself into the likeness of Jasodha he went to the king's wife and seduced her. Immediately the boon was lifted and Shiv was able to cut off Jasodha's head.

Harsil is also the setting for a more recent legend, the story of Frederick Wilson, who is said to be the inspiration for Rudyard Kipling's "The Man Who Would Be King." Like any myth, Wilson's story has many different versions and it is difficult to unravel the truth even though he died just over a hundred years ago. By some accounts he was a deserter from the Indian army, who set himself up as an independent contractor in the kingdom of Tehri Garhwal. An enterprising man, Wilson is said to have introduced apples to the region and he is also believed to be the first person to float timber down the Ganga, beginning the process of deforestation. Though he was an Englishman, Wilson was clearly beyond the pale of Anglo-Indian society. He seems to have had little concern for colonial etiquette, marrying a Garhwali woman named Gulabi and building himself an impressive wooden mansion in Harsil. His fortune was made in the timber business and eventually Wilson grew so wealthy that he was able to mint his own rupee coins. By the end of the nineteenth century he seems to have established informal control over the upper reaches of the Bhagirathi Valley. One of his accomplishments was building bridges along the yatra route to Gangotri. Always looking for a commercial opportunity, Wilson charged pilgrims a toll for crossing these bridges. When they balked at the precarious construction, he is said to have demonstrated that the bridges were safe by galloping across on horseback. Though Frederick Wilson was ostracized by most of his British contemporaries, he also appealed to the forbidden side of the colonial adventure. He was a colorful and controversial figure who was given the epithet "Pahari," which means man of the mountains.

The palace that Wilson built for himself in Harsil burned down ten years ago and the wooden bridges he constructed have long since been replaced by more permanent spans of steel and concrete. Little remains of his legacy, except for the deforestation. Two photographs survive, one of Frederick Wilson and the other of his wife, Gulabi. With a bald head and gray beard Pahari Wilson hardly appears to be a swashbuckling adventurer. In his eyes there is a hint of visionary defiance though he looks more like an elderly bank clerk than a man who would be king. Gulabi's face is turned demurely away from the camera. She is much younger than Wilson, with smooth, clear features. Her hair is wrapped in a scarf and around her neck are strands of silver chains.

Harsil is now an important military outpost, with a small bazaar and even a bank. The main temple, on the far side of the river, is the winter home of the goddess Ganga, who is carried down from Gangotri in late October and resides here in seclusion until the snow has melted in the spring. Because of the army presence foreigners are not allowed to spend the night in Harsil and I was told that I had to go several kilometers upriver, beyond the village of Dharali, before I would be permitted to pitch my tent.

While Surya represents the sun, Soma is the lunar deity, his myths recounted in the Puranas. He rides across the sky in a chariot with three wheels, drawn by ten white horses the color of jasmine blossoms. Like Surya he has many names: Chandra, Indu, Sasi (marked like a hare), Nakshatra-nath (lord of the constellations), Mriganka (marked like a deer), Shiv-sekhar (crest of Shiv), Kamuda-pati (lord of the lotus).

Hindu lore offers various explanations for the phases of the moon. In one myth Shiv cuts Soma in half with his trident. In another Soma marries the twenty-seven daughters of Rishi Daksha. When jealousy arose among the sisters they appealed to their father, who cursed Soma so that each month he gradually decayed before regaining his full brilliance.

In the Vedas, Soma is the elixir of the gods, extracted from a celestial herb. This plant has a milky white juice that, when fermented, induces the purest form of intoxication, with visions of immortality. The Rig Veda in particular contains a number of hymns to Soma and even the stones that are used to crush the juices out of this plant sing its praises. Of all the Vedic deities Soma is perhaps the most enigmatic. In many ways he is a metaphorical representation of ecstatic spiritual experience and the mind-altering drugs used by sadhus and rishis. Celebrated for the sublime hallucinations he brings on, Soma is also referred to as the king of plants. In certain hymns Soma is compared to the milk and butter that flows from the udders of Surabhi, the cow of plenty. Though he was obviously an important deity in early Indo-Aryan culture, contemporary Hinduism takes little notice of Soma, except for the reference to Somvar, or Monday—the day of the week assigned to the moon.

In Hindu scriptures, the connection between Soma juice and the moon remains obscure, illustrating the fluid nature of mythology as it is translated from one tradition to the next. The Rig Veda contains only one reference to Soma as a lunar deity, though the moon itself has always had liquid connotations because of its milky color. By some accounts, Soma was created out of the churning of the primordial sea but in a much more tangible sense moonlight can be considered a distillation of the sun's energy, the purest form of illumination.

On December 22, 1999, the full moon coincided with the winter solstice. It was predicted to be the "largest" moon in over a century, an astrological phenomenon that ushered in the new millennium. Having read about this event before starting my pilgrimage I was hoping for clear skies. On earlier nights the moon had looked enormous, a lopsided orb that floated above the mountains. But tonight it would be complete, a full circle. As I walked along the road above Harsil I kept looking up at the sky. There were only a few plumes of feathery cirrus drifting above the snows and the late-afternoon sun was slanting across the ridges.

As I came to a bend in the road beyond Dharali, I could see a patch of open ground beside the river. It seemed an ideal place to camp with forests of deodar trees on either side and a view of the snow mountains at both ends of the valley. Having crossed through the bulwark of the Himalayas it seemed as if I was now in the heart of the mountains. A thousand feet above me lay the tree line, where the forest ended and the mountains turned to rock, then snow. It was much colder here than lower down the Bhagirathi. There was hardly any wind but the slightest breeze cut through my clothes and whenever I stopped walking I began to shiver.

Near the campsite grew a jungle of thorny shrubs, which had cast off their leaves though the branches were covered with bright orange fruit. In the amber sunlight, it looked as if these bushes were in flames. The shrub is a kind of buckthorn, called ameel in Garhwali, and its berries, which ripen with the onset of winter, have a sharp, astringent flavor. They are used for making chutney and sometimes added to curries as a spice.

Scrambling down from the motor road I pushed my way through the ameel bushes and selected a place to pitch my tent, clearing away rocks and piles of dry cowdung. A few feet away was a small stream and despite the direct sunlight it was rimmed with ice. The rocks that bordered the stream were coated white and icicles hung from the branches of the ameel bushes at the water's edge, their orange berries encased in clear, brittle sheaths. This stream flowed directly into the Bhagirathi, about thirty meters from where I camped. The shallow pools along the river's edge were frozen and the rocks were slick with ice. The sound of the Bhagirathi was a wintry murmur, like the rustling of dry leaves.

By the time I finished erecting my tent the sun had disappeared though it continued to reflect off the upper ranges for another hour, before the shadows met the sky. I gathered together a pile of firewood, mostly dead twigs from the ameel bushes, as well as deodar branches that lay in the riverbed. These were white and smooth as bones, the bark stripped off and the wood twisted into contorted shapes. I also collected dry cowdung to use as fuel and built an open hearth with three large stones. There was plenty of tinder so that soon I had a small fire going to keep me warm. Though I used my petrol stove to cook on, it was comforting to sit beside a fire, tending it carefully so the flames did not blaze too high or burn down into ashes. This required my constant attention but there was little else for me to do, and I have always enjoyed the meditative quality of tending a fire, a sense of contentment that comes from keeping the flames alight. Each type of wood burned differently, the thorny sticks from the ameel bushes giving off a lot of smoke, while the deodar had a cleaner, more constant flame. The cowdung smoldered like peat, burning steadily with only the faintest glimmer of combustion. I had also collected pinecones, which snapped and popped like firecrackers as pockets of resin exploded.

Across the river and half a kilometer downstream lay a village of ten or twelve houses and a whitewashed temple but on my side of the valley there was no sign of habitation. It was a lonely, silent spot, made all the more secluded by the envelope of firelight that surrounded me. Whenever I glanced up from the flames it looked as if there was nothing but darkness on all sides until my eyes adjusted and the black profiles of the ridges revealed themselves. Some of the stars and planets had come out but within half an hour of sunset the sky began to brighten once again.

Feeding twigs into the fire I noticed a pale aura beyond the mountains at the head of the valley. Behind me the snow peaks grew steadily whiter, reflecting a lunar glow. I was impatient to see the full moon rise but it took over half an hour. The air had grown even colder now and only the front of my body was warm as I faced the fire. My shoulders and back were chilled, my knees and legs numb with cold. Moving closer to the flames I closed my eyes as the smoke blew into my face. The crenellated profiles of the mountains were silhouetted against a penumbral sheen but when the moon finally came into view its brightness startled me, a circular blade of light that cut open the sky. Sliding upward it gradually revealed more and more of its circumference. By comparison my fire seemed insignificant, no more than a glimmering cinder, as a milky luminescence filled the valley. The higher the moon climbed the larger it seemed to grow and when it finally broke free of the mountains, it looked even bigger than the earth, bloated with light. It was perfectly round and white, except for the shadowy markings on its surface, dry seas and craters. But for all its beauty the moonlight offered no warmth and it seemed a sphere of snow, a crystalline ball, like one of the round river rocks coated in ice. Sitting there in the valley I felt entirely alone.

The symmetry of the full moon reminded me of Emerson's words: "The eye is the first circle; the horizon which it forms is the second; and throughout nature this primary picture is repeated without end. It is the highest emblem in the cipher of the world. St. Augustine described the nature of God as a circle whose centre was everywhere and its circumference nowhere."

By some accounts the moon is the true source of the Ganga, a circular vessel decanting her sacred waters into Shiv's long tresses. As the moon spills its oblation from the night sky it gradually wanes, like a bowl of milk that is emptied of its contents, only to be refilled again and again. Shiv is often depicted with a crescent moon in his hair or surrounded by a pure white halo. As I sat and watched the full moon rise above the Bhagirathi Valley, reflecting off the white snow peaks and flowing river, I couldn't help but imagine the goddess Ganga tumbling to earth, like a waterfall of light.

# FIRE AND ICE

ON THE WAY UP TO GANGOTRI I MET AN ELDERLY
sadhu walking in the opposite direction who could easily have
been a tantric incarnation of Santa Claus. His white beard was
twisted into two long strands, like the raw wool that Garhwali
villagers spin into yarn. On his head he wore an orange balaclava rolled down over his ears. He was dressed in a woolen
overcoat that reached to his knees and buttoned up to his neck.
The coat had originally been dyed a saffron color but the coarse
fabric had faded to a rusty tan. On his feet the sadhu wore a pair
of canvas army boots, into the tops of which he had tucked the
long underwear that covered his legs. Once upon a time these
too had been dyed saffron to match the rest of his attire. The old
sadhu was hardly overweight though the coat bulged around his
middle and he had a cloth bundle over one shoulder and a walking stick in hand. His face bore a ruddy cheerfulness, highlighted by streaks of ash across his forehead.

It was December 23, two days until Christmas. Greeting me
with a wave of his stick the sadhu explained that he was on his
way to Uttarkashi to get some supplies. He lived in Gangotri
and planned to return before the end of the month and spend
the rest of the winter there.

The walking trail above Harsil follows the west bank of the
Bhagirathi while the motor road lies on the east. They join

together near a bridge, five kilometers beyond Dharali, where the river comes out of a deep gorge that extends the rest of the way up to Gangotri. At this point the landscape changes dramatically. The valley narrows and the mountains seem to lean in upon each other, one ridge encroaching on the next. Forests of deodar and birch cover the lower slopes but as the cliffs grow steeper the trees disappear and the upper reaches of the mountains are barren rock and snow.

There is a forbidding beauty about this valley especially in winter when it is virtually deserted. While I was walking up from Dharali to Gangotri, only one vehicle passed me along the motor road, a military truck on its way to the Army Signal outpost at Lanka. The river had all but disappeared into the gorge and only at one or two places was I able to look down and see its blue waters slipping through sculpted walls of rock. In this part of the Himalayas the mountains are mostly granite, of which there are several different kinds. The higher cliffs are a dark metallic gray, enormous slabs of igneous stone with sharp edges whetted by the wind. Lower down in the gorge the granite turns a pale cream color, almost like marble. It is embedded with crystals that formed when the rocks melted for a second time under tectonic pressures that shaped the mountains. Geologists refer to these rocks as Gangotri Leucogranite because of their milky color, which has been polished to a smooth, glossy texture by the headwaters of the Bhagirathi.

Stones serve as a record of history that goes back to a time before man. We revere them for their strength and permanence because they are relics of cataclysmic events that formed this planet. The creative forces evidenced in stone suggest the origins of life, even though the rocks themselves are lifeless. Like water, wind, or fire, stones convey narratives that take our imaginations back to the genesis of life. These are the primary elements of myths, the minerals out of which we forge our faith.

Throughout my pilgrimage I was struck by the fact that so many rocks along the roadside had been painted, as if it were a basic human instinct to daub these stones. Some were simply splashed with whitewash to mark the edges of the motor road and reflect the headlights of cars at night. This seemed a prudent measure, particularly where the hill dropped away several hundred feet. But elsewhere the rocks had been painted with messages and slogans, most of them unnecessary. It may be the solidity of stones, their immovable nature, that invites us to deface these hard surfaces with images and words. I suspect it is a primitive impulse going back to a time when our ancestors decorated the walls of caves with stories of their hunting exploits.

On the roadside rocks in Garhwal, however, most of the painted messages reflect institutional authority. The Indian army's Border Roads Organization, which maintains strategic highways in the Himalayas, announces its presence on boulders that bear inscriptions like, WE WORK TODAY FOR YOUR TOMORROW. There is also a good deal of doggerel that is supposed to warn drivers about the dangers of the road:

THE ROAD IS HILLY, DON'T DRIVE SILLY.

IF YOU SLEEP YOUR FAMILY WILL WEEP.

THIS IS NOT A RACE OR RALLY, DRIVE SLOW AND ENJOY THE BEAUTY OF THE VALLEY.

In addition to these warnings, the state police have added their own words of admonition:

BLOW HORN!

STAY LEFT!

BEWARE OF FALLING ROCKS!

At one point, just short of Gangotri there was a sign, WE ARE HERE FOR YOU ALWAYS. UTTAR PRADESH POLICE, though the last constable I saw was in Bhatwari, fifty kilometers downstream. Not to be left out, the forest department has also adopted the practice of painting on rocks though their messages follow a

more ecological vein: CLEAN, GREEN HIMALAYAS and PREVENT
FOREST FIRES. Predictably, there were plenty of religious slogans as well. AAP KI YATRA MANGALMAI HO! (May your pilgrimage be full of joy!), "SATYAM, SHIVAM, SUNDARAM" (Truth,
Peace, Beauty), and the enigmatic GOD IS NOWHERE. Added to
these were more disturbing expressions of fundamentalist rhetoric, where the Vishwa Hindu Parishad had painted rocks with
jingoistic political refrains: GARB SEY BOLO HUM HINDU HAIN!
(Affirm with pride that we are Hindus) and BHARAT HINDU
RASHTRA HAI! (India is a Hindu state).

As I made my way up to Gangotri, through mountain ranges
that have remained unspoiled for centuries, I found myself
angered by these painted rocks and the imposition of absurd
warnings, exhortations, and threats. Aside from the ugliness of
the signs there was something corrupt and intrusive about these
messages, as if the immutable granite surfaces had been sullied
by the pointless babble of the modern world.

Until twenty years ago the motor road went only as far as
Lanka and from there pilgrims had to walk the last ten kilometers to Gangotri. The reason for this is a spectacular gorge
where the Jadganga joins the Bhagirathi, their confluence hidden from view by deep chasms. A broad cement bridge now
crosses the Jadganga at a height of several hundred feet and
most pilgrims today are blissfully unaware of the dangerous
drop beneath them, the straight walls of rock descending to a
raging torrent. At one time, however, there was only a narrow
footbridge that swayed over this gorge. It was such a frightening crossing that many pilgrims were said to crawl from one side
to the other on their hands and knees. Next to the new motor
bridge one can still see the huge wooden posts that once supported this suspension bridge, which is said to have been built
by Pahari Wilson. Before the footbridge was constructed there
used to be a trolley on a grass rope with pulleys. One pilgrim at

a time was hauled across the gorge, dangling above the Jadganga like an acrobat on a high trapeze.

At Bhairon Ghatti, which lies on the opposite side of the Jadganga, a tea shop owner told me the story of how the trolley was finally dismantled. According to him, one of the wives of the Maharajah of Tehri had come on a pilgrimage to Gangotri. She was pregnant and undertook the journey in order to pray for the health of her child. When she reached Lanka, the maharani was placed in the trolley and pulled across, but as soon as she looked down and saw the terrifying depth of the gorge, the queen was so frightened that she suffered a miscarriage. When the maharajah heard what had happened he was enraged and ordered that the trolley be torn down immediately. In its place a footpath was constructed that led down into the gorge, across a bridge, and up the other side. This trail still exists though it is seldom used now that the motor bridge has been built.

In the *Himalayan Gazetteer,* a geographical encyclopedia of Garhwal and Kumaon first printed in 1886, Edwin Atkinson records the impressions of British travelers who visited the gorge in the middle of the nineteenth century.

> Hodgson described it as "a most terrific and awful-looking place" . . . [He] states that he has never seen anything in the hills to be compared with the scenery around Bhairon-ghati for horror and extravagance. Both the Jadh-Ganga and the Bhagirathi are here confined within high and perpendicular rocks of solid granite and in the acute angle formed by the confluence a lofty massive rock projects downwards between the streams like an enormous wedge. . . . Hodgson compares this scene of terrific sublimity to "the appearance that the ruins of a Gothic cathedral might have on a spectator within them, supposing that thunderbolts or earthquakes had rifted its lofty and massy towers, spires, and buttresses; the parts left

standing might then in miniature give an idea of the rocks at Bhairon-ghati."

Fraser, too, describes it as a very singular and terrible place. The course of the river has continued foaming through its narrow rocky bed, and the hills approach their heads as though they would meet at a prodigious height above. "Here both rivers run in chasms, the depth, narrowness, and rugged wildness of which it is impossible to describe; between them is thrust a lofty crag, like a wedge, equal in height and savage aspect to those that on either side tower above the torrents. The extreme precipitousness of all these, and the roughness of their face, with wood which grows near the riverside, obstructs the view, and prevents the eye from comprehending the whole at a glance; but still the distant black cliffs, topped with lofty peaks of snow, are discovered, shutting up the view in either of the three ravines . . .

By all accounts the gorge between Lanka and Bhairon Ghatti was never a place for the faint of heart and even today, glancing over the concrete railings of the motor bridge, one can easily appreciate the terror and awe that this natural barrier inspired. On safely reaching the other side, pilgrims worshiped at the shrine of Bhairon Devta, a popular deity in Garhwal. His temples traditionally guard the approaches to each of the major pilgrimage sites and Bhairon is usually depicted as a warrior, with a sword or trident in one hand. He represents the martial aspects of Shiv, a fearsome and unyielding god who protects the sanctity of mountain shrines with his lethal weapons and fierce demeanor. It isn't difficult to understand why Bhairon's temple is situated above the gorge, as if he himself had cut this trench through which the river flows, a last defense against incursions of the outside world.

Knowing how difficult and forbidding the journey used to

be, it would seem that something essential has been lost with the construction of a motor bridge. Today the accessibility of this route has taken away much of the mystery and remoteness of the valley, that sense of nature's "horror and extravagance." Pilgrims can now drive to within a few hundred meters of the temple at Gangotri and though the cliffs and gorges may still seem frightening viewed from the window of a bus, this experience can never compare with the dangers and challenges of negotiating the valley on foot.

Just beyond Bhairon Ghatti a military road branches off to Keylong and the Tsang Chokla Pass. A signboard declares this route off-limits to everyone but military personnel, for the Tibetan border is less than twenty kilometers away. Tensions in the region remain from India's war with China in 1962. Though the main pass from Garhwal into Tibet lies to the east, above Badrinath and Mana, the Tsang Chokla Pass has always been one of the traditional trade routes across the Himalayas. It was up this valley, along the Jadganga, that Heinrich Harrer escaped into Tibet at the beginning of World War II. An Austrian mountaineer who was incarcerated by the British as a prisoner of war, his adventures are chronicled in the book *Seven Years in Tibet*, recently made into an unconvincing movie that fails to capture the dramatic landscapes of the Himalayas.

The Jadganga tributary is also known as Jahnavi, or the daughter of Jahnu, and this name is sometimes applied to the Ganga as a whole. The Puranas contain a myth about a rishi named Jahnu who was meditating in the Himalayas soon after Ganga was released from the tangled locks of Shiv's hair. The loud roar of her waters disturbed the rishi as he was performing tapasya and in his anger he swallowed up the river. Alarmed by this event, the gods immediately tried to placate Jahnu and only after much persuasion did he agree to let the river flow out of his ear.

A variety of different myths are associated with the origins of the Ganga. The most famous, of course, is the legend of King Bhagirath, who did penance for his ancestors and brought the sacred river down to earth. But there is also the story of how Ganga was first formed, flowing out of the toe of Vishnu. This legend involves Narada, the messenger of the gods and a comic figure in Hindu mythology. He is also a musician and credited with inventing the veena, a stringed instrument, to accompany his songs. Though Narada was an accomplished singer by human standards his voice could never compare to the celestial music of the gods. Vishnu once teased him by placing his veena in the paws of a bear. When the animal touched the strings with its claws the notes it produced were much more sublime than anything Narada had ever played.

One day, as Narada was wandering through the Himalayas, playing his veena and singing hymns, he met a group of beautiful men and women, each of whom was missing some part of their body. One had lost an arm, others a foot, a hand, or an eye. Puzzled by their appearance, Narada asked what had happened and he was told that they were Ragas and Raginis, the divine spirits of music, whom he had mutilated through his singing. Appalled that he was responsible for their injuries, Narada asked what he could do to make them whole again. They replied that only if Shiv were to sing would their limbs be restored by the perfection of his music. Immediately Narada went to Shiv and asked for this favor. Mahadev agreed but said that he could only perform in the presence of a perfect audience. Narada then persuaded Brahma and Vishnu to listen to his songs. Shortly after Shiv began his concert the Ragas and Raginis were miraculously healed. As Shiv continued singing, Vishnu became so absorbed in the music that he began to melt. The stream of liquid that flowed from his toe became the Ganga and this explains the purity of her waters.

Most pilgrims consider Gangotri to be the primary source of the Ganga. It was here that King Bhagirath came and did tapasya, luring Ganga down from the heavens with his acts of piety and devotion. Even the geographers and geologists agree: Of the Ganga's four main tributaries, the Bhagirathi reaches farthest back into the mountains, beyond the central thrust of the Himalayas to the most remote point of origin.

At one time the Gaumukh Glacier, which feeds this river, must have extended all the way down to Gangotri, at the upper end of the Bhairon Ghatti gorge. Over several centuries, however, the ice has receded eighteen kilometers upstream. For this reason the temple at Gangotri no longer marks the true source but instead overlooks a sizable river that drains from farther up the valley. Forests of deodar trees converge at the head of the gorge, which opens out into a relatively broad passage between the mountains, granite cliffs giving way to glacial moraine.

Despite the changing topography of the valley, Gangotri still retains its religious significance. The main temple is said to have been built around 1800 by Amar Singh Thapa, a Nepali general who conquered Garhwal. It is constructed on top of a stone that is believed to be the site where King Bhagirath performed his tapasya. The temple also houses an image of the goddess Ganga, ornamented with a golden crown. Toward the end of October she is carried down to Harsil and locked away in her winter quarters. When I arrived at Gangotri in December the temple was sealed. It is an unusual structure, about thirty feet high, made mostly of granite blocks with a series of metal domes that are painted silver. The courtyard surrounding the temple is paved with slate flagstones and there are several smaller shrines for attendant deities.

I had been to Gangotri once before, over fifteen years ago, and was surprised and disappointed by the way it has expanded.

From the bus stand all the way to the temple stretches a long bazaar, with shops and restaurants on either side. Altogether there must be over fifty hotels and dharamshalas constructed on either bank of the river, as well as dozens of ashrams and minor temples. Some of these were here when I visited in 1984 but Gangotri has grown from a cluster of rest houses into a small town. Being December, though, everything was deserted. The restaurants were boarded up and the hotels locked. Only a handful of sadhus remain in Gangotri throughout the winter and none of them was out and about. Not one of the shops was open and most of the doors had padlocks sewn up in cloth and sealed with scabs of wax. The signs in the bazaar advertised everything from masala dosa to Fuji film but the main street leading to the temple was completely empty, like a ghost town.

I felt immediately uneasy on my arrival at Gangotri as if a plague or catastrophe had recently swept through the town and driven all of the inhabitants away. The weather too had changed for the worse. Though it had been bright and clear that morning when I left Dharali the sky was now overcast and the air had turned much colder. There were sheets of snow on the ground and it looked as if more were going to fall. A sharp wind had picked up, gnawing at the ragged corner of a plastic sheet that covered the roof of a hotel.

Scraps of paper and plastic bags were blowing about, even though I had seen a garbage incinerator near the bus stand. This had been set up by the Himalayan Environmental Trust, which lists a number of famous mountaineers as patrons, including Maurice Herzog and Edmund Hillary. During the pilgrim season the incinerator burns trash that accumulates in Gangotri but at this time of year it was not used and the streets were littered with the detritus of human habitation.

A series of cement steps led me down to a wooden bridge across the river. Taking shelter from the wind in the courtyard of a rest house, I lit my stove and prepared a meal of rice and dal. While it was cooking, I saw a lone sadhu emerge from one of the ashrams on the opposite bank of the river. He was bundled up in a saffron blanket and moved about like a furtive spirit haunting the empty buildings. After a minute or two he disappeared again. Later I saw smoke emerging from one of the ashrams but no other signs of life.

If there had been only a few buildings at Gangotri or nothing at all, the emptiness and desolation would not have bothered me, but being surrounded by so many locked and empty rooms was disconcerting. There was a feeling of abandonment about the place that made me want to leave immediately. My plan had been to spend the night in Gangotri and there were plenty of spots to pitch my tent, on level areas in front of the rest houses, but the longer I remained the more restless and uncomfortable I became.

After eating my meal I walked back down to the wooden bridge and tried to get as close to the river as I could. Some of the most dramatic physical features at Gangotri are the waterfalls and pools at the head of the gorge. Here the Bhagirathi drops through a series of pale granite cataracts that have been carved into surrealistic shapes by the force of the river. Both in color and texture the rocks look like whipped meringue even though they are as hard as bone. Because of the overhanging cliffs and arched chambers of stone, the Bhagirathi disappears at points, so that one could almost imagine that this is where the river actually begins.

Most of the year the water is a gray, soapy color because of silt carried down from the glacier, but for a few short weeks in winter the river clears. The pale rocks that line its bed give the Bhagirathi a bright turquoise hue. Added to the unusual granite formations are equally strange shapes where the water has sprayed up and frozen into weird conglomerations of ice, opaque tumuli that look like melted glass and dozens of crystal daggers suspended above the stream.

Just below the bridge lie several pools where the water has hollowed out deep reservoirs between the cliffs and the current circles in upon itself before the river tumbles over the next cataract. Three of these pools are known as Bhrahmkund, Gaurikund, and Vishnukund. Though the cliffs make it virtually impossible for anyone to reach the pools they are believed to be the most sacred place for pilgrims to bathe. The majority of devotees perform their ritual ablutions upstream where a cement bathing ghat has been constructed below the main temple. Only during winter, when the water is perfectly clear, can you see the submerged Shiv lingams that lie within these pools—large, naturally rounded rocks that protrude in phallic shapes and receive the continuous libations of the Ganga.

Unfortunately the recent construction of ashrams and hotels at Gangotri has overshadowed these natural phenomena. After looking down into the fantastic, labial shapes of the gorge and seeing the river in its nascent state, one looks up to see a messy clutter of cement walls and tin roofs, wooden balconies and gaudy signboards. Whatever inspiration a pilgrim might take from the natural artistry of these granite sculptures is immediately erased by rows of vacant windows and doorways, drains and gutters, staircases and painted stones. One sign at a hotel next to the bridge advertised ATTACHED BATHS with an arrow pointing to the river. Further downstream, an ashram located directly above Gaurikund had a makeshift washroom constructed on a rock overlooking the pool. A tin bucket on a rope could be lowered into the river to collect the necessary supply of Gangajal, with which to rinse away your sins.

The inhospitable atmosphere at Gangotri and the threat of an impending snowstorm made me decide to retreat down the valley and camp at Lanka for the night. This meant another ten kilometers of walking but I was glad to turn my back on the deserted hotels and restaurants, the empty shrines and haunted streets. Earlier in the day, I had stopped at Lanka on my way upriver and drank tea with another sadhu who lived by the roadside. He seemed an interesting character and our brief conversation made me want to talk with him some more. The tin hut where this sadhu lived was situated in the middle of a grove of deodar trees and there were plenty of places nearby to pitch my tent.

Unlike the white-bearded mendicant I had passed that morning, the sadhu at Lanka had a wild, untamed appearance. His hair and beard were teased into a dark, unruly mane and his clothes and skin were blackened with soot. He looked as if he had just emerged from a coal mine and the whites of his eyes were alarmingly bright. The reason for his sooty features, I discovered, was a fire that burned continuously in his hearth. The interior of the sadhu's hut was completely black as well and looked like a chimney that had never been cleaned. Despite the baba's threatening demeanor he was a gentle and generous man, who hailed me with a loud, *"Hari Om!"* when I returned that evening. Once I had set up my tent, I went into his hut to warm myself by the smoky fire.

The baba asked me whether I had reached Gangotri and when I told him about my experience there, he shrugged indifferently.

"I have been living here at Lanka for more than two years," he said, "but I have never been to Gangotri."

Surprised, I asked him why.

"This is where I have chosen to do my tapasya. Why should I go anywhere else?"

"But wouldn't you want to visit the Gangotri temple and the source of the Ganga?"

He shook his head and laughed

"God is everywhere," he replied.

The sadhu expressed a sentiment that I heard echoed on many different occasions over the course of my pilgrimage. Though each of the main temples in Garhwal is imbued with mythological and spiritual resonance, most Hindus would argue that God is not located in a specific place. Many would claim that the most accessible form of the deity exists within ourselves. This is the paradox of any pilgrimage—the devotee undertakes a spiritual quest, knowing full well that the object of that search lies within himself. A specific destination like Gangotri may signify the completion of a journey and a desire to receive darshan from a material form of the deity but at the same time it is acknowledged that truth can be discovered anywhere along the pilgrim's path.

Later that evening the sadhu explained to me that Lanka got its name from the city of demons in the Ramayana and that this was the place where Ravan had come to do tapasya, before he abducted Sita. In many ways the baba himself looked like a benign demon with his sooty features and tangled hair.

His hut contained two shrines. One was a closetlike space with a shelf displaying pictures of the gods. The most prominent of these was of Krishn playing his flute. Two empty rum bottles stood on either side of the shelf with candles stuck in the tops. The floor of the shrine was also full of empty bottles that the sadhu had collected from the army signal depot in Lanka. The second shrine was dedicated to Shiv and located outside the main shelter, under an awning of tin sheets. It consisted of a large stone lingam, guarded by two tridents and a metal cobra. Hanging directly above the lingam was a brass pot of Gangajal.

The fire, which burned continuously inside the hut, was also treated as a shrine. Whenever he tended his hearth, the sadhu muttered a prayer and he referred to the flames as Agni, the

Vedic god of fire. For fuel the baba had a dry deodar log, about six feet long, which was smoldering at one end. Behind the shed was a stack of dry wood collected from the forest. Whenever he wanted to make tea or cook his food, the baba added a few sticks to the coals and blew on these to get a flame going. An iron tripod was used to position his pots and pans and each time any tea or food was prepared the baba ceremoniously offered the first spoonful to the flames, mumbling an invocation. For him the fire was not only a necessity in winter but a symbol of energy and life. Most of the time he sat directly beside the hearth and as the log burned down the baba moved it forward gradually. Whenever he lit a chillum of ganja, which he did at frequent intervals, the sadhu used a pair of tongs to pick up a coal from the fire. Once again he would make reverent utterances to the flames, exhaling the smoke with a heartfelt "Om!" In many ways he seemed a part of the fire himself, covered as he was in soot and wreathed in smoke.

Like many sadhus he was something of a showman, performing his rituals with a dramatic flourish. In the middle of our conversation, he would suddenly pick up a small drum from the shadows behind him and beat it with one hand to emphasize a point. From time to time he'd wave a burning stick about like a sacramental taper, as if he were searching for mystical omens in the smoke. Many of these gestures were obviously improvised for my benefit but unlike some sadhus I met, who demanded my attention (and my money), the baba at Lanka had an endearing, inoffensive manner.

He told me that he had traveled for many years before coming to Garhwal and described the places he had seen in other parts of India—Varanasi, Calcutta, Rajasthan. The baba also recounted other pilgrimages I should make, almost as if he were a spiritual travel agent recommending religious itineraries.

"I've been abroad as well," he said, with an offhand gesture. "Ten, twelve years back."

"Where did you go?"

"England. Italy. Cyprus. Lebanon. Egypt." He counted the countries on his fingers.

When I told him that I used to live in Egypt myself, he immediately threw out a few phrases of simple Arabic and for the rest of the time he called me Habibi.

"What made you visit all these places?" I asked, intrigued.

"There were two foreigners I met in Varanasi," said the baba, "one Italian and one Australian. They got me a passport and a ticket and took me with them. I am a sanyasi. I had no interest in going abroad but they insisted. We flew directly to London from Delhi. From there we went overland by train and bus. We took a boat to Cyprus and on to Lebanon. But I liked Egypt best of all. Cairo is a great city. The Egyptians asked me, Where have you come from? When I said India, they were very happy. *'Al Hind,'* they said, *'Ahlan Wa Sahlan. Habibi.'* Being vegetarian it was difficult to get proper food but I loved to eat tamia and ful beans. I also ate plenty of pizza."

He rambled on about his journey for almost an hour and told me how he and his companions had been arrested in Beirut because they didn't have visas. The sadhu had finally persuaded the police to let them go because he was a sufi.

"No matter where you go in the world people recognize a man of faith. Even if I am a Hindu and they are Muslims. What does it matter? We all believe in God."

By this time it was growing dark and I was surprised to see two figures appear in the doorway of the hut, for I had assumed that there was nobody else around. As the men removed their shoes and came inside I could see they were soldiers.

The two men greeted the baba with folded hands and he told

them to sit down beside the fire. After I had introduced myself
the soldiers explained that they were with the Army Signal
Corps. A radio transmitter at Lanka is used to communicate
with other army posts in the region and their job was to monitor
the road that goes up to Keylong, near the Tibetan border. In
winter three soldiers were posted at Lanka and while one was
on duty the other two often came to the baba's hut and ate their
evening meal with him.

Both men were from the plains, one from Punjab and the
other from Haryana. They complained about the cold and the
boredom of their job but otherwise seemed content. The army
kept them well supplied with rations and the soldiers shared
whatever they had with the sadhu. Soon after their arrival they
began to prepare our dinner, setting a pressure cooker of dal on
the fire and kneading dough for chappatis. As they worked the
baba gave elaborate instructions on what spices to put in the
dal. From his larder—a metal trunk hidden away in a corner of
the shed—he produced a tin of butter that was opened in my
honor. Though the two soldiers were respectful toward the baba
they also teased him with gentle banter, playfully referring to
themselves as his disciples.

Once the sadhu was satisfied that preparations for dinner
were properly under way, he arose from his place by the fire and
announced that he was going to perform his evening aarti. The
darkness was almost complete and there was only the glow of
firelight inside the hut. First the baba lit candles in the inner
shrine, then a small oil lamp that he waved in front of the pictures of the gods. He began chanting a Sanskrit prayer and his
voice had a musical quality that gave the words an added resonance. Slowly at first, but picking up the tempo gradually, the
baba began to dance in rhythm with his prayers. His right hand
held the oil lamp and in his left he had a pair of tiny brass cymbals that kept time with the cadence of his words. As he spun

about and leaped from one side of the hut to the next, his shadow followed him across the walls. For a minute or two he would address himself to the shelf of deities in the shrine, then swoop down in front of the hearth and chant into the flames, the lamp orbiting around the fire and the cymbals flickering like flying embers. I couldn't understand most of what he said but much of the prayer seemed to list the names of different Hindu gods, though he also included Jesus Christ and Allah.

While this was going on the two soldiers and I sat in silence, watching the performance taking place around us. Sometimes it seemed as if there was more than just one sadhu dancing, as if he had separated into several figures. His voice rose in volume and within the enclosed space of the hut it sounded like a chorus. After a quarter of an hour the baba abruptly went outside and danced in front of the Shiv lingam for a while, lighting two more oil lamps that were suspended from the rafters. Finally, his voice erupted in a loud *"Om Nam Shivam! Om!"* I had noticed earlier that he didn't use a conch shell but instead he bellowed out the sacred syllable with the full force of his lungs. When the sadhu returned inside he brought the oil lamp in front of each of us, so that we could run our hands over the flame and receive its blessing.

He concluded the aarti with a final prayer to the fire, then applied a generous tilak of ash to his forehead. After that he settled down by the hearth once again and lit another chillum of ganja, which he smoked in silence for several minutes, ignoring the soldiers and me completely. Outside the hut there was no sound except for the distant roar of the Ganga flowing through the Bhairon Ghatti gorge.

# III
# REFLECTION

*Who sees all beings in his own Self,*
*and his own Self in all beings, loses all fear.*

ISA UPANISHAD

# THE COW'S MOUTH

GANGOTRI WAS UNRECOGNIZABLE WHEN I WENT
back in the middle of May, four and a half months after my winter pilgrimage. Hundreds of cars and buses sped along the
motor road and soon after the taxi I was riding in crossed the
bridge at Lanka, we found ourselves in a traffic jam. Vehicles
were lined up in both directions and yatra buses were parked
bumper to bumper along the roadside. Half a dozen policemen
were trying to direct traffic but all they could do was blow their
whistles and wave their arms as the drivers edged forward, a
few inches at a time, squeezing past each other on the narrow
turns. In the end I abandoned my taxi about two kilometers
below Gangotri and walked the rest of the way, dodging back
and forth between the vehicles, until I reached the main bazaar.
Crowds of pilgrims were milling about the lanes, which had
been completely deserted in December. All of the rest houses
and ashrams were fully occupied and rooms were being rented
for exorbitant rates. Unable to afford accommodation, many of
the yatris had camped out in the open. Some had constructed
temporary shelters using plastic sheets, while others found
refuge under trees and rocks. The sanitary facilities provided by
the state government consisted of rows of temporary latrines.
These were made of burlap curtains stretched over bamboo
frames, which offered minimal privacy and no running water.

The area surrounding the latrines was sprinkled with powdered lime, which serves as a disinfectant, though the smell of urine and human ordure was sickeningly pungent.

Lines of beggars sat along the edges of the bazaar and next to them were money changers with mountains of coins, recycling the alms doled out by pilgrims. Dozens of itinerant vendors had also staked out their positions at the side of the street, displaying rings and necklaces of semiprecious stones, conch shells, rudraksha beads, and medicinal roots. Several of the vendors were selling what they claimed to be musk deer glands, though these were nothing but dried goat scrotums stuffed with sawdust and scented with cheap perfume. When I asked the price one man quoted five hundred rupees and handed me one of the balls to sniff. It smelled like rose water and was so obviously fake I couldn't believe that anyone would seriously think of buying it. However, many of the pilgrims who come to Gangotri seem to have suspended any sense of rationality and readily accept the prescriptions and pronouncements of these charlatans and touts. Preying on the gullibility of yatris the vendors hawk medicinal herbs that are either spurious or adulterated—desiccated dahlia bulbs sold as aconite roots, or powdered nostrums that are said to cure everything from dyspepsia to diabetes. During the pilgrimage season diseases flourish at Gangotri, particularly amoebic dysentery and gastrointestinal infections spread by unpurified water.

In May and June most of the sadhus and rishis emerge from their winter hibernation and dozens of mendicants migrate up to Gangotri for the summer, collecting donations and providing spiritual counsel. In front of one ashram I saw a sign announcing that the "Mahatma" who resided there was only available for public audience from 4:00 to 4:30 every afternoon. There was also a stern warning that absolutely no accommodation was available at this ashram. Though each of these holy men has taken sanyas and renounced the material world, many of them collect a good deal of money for their austerities. Plenty of genuine mystics live in the Himalayas, but there are an equal number of frauds, like one sadhu I met near Gangotri.

He was a vigorous, well-built man in his early thirties with an oiled black beard and heavy wooden earrings. Greeting me with a loud *"Hari Om!"* he blocked my path and demanded that I give him money. When I refused and pushed my way past, the sadhu shook his trident in a threatening manner and cursed me for showing him no respect. At first I wasn't particularly worried but a few corners ahead, I found myself surrounded by a cloud of bees. For a moment I thought that the sadhu had used his powers to summon the swarm. Fortunately they did not attack, circling around me harmlessly before flying off into the valley.

The temple at Gangotri had a queue that stretched across the courtyard and down the steps to the bathing ghat. Pilgrims stood in line for hours to perform pooja, holding trays of coconuts, rice, flower petals, and incense. The trays are sold at shops near the entrance to the temple. Priests lie in wait for each pilgrim bus, as it disgorges another group of unsuspecting devotees. These brahmin pandas, who hold the ancestral rights to conduct religious ceremonies at Gangotri, attach themselves to yatris and lead them through the complicated steps of worship. Often they will meet pilgrim parties in Devprayag or Uttarkashi and travel up to Gangotri with them, taking on the role of spiritual tour guides. Years ago, before the motor roads were built, these pandas often escorted pilgrims as they walked along the Char Dham route. Now they have had to adapt to the changing pattern of the pilgrimage. Traditionally the pandas recounted the myths and legends of Hindu shrines, providing an accompanying narrative for the journey. Today their importance has diminished and one of the pandas I met in Gangotri complained that his livelihood was threatened because the pilgrims were no longer interested in hearing his stories.

"Haven't you seen?" he said. "Now all of the pilgrim buses are video coaches and instead of listening to the tales and legends from the Ramayana, the yatris are entertained by Bombay films. Rather than go to the temple or bathe in the Ganga, many of them prefer to sit in their buses and watch movies."

Once again I had no desire to spend the night in Gangotri and I headed directly up the valley, on my way to Gaumukh Glacier and Tapovan. A bridle path runs along the northwest bank of the Bhagirathi and during the pilgrim season it is heavily traveled. In recent years efforts have been made to protect the valley from pollution and deforestation. The Himalayan Environmental Trust, a nonprofit organization, collaborates with the forestry department to control the problem of litter. It is a remarkably simple but successful project. A forest checkpoint has been erected about a kilometer above Gangotri where pilgrims on their way to Gaumukh are asked to write down the number of plastic bags and bottles they are carrying. On their return they must show that they have brought these back with them. In addition to this garbage bins are located at each of the halts along the route. In comparison to many of the other pilgrimage sites in Garhwal, the trek from Gangotri to Gaumukh is relatively free of rubbish.

The valley itself offers one of the most accessible and scenic walks in the Himalayas, with high snow peaks on either side and the river bordered by forests of deodar, pine, and birch. The sides of the trail are draped with pink and white musk roses that bloom in May and June. Despite the seasonal influx of pilgrims the valley has been spared most of the destructive encroachments that have ruined Gangotri. When I stopped at the checkpoint I asked how many pilgrims went up to Gaumukh and the guard told me that 187 people had passed through the gate the day before. He said this was an average number for that time of year. Some of the pilgrims ride on ponies and mules but most make the journey on foot, walking up to Bhojbasa where they spend the night, then continuing on to Gaumukh the next morning. Altogether it is a distance of eighteen kilometers from Gangotri to the glacier, a gradual but steady climb.

I started late in the afternoon and stopped at Chirbasa, eight kilometers above Gangotri, where I camped in a grove of pine trees below the path. There are tea shops and shelters at Chirbasa but I was able to pitch my tent in a secluded glen just above the river. After the traffic jams and crowds at Gangotri, it was a relief to be alone at last.

As I sat in front of my tent and boiled a pot of water to cook rice, the sun was still gleaming off the snow peaks, though the valley lay in shadow. The air was cool but the temperature remained well above freezing. Flowers were blooming among the rocks and the resinous scent of pine and juniper sweetened the air. Below me I could hear the gnashing of the river as it cut through rocky moraine, eroding away layers of debris that the receding glacier has exposed. In certain places like Chirbasa, trees and plants have taken root, while in other areas there is no vegetation, only a barren expanse of stones and rubble. Looking down the valley I could no longer see Gangotri for it was hidden behind a ridge. In the opposite direction, at the head of the valley, were the three Bhagirathi peaks that stand sentinel over Gaumukh.

There was something raw and unfinished about the landscape, as if the river was still struggling to establish its course. The mountains looked as if they had been freshly chiseled, sculpted into jagged shapes, with flakes of stone scattered at their feet. The sheets of snow that covered the summits of the highest peaks made them look like statues yet to be unveiled.

Even the pine forest where I camped seemed to have grown up only recently. As the sunlight faded and the shadows converged, I was aware of an elemental tension in the terrain—the tidal pull of the glacier as it receded, the indomitable current of the river surging downstream, the ever-changing shapes of ridgelines and ravines, all of the conflicting forces in nature that leave their signatures on the valley from one season to the next.

Chirbasa means "place of the pines" and the forest that covers this ridge is now protected. Seven kilometers farther on lies Bhojbasa, "place of the birches," though none of these trees remains because they have been cut for fuel by pilgrims. In the last two decades a number of tea shops and rest houses have sprung up at Bhojbasa, but originally there was only a single dharamshala run by an eccentric and temperamental sadhu named Lal Baba. Though he styles himself as the protector of this site, Lal Baba and his retinue have been accused by some environmentalists of destroying the forest at Bhojbasa. Efforts are under way to replant the birch groves, and the forest department has established several nurseries. It is a difficult task, however, for Bhojbasa lies at the extreme edge of the timberline and winters at this altitude are severe. Even lower down the valley, wind and snow twist the trees into crippled shapes.

Himalayan birches have a special significance in Hindu mythology for the bark of these trees, known as bhoj patra, is said to have been used by ancient sages to record Hindu legends and scriptures. Though few of these written texts have survived, the popular image of a saintly ascetic inscribing sacred verses on birch bark reinforces the belief that wisdom can only be acquired through an escape into nature. Just as Vyasa and Valmiki sought exile in the forest to compose their oral epics, other holy men retreated to the high Himalayas and transcribed their spiritual discoveries on the papery bhoj patra. Some of the birch trees grow to ten or twelve inches in girth, and the bark peels off in leathery strips. Though the outer layers are a silvery white the inner surfaces are a pale salmon color and smooth as parchment.

The next morning, as I approached the tea shops at Bhojbasa, I was startled to see a foreigner running down the path to meet me. He was English, about sixty years old, with a flushed red face and sparse white hair. His eyes were wide with alarm and at first I thought there had been some sort of accident. Waving his hands anxiously, he blurted out, "I say, have you got any camera batteries? Mine have gone dead and I didn't bring any spares."

Startled by the intensity of his gestures I shook my head.

"Damn it! Trip of a lifetime," he said in flustered disappointment. "Now it's completely ruined."

There was something both pathetic and absurd about the Englishman's behavior. The fact that he had forgotten to carry an extra set of batteries seemed foolish enough but his assumption that the success of his journey depended on the photographs he might have taken was altogether ridiculous. If he had been less concerned about the failure of his camera, he probably would have discovered that his own eyes gave him a much greater appreciation of the mountains and a more vivid set of memories.

In the past I have taken my camera on other treks but as I prepared for this pilgrimage, I made a conscious decision to leave it behind. Part of the reason was practical, for photography takes a lot of time and effort if the results are to be at all worthwhile. There is nothing more frustrating and time consuming than stopping every hundred meters to take a picture. More important, however, I wanted to focus on the immediate experience of my pilgrimage rather than trying to preserve fragmented images for posterity. When one is looking at everything through the viewfinder of a camera, worrying about shutter speeds, f-stops, and depth of focus, the innate beauty of a scene is often lost. The lens through which a photographer observes the world may capture a spectacular vision of the mountains but it can never compare with the human eye. Not having a camera forced me to look at the mountains more carefully, to observe the details of a scene and commit them to memory.

Whenever I study photographs of places I have visited, I am aware of what has been left out. This has less to do with the framing of a photograph than the way in which we see the world. It is not a flat, two-dimensional image. There are no borders. The colors have a greater range and depth. But more than that, the landscape changes—the light, the perspective, the arrangement of objects. Our eyes are able to absorb all this and take in the complexities of nature that a camera can only suggest. After all, the shutter opens for less than a hundredth of a second, while we can look at a scene for hours. Walking up and down the Gangotri Valley I was able to observe each peak from different angles and at different times of the day, so that not only were my memories recorded in three dimensions, but over time as well.

Gaumukh. The cow's mouth—or translated more accurately, its facial features. Scholars trace the significance of cows in Hindu tradition back to the Aryan herdsmen who shepherded their cattle over the Himalayas when they first came to India. The Vedas contain the legend of Surabhi, the cow of plenty, who was created out of the churning of a primordial ocean, which also produced fountains of milk and curd. Surabhi gave birth to a calf named Nandini, who belonged to the sage Vashishta. As munificent as her mother, Nandini provided Vashishta with everything he desired.

In subsequent myths, the avatar of Krishn has reinforced

the cow's place in Hindu culture. As a child he drank milk directly from the cow's udders and stole butter from a churn. In later life, Krishn is often depicted as a herdsman, playing his flute while docile white cattle graze in the meadows and sacred groves of Brindavan. Unlike the buffalo, which is often a demonic symbol, the cow is seen as a gentle, benevolent beast, whose milk represents maternal sustenance and purity. The ghee, or clarified butter, from cow's milk fuels the lamps in many Hindu temples. Even cowdung and cow urine are believed to be pure and to kill a cow is one of the greatest sins, which leads to punishment in future lives. Over the course of the twentieth century, cows have taken on political as well as religious overtones. Leaders like Mahatma Gandhi and Vinoba Bhave reasserted traditional Hindu beliefs regarding their protection and sanctity, while using them as emblems of self-sufficiency and social change.

Water from the Ganga is often compared to cow's milk on account of its purity and cleansing qualities. As the Bhagirathi emerges from Gaumukh Glacier, it actually has the appearance of milk, though instead of being white it is a viscous gray color. The silt that mixes with this stream is sometimes referred to as "glacial rock flour," a description that more accurately reflects the color and consistency of the water. I found that even when I left a bottle of Gangajal sitting overnight very little of the sediment settled to the bottom and it retained the opacity of milk. Only during winter, when the glacier stops melting and the river is reduced to a narrow stream, does the Bhagirathi become absolutely clear.

There is no temple at Gaumukh, though a few temporary shrines have been erected near the source. The trail from Gangotri ends about half a kilometer below the snout of the glacier and pilgrims must clamber over rocks and boulders to reach the river's edge. A detour across the glacier continues on to Tapovan, which lies five kilometers higher up. The Bhagirathi issues out of a frozen cavern at the center of a gray-blue wall of ice, about four hundred meters across. At its source the river is roughly thirty feet wide, a large, fast-flowing stream. The water is freezing cold and when I stepped into a shallow pool at the foot of the glacier, my toes and ankles felt as if they had been gripped in a vice. Though I lacked the courage to submerge myself in the river, I did perform a brief ablution, splashing the water upon my face. In Garhwali there is a saying, *"Panch snaan, mukh gyan."* (Bathing the five facial features gives you the facade of wisdom.)

Scooping up Gangajal in my cupped palms I drank from the source, feeling first the sharp coldness in my teeth like bits of ice drilling into my skull, a throbbing in my temples. It took a few seconds before I could taste the minerals on my tongue—a clean, bitter flavor, almost medicinal, with a silty residue. At the back of my throat I could feel a cold numbness long after I swallowed and this sensation spread throughout my body, as if the water had been absorbed directly into my veins.

On either side of me the cliffs of ice were melting. Every few minutes a slab of the glacier broke free and tumbled into the water with a resounding splash. Meanwhile, the rocks that form a crust on top of the glacier also kept crashing down into the river. One of these, about the size of a basketball, missed me by a few feet. Most of the pilgrims kept a safe distance, filling their water bottles with Gangajal well below the cliffs of ice, but there was one young man who had climbed as close to the glacier as he could. Sitting on a rock at the water's edge he was writing in his journal, unperturbed as chunks of ice and stone crashed down around him. The only other person, besides myself, who was foolish enough to go that far was a gaunt-looking sadhu, carrying a cloth bundle on his shoulder along with a trident and a pair of iron tongs.

He beckoned to me as I was making my way back down to safety. Though the sound of the river was so loud we couldn't hear each other speak, the sadhu indicated through gestures that he needed a match. When I produced a box from my pocket, he immediately squatted down and took out a chillum full of ganja, holding it cupped between his hands. There was a sharp breeze blowing off the glacier that made it difficult to light the chillum but after using up half my box of matches we finally got it going. Inhaling a cloud of fragrant smoke, the sadhu offered me the chillum, then grinned when I shook my head. Leaving him contentedly puffing on his ganja, I retrieved my pack and scrambled up the rocks until I reached the path to Tapovan.

Here I stopped to rest and get my bearings. The glacier filled the valley above Gaumukh though very little of the ice was visible for it was covered with debris, a rough moonscape of stones and gravel. Straight ahead were the trio of peaks, Bhagirathi I, II, and III, like gleaming white turrets at the head of the valley. In the opposite direction, about three kilometers lower down, lay the tea shops at Bhojbasa where I had met the distraught photographer. It was now late in the morning and the sun was directly overhead. On the opposite side of the glacier, roughly southeast, I could see the top of Shivling peak, a spire of snow and ice. In front of this mountain stood a wall of crumbling moraine that rose about eight hundred feet above the glacier. A stream of water was flowing down this slope and it had gouged a crooked ravine in the exposed soil. At places I could see signs of a trail and the top of the climb was marked by a flagpole with a tattered strip of cotton waving in the wind. Each year the path across the glacier has to be reconstructed because the winter snow and shifting ice destroy whatever route was laid out the summer before. To call it a path is somewhat misleading. A series of small cairns—five or six rocks piled on top of each other—outline the safest route, skirting crevasses and avoiding unstable sections of the glacier. At many places pilgrims have to leap from one boulder to the next or crawl through fissures in the ice. Though the crossing is not particularly dangerous, it is easy to get lost for the cairns have a way of disappearing at places and there is no defined trail, other than a few scattered footprints.

Just as I was about to set off I saw the sadhu coming toward me. He was walking with an energetic stride, obviously fired up with the ganja he had smoked. Hailing me he shouted, *"Bolo Bam Bam Bolo!"* and raced on in the direction of Tapovan. Not even trying to keep pace with him I followed slowly, picking my way over the rutted surface of the glacier. The altitude at Gaumukh is about twelve thousand feet and even the slightest climb takes some effort, particularly when the rocks provide uneven footholds over the furrows of ice. My pack seemed to weigh twice as much as usual and my boots felt as if they were filled with sand.

Focusing my eyes on the cairns I tried to avoid looking up at the final ascent to Tapovan, which seemed to grow steeper and steeper the closer I got. Halfway across the glacier, I caught sight of the sadhu about a hundred meters off to my left. He had obviously wandered away from the trail and was working his way back in my direction, slipping on the loose stones and gesturing frantically for me to wait. Eventually the two of us met up again in a shallow trough between two ridges of ice. The sadhu immediately collapsed against a rock and his bloodshot eyes betrayed his exhaustion. The effects of his chillum had clearly worn off and I tried to revive him by giving him some water to drink and biscuits to eat.

The sadhu spoke very little Hindi and I learned later that he came from Assam. Having abandoned his wife and two children a year ago, he had traveled all the way from Gauhati. He told me that he had come "to find my death," as he put it, in the mountains above Gangotri. Leaning back against the rock with his eyes glazed and his mouth agape, he looked as if he was about to expire. I tried to persuade him to go back down to Bhojbasa but the sadhu insisted on accompanying me to Tapovan. With great difficulty he got to his feet again and leaning on his trident he kept coughing and wheezing. After every few steps I had to stop and let him catch up. Whenever we sat down to rest the sadhu complained about the climb, as if it were my fault, and before we were halfway to the top he had emptied my water bottle.

From the edge of the glacier up to Tapovan our trail followed the shortest possible route, cutting back and forth across the slope to avoid treacherous sections of moraine. It was a dangerous climb and the slightest misstep would have sent us cartwheeling onto the rocks below. With the sadhu staggering behind me I kept trying to imagine what I would do if he fell. By this time I was so irritated by his complaints that I wondered if I would even try to rescue him. Whenever I got more than twenty feet ahead the sadhu called out in a pitiful voice, asking me to wait. The ascent was difficult enough as it was but with the sadhu in tow it took me over an hour and a half to cover a distance of two kilometers. On our way up we passed a couple of Germans who were coming down from Tapovan. One of them grinned and said, "Very steep," as if I hadn't noticed. When we finally arrived at the top, the sadhu dropped to his knees near the flagpole, moaning, *"Har Har Mahadev!"* and holding his head in his hands.

The word Tapovan suggests a forest retreat where tapasya is performed, and there are several places in Uttarakhand that bear this name, the most famous of which is a sacred grove near Rishikesh. At Tapovan, above Gaumukh, there are no trees though the landscape changes dramatically. Instead of the barren, rock-strewn surface of the glacier and the perpendicular slopes of loose moraine, there is a broad plateau, almost as level as the baize surface of a billiards table. Through the middle of this meadow runs a meandering stream that glides between fields of grass without a ripple on its surface. Near the point where the path crested the ridge, I saw two bharal, or blue sheep, grazing on the meadow. They were only a hundred feet away but ignored the sadhu and me as we sat and rested on the grass. About the size of domestic sheep, the bharal had grayish wool and looked as if they were molting. The Gaumukh Valley is a wildlife sanctuary and closed to shepherds. Bharal and Himalayan thar, a species of mountain goat that also live here, have these high pastures to themselves and are relatively tame. Being above the tree line, there aren't many birds or animals that can survive at this altitude, though I did see flocks of snow pigeons, their white wings flashing as they wheeled above the exposed rocks.

On a large boulder near the top of the path is a memorial plaque for a mountaineer named Rajiv Raj who died in 1990 while climbing Kirti Stambh, one of the mountains above Tapovan. These meadows are used as a base camp for expeditions to the surrounding peaks and in the distance I could see a dozen or more tents pitched at the far side of the plateau. Straight ahead was Shivling peak, which rises directly out of the meadows. This mountain is often compared to the Matterhorn in shape and stature, a tower of rock and ice that punctures the sky with its tapered summit. Worshiped as a representation of the phallic form of Shiv, the mountain dominates the skyline, even though it is not as high as many of the surrounding peaks.

On reaching Tapovan my first concern was to detach myself

from the sadhu, who seemed to think that I was responsible for his continued survival. A short distance from the edge of the meadow, we found a couple of stone sheds, one of which was a dharamshala. With some difficulty I was able to persuade the sadhu that he should stay here for the night rather than sharing my tent. He was obviously feeling the altitude and kept pressing his temples gingerly. I gave him a couple of painkillers for his headache and left him in the care of two other pilgrims who had arrived ahead of us. As I set off to find a place to camp, I noticed the sadhu had already cadged a cigarette from them. He was the kind of needy, aggravating person who is completely dependent on others and I was glad to see the last of him.

Several mendicants live year-round at Tapovan. One of these men, known as Simla Baba, has been there for over fifteen years. During the summer months he looks after the dharamshala and provides food and shelter for the few pilgrims who come to Tapovan, freely distributing whatever he receives as donations. From October until April he lives in isolation under a blanket of snow. I met Simla Baba briefly the next day and he impressed me as a quiet, self-sufficient ascetic, with a dignified and saintly appearance, the complete opposite of the sadhu from Assam.

At Tapovan I also met a man named Pradhuman Panchmia, who had come all the way from Calcutta to spend a two-weeks' holiday in Garhwal. He was a Jain and not a Hindu, as I first assumed, though after we had been talking for a while Pradhuman confessed that he was a "nonbeliever." The Jain religion teaches us that every form of life is sacred and orthodox members of this community are strict vegetarians who cover their mouths with cotton masks so that they will not breathe in any insects. Closer in theology to Buddhism than Hinduism, the Jain faith has survived in India for centuries, even though it is represented by a very small minority.

Pradhuman and his wife had arrived in Tapovan the day before. Though both of them were suffering from the altitude and hadn't been able to sleep all night they spent the day strolling about the meadows and gazing up at the magnificent heights of Shivling peak. We sat together on the rocks near my tent and chatted for a while. They told me that they had three daughters and were proud of the fact that the eldest girl had a Jain name, the second a Hindu name, and the third a Buddhist name. Being a skeptic, however, Pradhuman was suspicious of popular religion. He told me that his favorite author was Bertrand Russell, though he also enjoyed reading the stories of W. Somerset Maugham. Despite being a self-described rationalist, he recognized the sanctity of nature.

"I don't come here to pray at the temples," he said. "I come here for the mountains. Instead of worshiping gods and goddesses, we should worship nature."

The meadows at Tapovan are similar to arctic tundra, a thick, spongy layer of earth and matted roots that is saturated with moisture and remains frozen throughout winter. Even in the middle of May the ground hardened at night and thawed out around noon. The stream that winds its way through the meadow channels water down from the snow peaks and the entire plateau serves as a reservoir, a high-altitude aquifer hidden beneath a carpet of grass. Later in the year, during the height of the monsoon, Tapovan comes to life with a profusion of wildflowers. While I was there, however, it was still too cold for anything more than a few hardy gentians blooming close to the ground. The grass was not as lush as it would be in another month and when I looked at it closely I could see where the green blades had been scorched by frost.

The spot where I chose to camp was slightly higher than

most of the surrounding area, though it was close to the stream. A few feet away was a low escarpment that served as a shelter from the wind. What I hadn't anticipated was that the water level rose every night with the melting and freezing of the snow. Though the area around my tent was dry when I went to bed, the next morning I woke up to find my tent surrounded by a shallow pond of ice. The circle of rocks I had constructed to shield my stove the night before was partially submerged, for the water had risen nearly six inches. At dawn a heavy frost lay over the meadow like a dusting of confectioners' sugar and when I got up my tent was completely white.

Though Gaumukh Glacier is considered by most people to be the primary source of the Ganga, an argument can easily be made that the origins of this river lie higher up, near Tapovan and beyond. In fact, at each of the four main sources of the Ganga—Yamnotri, Gangotri, Kedarnath, and Badrinath—pilgrims are confronted with the paradox of a source that is not a source. All of the major tributaries seem to flow from somewhere farther back in the mountains. Even if we followed every stream to its point of origin and measured and mapped the terrain, there would still be no way of asserting the precedence of one source over the other. Each has its season—while one stream may seem larger in the spring, others grow stronger during the monsoon, and only a few continue to flow during winter.

Finding the source of a river is just as impossible as marking the point where a circle begins. Yet it seems to be one of the guiding principles of modern geography. In the nineteenth century, European explorers displayed an obsession for searching out the sources of rivers that flowed through their colonies. Part of our fascination with the origin of rivers may stem from these myths of adventure but there is also a spiritual dimension to the quest that goes back much further. For the pilgrim who travels to the headwaters of the Ganga, this journey upstream mirrors his search for God and the ambiguities of the source suggest the ultimate enigmas of the soul.

Why then should we assign any importance to a source? Wouldn't it be more sensible to worship the Ganga at its widest point or bathe exactly halfway between the mountains and the sea? There is no reason to believe that one section of the current is more sacred than the next, when it is constantly flowing in the same direction. Part of our fascination with sources may come from a belief in the essential spirit of a river, that imaginary point of distillation, the purest drop, from which all other drops are formed. But where exactly is that seminal essence to be found? Does it lie deep within the marshy soil at Tapovan or is it frozen in the ice at Gaumukh? Does it seep out of the rocks at the foot of Shivling peak or is it suspended in the clouds that crown its summit?

Then again, perhaps there is another reason for this quest, a further paradox that cancels out the first and tells us more about ourselves than it does about the river. It could be that we seek the origins of the Ganga so that we can go beyond that point to a place where the river does not exist.

# THE SHAPE OF A STONE

IN 1844 AN ENGLISHMAN WHO IDENTIFIED HIM-
self only by the pen name "Pilgrim" published an account of his
travels through Garhwal. The book is titled *Wanderings in the
Himmala* and it reveals as much about the prejudices and per-
versions of British colonialism as it does about the territory he
covered. Starting from the hill station of Mussoorie, Pilgrim
headed up into the Bhagirathi Valley. Instead of going to Gangotri, however, he and his party crossed directly over to Kedarnath and Badrinath, by way of Belak, Buda Kedar, and Panwali.

This expedition consisted of three white "sahibs" and seventy-
five Garhwali porters, as well as twenty assorted staff and ser-
vants—a party roughly a hundred strong. At the beginning of
his book Pilgrim writes, "With such a large number of men for
carrying our baggage . . . you will be rather surprised, I dare
say, to be told that I was so hard pressed for conveyance, as to
be compelled to leave behind a great number of articles, which,
under ordinary circumstances, you would consider indispensa-
ble." One of the items he regretted not taking with him was a
three-volume encyclopedia of geology, which would probably
have made up one porter's load on its own.

Reading Pilgrim's account of his "wanderings," I cannot
help but be struck by the excessive accoutrements of expeditions like this and wonder at the purpose of all those men and

equipment. Though he speaks of the dangers of "starvation" along the route, it wasn't as though he was traveling through a wilderness. In fact much of the journey followed the traditional yatra route and basic provisions must have been available in larger villages and towns. The logistical nightmare of organizing so many porters would seem to have overshadowed the comforts of eighty-pound tents, washbasins, thunder boxes, folding beds, and camp chairs that they carried on their backs. At the same time it is obvious that part of the reason for this journey was to be in command; Pilgrim was a man who clearly relished his own sense of superiority. Throughout the book he treats his Garhwali porters with disdain. "Altogether the natives of the hills far excel those of the plains in the fabrication of complaints, which have little or no foundation. They are, I think, the most fickle and changeable race under the sun."

Yet these are the same men who faithfully carry Pilgrim in a sedan chair when he comes down with malarial fever. Once he recovers, the Englishman devises a unique method of negotiating the steeper climbs. He harnesses four porters to ropes that are then fastened to a broad leather belt around his waist. In this way he is dragged up the path by "four hill men on whom now devolved the delightful duty of supporting me in an upright position, leaving me little to do, but move on the legs. The relief accorded by this was beyond all conception, and I recommend any one, similarly situated, having recourse to this simple contrivance."

The arrogance and absurdity of this adventure, which involved plenty of hunting along the way, is difficult to reconcile with the idea of a pilgrimage. Despite his sanctimonious pseudonym the author provides a ready disclaimer. "In case some readers should suspect me of belonging to the Hindoo religion . . . I take the opportunity of denying it, and assuring them that I was not a party to any of the rites and ceremonies connected with the worship of Siva and Vishnoo." In fact, he has little to say about the shrines along his route and the few Hindu myths he recounts are garbled beyond recognition.

While he spends a good deal of time denigrating the people of Garhwal, Pilgrim's book is predictably full of praise for the Himalayan landscapes he encounters. Most Englishmen that ruled India clearly preferred picturesque scenery over the populace of their empire. "The contemplation of the stupendous works of nature leads us to imbibe a taste for pursuits, which otherwise might not have suggested themselves to us; it inspires us with resolution to overcome difficulties, and combat with adversity; it gives renewed vigour to the body, and softens the heart and mind; and awakens associations, which by directing our thoughts more impressively towards the first great cause, give us fortitude to bear disappointments and afflictions, and furnish new impulses to the anxious and inquiring mind."

This is one of the few sentences in his book that suggests any spiritual motives. It would seem that Pilgrim might have been better able to "contemplate" nature if he had traveled alone and carried his own load rather than relying on an army of porters he despised. Though the accounts of English travelers and mountaineers—many of whom are far more reliable and sensitive than Pilgrim—provide us with a record of Garhwal's recent history and geography, they must always be read with a degree of caution. Like any myths, these narratives contain heroes, gods, and demons but sometimes it is difficult to tell which is which.

At dusk the sound of drums reverberates throughout the valley. On the ridge across from me lies the village of Sulla where the Bajgi drummers are beating a final tattoo, calling the faithful to gather at the temple and waking the gods from their primordial sleep. After days of walking within earshot of the Ganga's constant roar, I have left the river behind. Now there is silence, except for the drums. It is like hearing the pulse of the forest, a steady throbbing that echoes between the ridges and brings the day to a close.

I have pitched my tent in an abandoned field beside a spring. Nearby is a grove of Himalayan tun trees—*Cedrella serrata,* the Latin name assigned by British botanists. These trees grow close together, their tall, straight shapes opening out into a parasol of branches. Picking a leaf from one of the saplings I crush it between my fingers and recognize the sour, slightly fetid scent of tun. Wood from these trees is used for making drums, their smooth trunks hollowed out and carved into tapered cylinders. Both ends are covered with goatskin, a taut, dry membrane that rustles at the slightest touch. With a pair of curved sticks the drummers beat a syncopated rhythm.

Standing alone in the forest, beneath the overlapping shadows of the trees, I listen to the sound of temple drums as they give voice to the secret vocabulary of the tun.

From Gangotri the pilgrim trail to Kedarnath retraces its route down the Bhagirathi to the village of Malla. After crossing the river, a broad footpath climbs eastward over a series of forested ridges. More than any other section of my pilgrimage, this part of the journey preserved and evoked the traditional spirit of the Char Dham Yatra. Motor roads have encroached on only a few segments of the trail and during summer, a trickle of pilgrims continue to use this route between Gangotri and Kedarnath. Leaving the Bhagirathi Valley the path goes up to a pass at Belak then crosses over to the village of Buda Kedar in the Bal Ganga Valley, roughly a two-days' walk. Though the climb is strenuous, the old chey-footia trail—seemingly unchanged for centuries—is easy to follow and there are several dharamshalas along the way, in various stages of disrepair.

Unlike the stark, rock-strewn landscapes around Gaumukh, most of the route between Malla and Buda Kedar passes through relatively lower altitudes, between six and nine thousand feet above sea level. The forests are verdant and humid, the mix of trees changing from one elevation to the next. As I ascended through thickets of ringal bamboo and bauhinia into open stands of long needle pine, then on to groves of tun and maple, I could estimate the height of the mountains. Each different species represented an increment in altitude—cassia giving way to ash, rhododendron, deodar, yew, and oak. In this way I could measure my progress and when I saw that the banj oaks had been replaced by moru, I knew that I was nearing the crest of a ridge. Similarly, as I dropped down the other side the forest changed from one level to the next, variegated bands of foliage like the rock strata in a cliff.

The largest and most dramatic trees along this trail were horse chestnuts, known in Garhwali as pangar. Nowhere else in the Himalayas have I seen chestnut trees as plentiful and as large as those on the ridges below Belak. They were growing at altitudes between seven to eight thousand feet, on the north side of the mountain. Some of the biggest trees were over eighty feet high and twenty feet in girth. The roots were like muscular arms that reached down into the soil, supporting the trees at an angle from the slope. Knotted, bulbous shapes grew at the base of the chestnuts, though higher up the trunks became round and smooth before branching out into expansive limbs. The largest of these trees must have been over a hundred years old and all of them were flowering, with bouquets of white blossoms high overhead. A sprinkling of petals had been shed on the ground beneath the trees and it was difficult to believe that something so huge and stately could produce flowers as delicate as these.

The first couple of hours after leaving my campsite, I had the trail to myself. Few experiences are more pleasurable than walking alone through a Himalayan forest just after dawn. A pale gray light filters in between the trees, sharpening the edges of the shadows and giving the shapes of branches a subtle adumbration. The air is clean and moist; the sultry weight of a summer night has lifted with the darkness. Birdsongs erupt from all sides: the whistling shrieks of scimitar babblers, the shrill pizzicato of bushchats, the hilarious cries of laughing thrushes, and the chuckling call of a koklas pheasant provide an overture for the day.

Turning a corner of the path I saw an animal standing thirty feet ahead of me, partly hidden in the dappled shade. As the creature moved forward into the sunlight I realized it was a kakar or barking deer. No more than thirty meters ahead of me, the kakar's head was turned away and I could see the stooped curve of its back and the russet color of its coat. Less than three feet tall, with delicate legs, the barking deer is one of the most timid creatures in the Himalayan forests. It gets its name from a sharp cry of alarm that sounds like the yelp of a dog, repeated at regular intervals. These deer have good reason to be afraid, for they are a favorite prey of leopards, but kakar often frighten themselves, barking at the slightest movement of a leaf or the distant sound of a woodcutter's ax. This one, however, was totally unaware of my presence and I watched it for several minutes as it grazed at the side of the trail. After a while the deer lifted its head and I could see its horns. The antlers on a kakar look like a pair of tongs, the ends curving in toward each other, with two smaller tines at the base. On older males the horns extend in a furrowed ridge, all the way down the forehead to the nose, giving the kakar a perpetually worried expression. Like the musk deer, an adult kakar has two sharp canine teeth that it uses for rooting in the soil. These often make a clicking sound as it feeds. Standing motionless, I watched the barking deer take a few more steps along the path before it silently climbed up the side of the hill and disappeared into the underbrush. Even with its red coat it seemed to melt away into the morning shadows. I waited for a few minutes to let it go, then carried on, expecting to hear a cry of alarm, though the kakar remained silent and probably never suspected that I was there.

Farther on, at a spring beneath a large chestnut tree, I stopped to fill my water bottle and saw a young man coming up the path behind me. He was about sixteen years old and carried a woven bamboo basket over one shoulder. Using a length of wire as a leash, the boy was leading a black bhootia puppy, which followed reluctantly at his heels.

"Last night I saw your tent across the valley from our village," he said, after we had greeted each other. "Why are you traveling by yourself?"

When I explained that I enjoyed the solitude he looked perturbed.

"I hate to walk alone in the forest," he said. *"Bahut juldi* bore *ho jata hun."* (Very quickly I get bored.) In Garhwal many expressions have been co-opted from English, the word "bore" being one of them. As far as I know, there aren't any synonyms for boredom in Garhwali, probably because most farmers in these hills don't enjoy the luxury of spare time.

The young man's name was Jaggat Singh and he came from Sulla, where I had heard the drums the night before. He attended high school in Saura, seven kilometers lower down the valley, and had just finished tenth class. A year ago Jaggat Singh had enrolled in a summer course at the Nehru Institute of Mountaineering in Uttarkashi and he had ambitions of becoming a guide for a trekking company someday. When I asked where he was going, he said that his family chaan lay farther up the path, where they kept their buffaloes in summer.

"I have two older brothers," he said, with a shrug. "That means I won't inherit much. Besides, these days it's impossible to make a living off the land. I need to find some other kind of work."

For a sixteen-year-old he was remarkably self-possessed and several times he asked if I could help him find a job. He said that he was willing to go anywhere to work, even as far away as Delhi. Though Jaggat Singh was planning to finish two more years of school and complete his intermediate degree, he didn't have much faith in the value of education.

"It won't do me any good," he said. "There are plenty of young men in our village who have their M.A., and what are they doing? Sitting at home and milking their buffaloes."

We walked together for about an hour and the time passed quickly in conversation. At one point the puppy sat down and refused to go any farther until I fed it some biscuits. Jaggat Singh claimed that once the bhootia grew up, he'd be able to sell it for two thousand rupees.

His chaan was located near a place called Pangari Dondi, which means "ridge of the chestnuts." As we came to a clearing Jaggat Singh said good-bye and turned off in the direction of a thatch hut about half a kilometer away.

Continuing on, I found three chaans above the trail. At the second of these an old woman put her head out of the door and asked if I wanted some tea. She pointed to a door at the far end of her chaan and told me to have a seat inside. One half of the shed was used as a stable for cattle and the old woman was in the process of cleaning out the stalls. Her arms were covered with buffalo dung, up to the elbows, and the interior of the chaan was swarming with flies. Nevertheless, I sat down on the floor and waited as she washed up and lit a fire to brew my tea. The old woman told me that during the pilgrim season yatris occasionally stayed at her chaan. In this way she earned a little extra income but complained that very few pilgrims traveled this route any more.

"I remember when thousands of yatris used to go along this trail each day," she said.

"How long have you lived here?" I asked.

"Who knows?" she said. "But I've been coming to this place since I was a child. Now I'm old and my husband is dead."

"Do you live here by yourself?" I asked.

"No," she said. "I have a son and a daughter-in-law. They help me take care of the buffaloes. I'm too old to climb trees and cut fodder."

At the far end of the chaan I could hear the buffaloes chewing their cud, though it was so dark that only their shadowy outlines were visible.

"What kind of leaves do they eat?" I asked.

"Mostly oak," she said. "That produces the best milk but there are many other kinds as well. If anyone wants to see trees this is the place to come. This is Kailash!"

While we waited for the tea to boil the old woman listed the names of the trees — banj, moru, kharsu, papari, pangar, deodar, chir, thunair. She described each of their uses, telling me which species were best for fodder, for firewood, and for timber. Her knowledge of the forest was intimate and exact, based on necessity rather than science. But listening to her I became aware of a deeper connection as well. The widow recited the names of the trees as if they were part of a sacred litany. Remembering the garland of flowers I'd seen tied around the moru oak near Dodi Tal, I asked if people worshiped the trees. The widow shook her head.

"No, here we worship the Devi," she said, pointing to a shrine on the wall above the hearth. In a shallow niche were two framed pictures, one of Shiv and the other of the goddess Durga, with her ten arms, riding on a lion. Surrounding these pictures was a garland of dry leaves. When I asked what they were she leaned over and picked one, then handed it to me.

"It's a kind of burans," she said, using the Garhwali word for rhododendron. "The bush that these leaves come from grows higher up near the Khush Kalyani bugiyals and has small white flowers. In the old days these leaves were burned as incense. We still use them to worship the gods."

Though the leaf was dry and brittle it had a fresh, sweet fragrance, with a hint of camphor.

Belak is located on the main pass between Malla and Buda Kedar, about nine thousand feet in altitude. Here the trees are mostly moru oaks, many of their branches lopped for firewood and fodder. At places the forest opens out into rolling meadows but the views of the higher mountains are limited. One would have to climb farther up, toward the Khush Kalyani bugiyals, to see the panorama of snow peaks. About three hundred meters below the crest of the ridge was a spring, bordered on either side by a bright yellow swathe of marsh marigolds. Gentians and wild strawberries were also blooming on the meadows, scattered tufts of purple and white. The only temple at Belak is a crude shrine to Bhairon Devta, about four feet high and made of stone with a wooden roof. Inside were a couple of broken coconuts, a pair of iron tongs, and a rusty trident. Coins had been pressed into the wooden frame that supported the roof but the shrine looked as if it was seldom used and the deity was represented by a simple, uncarved piece of slate. Elsewhere I saw more elaborate images of Bhairon Devta, depicted as a Rajput warrior with sword and shield. He often guards the mountain passes as well as the approaches to major temples like Gangotri.

Below the shrine is a line of four tea shops and several chaans where pilgrims can get shelter and bedding for a few rupees. At one time there used to be a Kali Kambli dharamshala here but it has collapsed and most of the huts have been recently built. Arriving at Belak, I found an elderly man sitting in the sun, weaving a basket out of strips of ringal bamboo. His hands were gnarled, with swollen knuckles like knotted briers, but his fingers moved with dexterity as he twisted the bamboo into overlapping shapes. He owned one of the tea shops and urged me to come inside, offering to make tea and paranthas. By this time it was the middle of the day and the final climb from Pangari Dondi had left me exhausted and hungry.

The old man was crippled with arthritis and it took him a long time to get up from his seat in the sun and hobble inside. I had noticed that one of his eyes was blind and the other was filmed over with the beginnings of a cataract. When he poured my tea from the pan, he spilled half of it on the floor because he couldn't see what he was doing. But the paranthas he made were delicious, served with fresh buffalo ghee. While I was sitting in the tea shop a younger man came in and introduced himself. He was a priest from Buda Kedar and told me that he was on his way to Gangotri. Producing a receipt book from his shoulder bag, he explained that he was collecting subscriptions to help rebuild the temple in his village.

Five pilgrims were staying at Belak including one yatri from Madras who spoke only Tamil. He communicated mostly through gestures, reciting the names of places where he had been. From what little I could gather he had walked all the way from Badrinath and was headed up to Gangotri.

Leaving Belak the trail dropped down the other side of the ridge. After three kilometers or so, I saw two figures coming up the hill. Both were dressed as sadhus but as they approached, I realized that one was a European. The two men looked exhausted and I offered them some water. The European was tall and emaciated, his arms like sticks of bamboo. He had a graying beard and sunken eyes. It turned out that he was a schoolteacher from Holland and spoke English. Accompanying him was a young sadhu, hardly twenty years old, his hair gathered into a thick topknot and only a wisp of a beard on his chin. The two of them had been traveling together for several weeks though neither of them could understand the other's language. The Dutchman told me that he had been to India six or seven times but never long enough to learn Hindi. He had a guru in Hardwar who had instructed him to go on this pilgrimage. After visiting Badrinath and Kedarnath by bus, someone had told him about the walking route, though he now regretted having come this way because the climb was so steep. The Dutchman kept shaking his head as he looked up the winding trail, then asked me to explain to the sadhu that he came from a country without mountains.

"Please tell him," he said. "In the town where I live the land is completely flat and lower than the sea."

When I translated this for the sadhu he looked at the two of us with a skeptical expression, as if we were mad. In response he took three Cadbury toffees out of his pocket for us to eat.

Half an hour later I passed another party of yatris, four elderly men walking barefoot up the trail, with cloth bundles on their heads. By this time the sky had darkened and it looked as if there was going to be a storm. At Belak I had been told that I should spend the night at a place called Pangrana Chatti. I got there late in the afternoon and found a newly built hotel, which consisted of an open shed with a thatch roof and bamboo mats on the floor. The owner, who came from a village near Buda Kedar, told me that originally there had been a large dharamshala on this site, "with thirty-five choolas for pilgrims to cook their meals," but it had crumbled into ruins many years ago.

I pitched my tent on a grassy meadow just below the hotel

and accepted the proprietor's offer to prepare dinner for me. As we were talking two other pilgrims arrived, a man in his thirties with a shaved head and a saffron cloak. Following after him came a woman about fifty years old, who was carrying half a dozen shoulder bags that hung all around her like bulging cloth appendages. The two pilgrims were traveling together and at first I assumed they were mother and son, but it turned out they were not related. I also discovered that both of them were ardent fundamentalists.

The man with the shaved head talked nonstop, spewing out a constant stream of religious platitudes. He was so vehement and dogmatic in his faith that I got a sense he was mentally disturbed. Later he told us that he was married but had no job. His father, who owned a shop somewhere in Madhya Pradesh, had given him money to go on the pilgrimage, essentially to get him out of the house. The yatri explained that he kept losing his temper at home and after consulting a number of doctors and spiritual advisers they hit upon the idea of sending him on the pilgrimage as a form of therapy. The woman was equally bombastic and kept suggesting to the hotel owner that he put them up for free because they were pilgrims. The two of them seemed to have been paired together by fate for she was like a surrogate mother, badgering her companion the whole time and making him fetch and carry things for her. They were an odd pair and by that evening the proprietor of the hotel was exasperated with them. At one point, the two yatris launched into an impassioned justification for the 1992 attack on the Babri Masjid at Ayodhya, a Mughal mosque destroyed by Hindu fundamentalists who believe it is the birthplace of Ram. The proprietor bluntly interrupted their communal ranting and said that as far as he was concerned it didn't matter if Ram was born on the site or if a Muslim emperor had built the mosque, the best solution was to retract all claims and construct a hospital where the masjid once stood. That way, he said, at least somebody would benefit from the controversy.

Buda Kedar, which means "old Kedar," is the name of the main temple in the village of Tati Tatur. It lies at the confluence of the Bal Ganga and the Dharam Ganga, a stream that flows down from the ridges near Belak. Today most people refer to the village itself as Buda Kedar. As its name implies, this site supposedly predates the shrine at Kedarnath. Many of the myths surrounding Buda Kedar are related to the concluding episodes of the Mahabharata when the five Pandav brothers and Draupadi came to the Himalayas to do penance for killing their cousins in battle. They searched through the mountains for Shiv in the hope that he would absolve their sins, but the elusive Mahadev was reluctant to grant them darshan. At Buda Kedar he took the form of an aged rishi and sequestered himself in a cave near the confluence. Eventually the Pandavs caught up with him, at which point Shiv changed himself into a buffalo and escaped to the high pastures bordering the snows.

There are two temples at Buda Kedar, the larger of which is dedicated to Shiv. This stands at the upper end of the village, while the smaller Rajrajeshwari temple, housing the goddess, is situated lower down, on a knoll above the confluence. In between the two temples, at the heart of the village, is an open square known as Pandav Chowk, with a flagpole at the center. The weapons of the Pandavs — metal swords and tridents — are kept at the foot of the flagpole, wrapped up in red cloth and surrounded by a cairn of river rocks.

When I visited the Shiv temple I was greeted by a sadhu who lived in one of the rooms next to the main sanctuary. He was a frail-looking man, with a loose topknot of gray hair and an untidy beard that sprouted in all directions. His eyes were bloodshot and his teeth yellowed, like rotting kernels of corn. One ear was pierced with a ring of wood and silver. Over his saffron tunic and dhoti he wore an army surplus jacket of camouflage green.

After telling me the story of the Pandavs' pursuit of Shiv he led me over to the temple, which was being rebuilt. The original structure had been made of wood and stone, with clay masonry, but the new walls were constructed of granite blocks. Plastic and canvas tarpaulins were draped over the original roof, part of which was still intact. Though the ground was littered with building materials there wasn't any work going on and the sadhu said that they had run out of money and were waiting for more donations. One of the reasons for rebuilding the temple had to do with the new motor road that is planned, connecting Buda Kedar to the main highway up to Gangotri. After the Tehri Dam is completed this will become one of the main routes for yatra buses and the people of Buda Kedar are anticipating a large influx of pilgrims.

Because of gaps in the walls and roof there was more light inside the temple than in most Garhwali shrines. The sadhu led me into the central chamber, which contains a huge rock about fifteen feet in diameter. Its surface is a dark, greasy color, stained by centuries of incense smoke and libations of oil. In some ways it looks like a giant lump of hardened tar. Carved into the surface are various images including a Shiv lingam and Nandi the bull. There is also a carving of Ganesh; at his feet are four footprints, which the sadhu said represented the four main dhams of Uttarakhand. Also carved into the sides of the stone are images of the Pandav brothers and Draupadi. In each case the natural contours of the rock have been chiseled into mythological icons, giving the entire boulder an organic form. A scaffolding of wooden pillars and beams supports the roof and as the sadhu and I circled the interior of the shrine we had to crawl in and around these obstructions.

When we emerged outdoors again, the sadhu pointed out the Rajrajeshwari temple at the other end of the village. He explained that this shrine was dedicated to a form of the goddess worshiped by the maharajahs of Garhwal.

"Wherever there is Shiv, there is always Shakti," he said.

Following a statement like this the sadhu had a peculiar habit of holding his right hand up to his nose and sniffing the palm, as if it were scented with perfume. This affectation was obviously intended to make his words seem more profound.

He went on to explain that the Devi's temple housed the trisul, or trident, of Kaila Pir, a local deity worshiped only in Buda Kedar.

"Many years ago," said the sadhu, "the Maharajah of Garhwal ordered the men of this village to join his army and go to fight against the kingdom of Kumaon. They marched from here, all the way across the mountains to the east, beyond the Alakanada, where they defeated the Kumaonis. Meanwhile, their families remained here in the village and waited anxiously for news of the battle. This took place around the time of Diwali, in the month of Kartik, but because the men were away, nobody had any desire to celebrate the festival. Finally, after a month had passed the men returned victorious. As a symbol of their conquest, they brought with them the trisul of Kaila Pir, which they took from a temple in Kumaon. Once these fighters had returned the villagers celebrated Diwali. That is why, here in Garhwal, this festival is held one month later than on the plains."

Sniffing his palm once again, the sadhu described how the people of Buda Kedar celebrate Diwali by wrapping resinous splinters of pine into bundles and setting them alight. Attached to ropes these are twirled overhead like fireworks in a playful ritual known as bhaila khelna. During festivals like this the Bajgi bards recount Dhol Sagar legends of Garhwali warriors like Kunji Pal and Kirti Pal. The beating of drums accompanies these renditions of heroic history. Villagers also conduct a mock battle on Diwali to commemorate their victory over Kumaon. The trisul of Kaila Pir is mounted on a lance and paraded through the fields while celebrants throw straw and dust in the air, to represent the chaos of the battle. During the course of this festival a number of people are possessed by the deity and serve as oracles, giving voice to the demands or admonitions of Kaila Pir and his pronouncements for the future.

When I asked if I could see the Devta's trident the sadhu shook his head, explaining that for most of the year it was kept locked away in an attic of the Rajrajeshwari temple. As with many gram devtas, or village deities, Kaila Pir is only worshiped on specific occasions. Though the festival of Diwali commemorates events from several different myths, it is essentially connected to the harvest, which occurs during November in Garhwal.

As I was about to leave, the sadhu pointed out a cluster of stone markers at the edge of the temple complex. These were the samadhi stones of his predecessors, he explained.

"In the past many great sages and rishis lived here at Buda Kedar and did tapasya on this site. They used to practice what is called 'haryali asan,'" he said, which translates roughly as "green posture" in yoga. Sitting cross-legged on the ground the sadhu demonstrated this position.

"The ancient rishis would plaster their bodies with a mixture of mud, cowdung, and millet seeds," he said. "Then they would sit in this position for nine days, completely motionless and absorbed in meditation. After a few days the millet seeds began to sprout and soon their whole bodies were covered in green, as if they were part of the land."

Completing his story the sadhu inhaled the mysterious fragrances of his palm, then closed his eyes and remained absolutely still for several minutes. Despite his fraudulent gestures and melodramatic voice, the sadhu's army jacket made it look as if he was camouflaged in green foliage.

A motor road, built in the 1980s, connects Buda Kedar to Ghansali and Tehri. Eventually this road will continue on to Gangotri. The village is growing rapidly and a number of new houses are under construction, as well as a steel bridge across the Bal Ganga. Farther up the valley, at a place called Jhala Chatti, the original wooden bridge had been washed away in a flash flood and I was forced to ford the stream. One easily forgets how difficult the pilgrimage must have been when there were no permanent bridges along this route.

Half a kilometer below Buda Kedar lies the Lok Jivan Vikas Bharti ashram, founded by a Sarvodhaya activist named Bihari Lal, whom I had met fifteen years earlier at an environmental conference in Delhi. Unlike the area near the village, which has been denuded of trees, the ashram is surrounded by a flourishing orchard. Located on a level promontory, at a bend in the river, this grove of trees provides a lush contrast to the bare slopes and terraced fields along the banks of the Bal Ganga. Most of the lower sections of this valley have been stripped of forest because of cultivation.

The ashram consists of a quadrangle of single-story cement buildings with a temple facing the river. Compared to the crowded village at Buda Kedar, the ashram projects an aura of tranquillity. An unpaved path leads down through the orchard and into the main courtyard. When I arrived it was the middle of the day and there seemed to be nobody about, except for an old bhootia dog who lounged in the shade of the veranda and ignored me. Taking off my pack and removing my boots, I wandered about the quadrangle and knocked on several doors but the ashram appeared deserted.

Assuming that someone would arrive eventually, I walked across to the temple. It had a high, tapered dome like most modern Hindu shrines, though the central sanctuary was open on all four sides, with plenty of natural light. Brass bells hung above the entrance but there were no deities or priests in this temple. Most of the space was taken up by a square enclosure, like an unplanted flowerbed, at the center of which was a rock surrounded by damp earth. Oil lamps were positioned at each of the four corners along with the remains of incense sticks but no other religious paraphernalia—no tridents, no coconuts, no pictures of gods or goddesses. The rock in the center was two and a half feet in diameter and at first I thought it might be an old tree stump. It looked like petrified wood, a rusty brown color with curved striations on the surface. Unlike the boulder in the Buda Kedar temple there were no figures carved into this stone. Half buried in the soil, sections of the rock might even have been roots. Hesitantly, I reached out to touch it and found that the surface was rough, the texture of brick. Circling the inner part of the shrine I tried to find some clue as to the significance and meaning of this rock but it had a mysterious, unexplained quality, like a meteor or a fossil recently unearthed.

The walls of the temple were covered with verses in Devanagari script and I discovered these were prayers composed in Hindi. They represented different religions, including Hindu, Sikh, Christian, Buddhist, and Muslim prayers. Nowhere in the temple was there any icon or pictorial image, only the words that spoke of devotion, faith, love, and peace as perceived by each of India's major religions. The overall effect of these prayers, carefully painted on the whitewashed walls, was a dizzying abstraction of lines and letters, surrounding the natural form of the rock.

After I had been waiting for half an hour, I saw a man emerge from the far side of the courtyard. He seemed surprised to see me but when I asked if Bihari Lal was home, the man nodded and asked me to follow him. We went through a covered passageway to another building that overlooked the river. Inside I could hear the sound of a television and saw a flickering blue screen in the darkness. The room was filled with people, mostly children. They were watching a weekly serial called *Vishnu Puran*, a religious program in which actors assume the roles of gods. In many ways these television shows have taken over from oral traditions, recounting the myths and adventures of Hindu deities. I had arrived just at the end of the program and in the final scene Vishnu raised his hand in blessing as an advertisement for Pepsi Cola came on.

Immediately the television was switched off and the windows were opened to let in light. The audience, about forty children and ten adults, got up and filed outside. Bihari Lal was not among them but he appeared a few minutes later, an effusive man with graying hair and a youthful face. He was dressed in a white khadi kurta with the sleeves rolled up to his elbows. When I apologized for arriving unannounced and interrupting the program he waved me into a chair.

"The children insisted on watching television this morning," he said with a laugh, "even though our school is on holiday."

Buda Kedar and sections of the Bal Ganga Valley have electricity but the supply is erratic and for several days there hadn't been any power. The ashram, however, has its own micro-hydel project, a small generator that runs off the river.

"At this time of year we don't use it very much because all of the water is needed for irrigation, but today the children diverted the flow from their fields and made us turn on the generator. They will do anything to watch television."

Bihari Lal has been active in the Chipko movement and the agitation against the Tehri Dam. Unlike many environmentalists, however, he is more of a pragmatist. The micro-hydel project, for instance, powers an oil press and a sawmill, which help earn money to support the school and ashram. Bihari Lal believes that forest resources can be used in a careful, controlled manner, without threatening the environment.

"We have planted over a thousand trees in this area alone," said Bihari Lal, referring to the orchard. "Most of them are walnuts but we also have fruit trees, peaches, plums, and lemons."

He spoke in a gentle, deliberate manner, like an indulgent schoolmaster, explaining the Gandhian ideals on which the ashram was founded. When I asked him to define the term *Sarvodhaya*, he paused thoughtfully.

"Essentially, Sarvodhaya is a belief that everyone is equal. No one is less. No one is more. Gandhiji taught us this," he said, "and in our work we try to promote equality. We do not believe in caste or class. All religions are one."

The ashram operates as a commune, though Bihari Lal is clearly the leader and he is referred to as mantriji (minister) by other residents. His wife and two daughters live with him as well as a dozen other members of the ashram. The school, when open, enrolls about a hundred students. Most come from villages nearby, though some are from other parts of Garhwal. In addition to the government curriculum students are educated in Gandhian principles. They live together in the ashram and help tend the gardens and the orchard. Though most students return home after completing school a few of them have stayed on to continue working as teachers or staff. In recent years the ashram has been involved in relief work for earthquake victims. They have raised funds to provide everything from first aid and blankets to long-term assistance such as rebuilding houses. In fact, the day that I arrived at the ashram, a delegation had come from a village near Rudraprayag where Bihari Lal and his staff helped construct over 250 tin sheds to replace houses destroyed in 1991.

Though the ashram itself was not damaged by the earthquakes, it has suffered the effects of other natural disasters.

"In 1997 we had a flash flood that washed away our mill and micro-hydel project," said Bihari Lal. "This made it very difficult for us to remain self-sufficient. It has taken three years to get the generator running again."

The ashram has a couple of guest rooms and Bihari Lal invited me to spend the night. After a week of trekking, I was grateful for the opportunity to bathe and wash some clothes. In the evening, just at dusk, I heard singing at the temple and went across to see what was happening. A group of women were seated inside the shrine and the oil lamps had been lit. The hymns they sang were not traditional Hindu kirtan, but prayers composed during India's freedom struggle against the British. The women's voices carried over the murmur of the river while the flickering oil lamps illuminated the verses on the temple walls.

Later, as we were eating dinner together, I asked Bihari Lal about the shrine. For the first time he seemed uncomfortable.

"To begin with, you must understand that I believe in a secular society," he said, choosing his words carefully. "But most people need a place where they can bow their heads. That is why we have a temple here, though it is not a shrine for any specific faith."

I asked about the rock.

"It has always been there," he said. "While clearing the land to build the ashram, we were about to dig it up and break it into pieces but someone noticed it had an unusual shape. They suggested that we leave the rock where it was and after a while, it acquired a spiritual significance. The temple was constructed afterward. I don't believe in it myself but at the same time I am not opposed to it. After all, the Vedas teach us that God is everywhere, even in this rock. It has weight and substance. It contains some kind of power and if that satisfies a person's belief then I suppose there can't be any harm in it."

He paused for a minute to look around the group that was gathered in the dining room.

"I have no real problem with religion but so much of it has been taken over by *vested interests*," he said, speaking in Hindi but using the occasional English phrase. "Most forms of religion have become a matter of making money. The priests force you to pay for everything from pooja thalis to coconuts and they get rich because people believe in these rituals. If you asked me to go to the Buda Kedar temple with you, I would go, but not on my own. If you asked me to go to a church with you, I would go, but not on my own. I don't believe in these things but I don't condemn them either, except when someone exploits religion. Earlier, you asked me about Sarvodhaya. What does it mean? It means that everyone should be content. We should have our basic needs fulfilled. Food. Shelter. Family. Even our spiritual needs. That is all we are trying to do."

# THE GODDESS AND THE
# BUFFALO

TWENTY KILOMETERS DOWNSTREAM FROM BUDA Kedar, the Bal Ganga flows into the Bhilang River, which eventually merges with the Bhagirathi at Tehri. Of these two tributaries the Bhilang is considerably larger and has its source in Khatling Glacier, which gives the water a soapy gray color. The Bal Ganga, on the other hand, is fed by mountain springs and runs clear, except during the monsoon. Between these two rivers lie a series of ridges, going up to nine thousand feet. Most of this region is heavily cultivated and there are dozens of villages scattered over the slopes.

With a growing population and limited land, many of the men in Garhwal have migrated to towns and cities on the plains in search of employment. Though some have taken their families with them, the majority of women and children remain in the hills, tending cattle and working the fields. This separation of men and their families has been a fact of life in Garhwal for well over a century. Starting in the late 1800s, the British recruited a large number of Garhwalis into regiments of the Indian army, a practice that continues today. Returning home to their villages on leave for only a month or less each year, these men had little to do with the day-to-day operations of their farms until they retired. Though the majority of Garhwalis live together in joint family households under patriarchal control, the women of this region have been forced to become more independent because of the absence of their husbands. The vast majority of farm labor in Garhwal, from tending buffaloes to harvesting rice, is performed by women and the only traditional role strictly reserved for men is plowing the fields.

Widespread migration of the male population and the necessity for women to work in the fields have led to a variety of social practices that are unique to Garhwal. Unlike people on the plains of India, who still pay dowry, most Garhwalis exchange a bride price at the time of marriage. Instead of being seen as a liability, for which the husband's family is compensated, wives are considered a valuable asset and at most weddings the groom is required to reimburse the bride's parents for the loss of their daughter. In many cases, immediately after marriage, the husband returns to his army posting or to a job in the city while the wife remains with her in-laws, helping to work the fields and tend cattle. Couples are often separated for months at a time and see each other only briefly when the husband returns home on leave. Understandably, these circumstances often lead to tensions within a household, as the bride adjusts to the demands of her in-laws' home.

Whenever I think of the dilemma of men who are separated from their families, I remember a Garhwali waiter I once met at a restaurant in Delhi. After he learned that I was going to be trekking near his village, he eagerly described in detail the exact route to his home—the bridges he crossed, every turn and fork in the trail, each climb and descent that led him back to the slate-roofed house where his wife and children lived. From the expression on his face and the tone in his voice I could tell that he retraced that route in his imagination every day that he remained in Delhi.

At the same time I recall a young woman I saw boarding a bus in a rainstorm. She must have been returning to her in-laws' home after visiting her parents and the whole family had come to see her off. They were standing at a bend of the motor road, in the middle of a downpour, six people under two umbrellas. When the bus came roaring into view they flagged it down and the women hurriedly embraced. As the family said good-bye to their daughter she broke into tears, wailing as they pushed her into the open door of the crowded bus. The rain had soaked the new sari she was wearing and tears flooded from her eyes. She clutched her mother's arm, not wanting to leave until the passengers inside the bus finally dragged her aboard.

It could be that the sense of separation in the mountains is all the more intense because distances seem greater and the ridges themselves rise up like barricades, hiding whatever lies beyond. A day's walk beyond Buda Kedar I passed through a prosperous village that overlooked the Bhilang River. As I got to the fields at the lower end of this settlement, a voice called out to me, and I looked back to see a young couple coming down the path. The man was in his mid-twenties and his wife was eighteen or nineteen. He was wearing a collared shirt and trousers with a new pair of Bata sneakers. His wife was barefoot, though she carried plastic sandals in one hand. On her head was balanced an attaché case. As we walked together down the path, the young man told me that he worked as a driver in Vasant Vihar, one of the most exclusive colonies in Delhi. He had come home to his village for a few-days' holiday and was now returning to work, taking his wife with him to Delhi. The two of them were on their way down to the village of Ghuttu, where they would catch a bus to Tehri.

"I've lived in Delhi for over ten years now," he said proudly, "ever since I was fourteen years old. My uncle works there and I used to stay with him. Until now I haven't had my own quarters but recently I got a new job and the people I work for gave me a room of my own. Last year I got married and this allows me to take my wife with me."

The young bride did not say anything, following behind us and letting her husband do the talking. Below the fields the trail dropped steeply down to the motor road, which runs along the Bhilang River. The surface of the path was covered in loose gravel and very slippery. I was leading the way and lost my footing several times but managed not to fall. The young man's shoes, however, kept sliding out from under him and having been away from the hills for all these years he wasn't used to negotiating the path. He must have fallen about a dozen times, while his wife had no problem at all, even with their luggage on her head. At one point, in the middle of telling me about the different kinds of cars he'd driven, the young man suddenly gave a cry of alarm. When I turned around to see what had happened he was lying on his back in the middle of the path. Looking up I caught his wife's eye, as she drew the pullav of her sari across her face, trying hard to keep from laughing.

The last three kilometers of my trek that day followed the motor road, which ends at Ghuttu. It was late afternoon and a storm was building up, rumpled piles of dark clouds gathering over the mountains like heavy quilts. The humidity had been rising for the past few hours and now that I was down in the valley the heat was intense. When I arrived at Ghuttu there was a truck near the bus stop, half filled with gas cylinders. A line of villagers stood patiently with their empty tanks, waiting to exchange them for a fresh supply of fuel. The agency contractor stood at the back of the truck with a receipt book in one hand, hurriedly collecting money. A full cylinder weighs thirty kilos and instead of carrying these on their shoulders, the villagers rolled them down the hill and through the main street of

Ghuttu. The sound of metal grinding against stones was deafening and a number of young boys were chasing after the gas cylinders to keep them from careening into the shops. It looked almost like a game, though I kept expecting one of the tanks to burst. Above us, in the mountains, echoed the ominous sound of thunder as streaks of lightning sliced through the clouds with piercing brilliance.

The first drops of rain started to fall as I was finishing a cup of tea at one of the stalls near the bus stand. Hurriedly I retraced my steps to the Garhwal Mandal Vikas Nigam rest house a few hundred meters away. By this time the gas cylinders had all been distributed and the truck was being loaded with empty tanks. Within a few minutes the storm struck with a torrential downpour and I was drenched by the time I made it under the veranda of the rest house. The gutters were overflowing, spewing jets of water from all corners of the roof. Because of the intensity of the rain, I could not see the other side of the valley, but every few minutes there was a flash of lightning far above us and the cement walls trembled with the boom of thunder.

The manager of the rest house and I had to shout at each other to make ourselves heard but within a few minutes he gave me a room. There were cracks in the walls from recent earthquakes but at least it was dry. For the next two hours the storm continued without respite and through my window I could see that the motor road had turned into a muddy canal. Some of the most violent weather in the Himalayas occurs at this time of year, as the first monsoon clouds sweep in across the plains of northern India and collide with the mountains. The dry heat that lies over the subcontinent during May and June creates powerful thermal currents that propel rafts of moisture in the direction of the Himalayas and keep the rain from falling before it reaches the mountains. As these storms hurtle across the

Gangetic Plain they generate spectacular displays of lightning and thunder.

When the clouds reach the cooler air of the Himalayas they literally burst on impact. Later in the season, rainfall can be more prolonged but never as intense as these first few thunderstorms. Even after the dry months of summer the mountains cannot absorb all of the moisture and some of the most dangerous erosion occurs at this time of year, landslides and flash floods. The rain descends on the ridges with such violence that trees are uprooted and boulders are tossed free of the soil. Houses collapse under the onslaught of water and fertile fields are turned into barren terraces of alluvial debris. Paths and motor roads disappear, bridges are washed away, irrigation channels are choked with mud, and even the shallowest streams become impassable torrents.

When the storm finally ended, just before dark, I stepped out onto the terrace of the rest house at Ghuttu. The Bhilang River had risen three or four feet in a couple of hours. Instead of being the gray color of glacial silt, its water was chocolate brown, flooding the riverbank and foaming over submerged rocks. Farther up the valley, toward Khatling Glacier, I could still see intermittent flashes of lightning, though the thunder had diminished to a distant growl. Directly above me lay the ridges of Panwali, which I planned to climb the following day. In the brief twilight that followed the storm, the forested slopes looked dark and forbidding. A black ceiling of clouds still covered the tops of the mountains but halfway up the hill I saw a minuscule glimmer of light. It was much too far away to know exactly what it was, probably a lantern or a fire being lit in one of the chaans, though to me it looked more like a star dislodged from the sky.

———

There is a saying: *"Jo charba Panwali ki charbai, woh lara German ki larai."* Whoever has climbed to Panwali has fought in the war against the Germans. This aphorism dates back to a time when thousands of soldiers from Garhwal were shipped off to Europe to fight in the two world wars. Though most of these men are no longer alive, the climb to Panwali remains as steep and tortuous as ever.

The morning after the storm, I set off at first light and was able to keep ahead of the sun for the first two hours. All of the clouds had disappeared and though the path was muddy, the air was clean and brisk. About two kilometers beyond Ghuttu I had to ford a stream that was still swollen with rain. From here the climb began. Fifteen years earlier I had attempted this trek in early April but was forced to turn back below Panwali because of heavy snow. This time I felt more confident because it was the middle of June, though my memory of the climb was not encouraging. The path went up through a forest of banj oaks, snaking back and forth across the ridge in a steady, monotonous ascent. One of the challenges of this route is that there are no springs along the way until you reach the top.

After three kilometers the path briefly leveled off and circled around a spur of the ridge. Glancing down at my feet I saw a leopard's pugmarks in the wet clay. The impressions were perfectly preserved, a central pad about two inches across and each of the toes arranged in a symmetrical arc. It was not a large animal, though the pugmarks were considerably bigger than a dog's footprint and there was no evidence of the leopard's retracted claws. The cat had obviously walked along this path during the night or early morning, sometime after the storm. I followed the pugmarks for fifty feet or so until they disappeared off the edge of the trail. Just the sight of them was exhilarating and made the forest seem alive. Even though I was alone there was something strangely reassuring about knowing that this predator was near.

The villages and fields bordering the Bhilang River were a thousand feet below me now and though I passed a few chaans, I didn't encounter anyone along the trail for the first three hours. Soon after I saw the pugmarks, however, I came upon a lean-to shed made of oak branches and thatched with leaves. A middle-aged man was blowing into a fire, trying to get the flames started. It turned out that he came from the village of Gangi, ten kilometers above Ghuttu. Two days earlier he had arrived at this spot with plans to set up a tea shop. The shelter he'd made gave little protection from the rain and he showed me that his clothes were soaking wet. Despite his dampness the man was surprisingly cheerful and once the fire was lit he brewed me a cup of tea. While waiting, I heard the sound of mule bells coming up the trail, and a party of four men rode past. They did not stop, except to ask where I was headed. The riders were on their way to Kedarnath and said that they were going to hire their mules out to pilgrims. The rest of the way to Panwali I kept passing these men, as we stopped at different points along the climb. Though the Himalayas can seem as lonely and remote as any mountains in the world, below ten thousand feet one is never more than an hour or two away from human habitation.

After leaving the tea shop, I came across patches of hailstones at the side of the path. These were the size of mothballs and had collected in ravines. While lower down there had been heavy rain, above seven thousand feet the storm had turned into a cannonade of ice. Many of the moru oaks had lost their leaves while viburnum bushes and other shrubs had been shredded by the hail. Farther on I came to a thicket of rhododendrons, their pale mauve flowers ripped and scattered on the ground, as if someone had attacked the bushes in a vindictive rage. With the stillness of the morning it was hard to recall the violence of the storm, though the forest bore evidence of the furious battering it had received.

By the time I was nearing the brow of the ridge, both of my water bottles were empty and the sun had melted most of the hailstones. Though the ground was still wet there were no streams or springs on the south face of the mountain. The path kept twisting its way up the ridge and each time I thought I was nearing the top, another climb presented itself. By now I was getting thirsty and my legs were starting to ache. Looking across at the mountains on the opposite side of the valley I tried to gauge my progress and measure the altitude I had climbed. Sections of the route I remembered from fifteen years ago and eventually I recognized the place where I was forced to turn back, at a point where the trail circled onto the northwest flank of the ridge. A short distance ahead, I finally came to a spring that was gushing down the hill, as if the mountain had sprung a leak. In Garhwal the source of water is often unpredictable. A deep ravine or a sheltered hollow in the ridge that appears to be a perfect place to find a spring will be completely dry, while a barren-looking slope will unexpectedly yield a dozen streams.

As I was resting beside the spring I saw, coming down the path toward me, a group of four gujjars. Two men were leading a horse, on which was seated a young girl. Following after them was a woman, presumably her mother. The men had sharp, chiseled features and neatly clipped beards. Being Muslims, the gujjars have a distinctly different culture and style of dress from the Hindu villagers in Garhwal. They greeted me by raising their right hands to their foreheads, then placing them over their hearts. The woman was dressed in a green outfit, a loose shirt and pantaloons, somewhat like a salwar kameez. Her face was visible though she had a cloak draped over her head and shoulders. The girl was similarly dressed and she clutched the pommel with both hands as her horse made its way down the rocky path.

The older of the two men, who looked about fifty, with a face as dignified and rugged as a mountain crag, gestured toward the girl and indicated that something was wrong. When I spoke in Hindi and asked what the problem was, he seemed relieved and immediately came and squatted down beside me.

"My daughter is sick because of the storm," he said, in a quiet but troubled voice. "Last night there was so much lightning near our camp, she went into a panic and started to scream and wail. Then all at once she fell silent and hasn't spoken a word since then. Her jaws are clamped shut and we cannot get her to eat or drink. This morning we tried to force her mouth open but her teeth are locked together."

The girl, who was about twelve or thirteen, was watching us with a calm but baleful expression on her face, peering out from under her shawl.

"We're taking her down to the doctor in Ghuttu," said the gujjar. "You wouldn't have any medicine for her?"

I told him that all I had was pills for aches and pain, but nothing that would help the girl.

"Did your hut get struck by lightning?" I asked, wishing there was some way that I could help.

"No, but fifteen of our buffaloes were killed last night."

His voice remained calm though I could see the exhaustion in his eyes from the sleepless night.

"Where did this happen?" I asked.

"On the bugiyals this side of Panwali. At night our animals stay out on the meadows and when the storm began they huddled together. That's when the lightning struck them."

The younger man now spoke.

"We've suffered a lot of damage," he said. "If you have a camera, maybe you could go and take a picture of the dead buffaloes, so we can try to claim something from the government."

Once again, I felt completely helpless when I said that I wasn't carrying a camera. Fifteen buffaloes represent a fortune for these migrant herdsmen, whose only assets are their animals. The gujjars' first concern, however, was the girl and after a few minutes her father rose to his feet and said that they needed to get down the hill as soon as possible. As he turned to leave the herdsman lifted one hand toward the sky, in a gesture of resignation and faith.

Watching the solemn group head down the trail, I tried to imagine what must have happened to the girl. Thunderclaps and bolts of lightning; hailstones battering the thatch roof of their hut—terrifying, especially for a child. Even as she cowered under a quilt and hugged her mother there could have been no reassuring her that the storm would pass. At the same time I imagined the buffaloes on the open meadow, their black shapes gathered like a cluster of boulders, each flash of lightning brighter than the fullest moon. And that final burst of electricity, striking the center of the herd and instantly killing them all.

An hour later, when I reached the meadows, there was little sign of the storm. The sky was mostly clear, though clouds had started to gather. Groves of birch trees bordered the lower edges of the bugiyals, which unfolded into open fields of grass and wildflowers. Sunlight glistened off the green pastures and the alpine scenery was idyllic, with vistas of the high snow peaks—Jaonli, Pithwara, Kedarnath, Chaukhamba, and to the east, Nanda Devi and Trisul. Above me, near a brook that came tumbling down a crease in the meadow, stood a mare and her foal. Farther on were cows and buffaloes grazing calmly, as if nothing had happened. The gujjar huts lay several kilometers off the main trail, along a separate arm of the ridge.

Panwali Kanta, which means thorn or barb, is a rocky pin-
nacle that juts out of the bugiyals. The altitude here is about
twelve thousand feet and after the steady ascent from Ghuttu
this last few hundred meters is particularly tiring. When I
finally made it to the top I collapsed against one of the exposed
rocks and waited until my lungs stopped heaving. There is no
temple at Panwali Kanta, though there are several plaques
inscribed with the names of villagers from the Bhilang Valley.
These are unusual, for most Hindus do not build memorials to
the dead. At the pass there was also a flagpole and a brass bell to
mark the top of the climb. Half a kilometer below I could see the
chaans and dharamshala at Panwali. By this time the clouds had
started to close in and the snow peaks were already hidden from
view. It was obvious there would be another storm.

As soon as I started down the path to Panwali, I saw a curious sight on the slope of the ridge to my right. There was a
stream flowing through the center of a meadow and on the far
side were a series of low mounds. At first I thought it was the
ruined foundations of a cowshed or a line of cairns. As I drew
closer, however, I could see about two dozen tumuli, edged with
pieces of slate. A red horse was grazing near the mounds and
when I left the path to investigate he raised his head and shook
his mane, moving nervously away. It was only when I got within
a few feet of the site that I realized these were graves. The gujjars, being Muslims, bury their dead and though the kabristan
was spare and simple, it was one of the most moving cemeteries
that I have ever seen. There were no names or carved head-
stones, only the uneven slabs of rock bordering each mound of
earth. No trees stood at this spot though there was a large
juniper bush growing nearby. As I lingered there, the shadows
of the clouds raced over the meadow and it felt as if the grass
was flowing downhill. At least half of the graves were those of
children, some of them no more than two or three feet long.

Wild irises had been planted on several of the mounds, their slender leaves and delicate flowers waving in the wind like a subtle but defiant gesture against death.

The four mule tiers from Ghuttu had arrived half an hour ahead of me and taken shelter in the dharamshala at Panwali, which is a relatively large, two-story building. They encouraged me to stay in one of the rooms but these were dark and airless, like monastic cells, and the dharamshala looked as if it was infested with rats and insects. A chowkidar took care of the building and he had a chaan nearby where he cooked meals for pilgrims. Everyone at Panwali had heard about the gujjars' buffaloes and warned me that there would be more lightning that night. Already the sky was overcast with dark, unruly clouds.

Reluctant to sleep in one of the claustrophobic cells, I made my way across the meadows to a stand of oak trees well below the shoulder of the ridge. Here I found a level patch of ground about thirty feet from a spring that seemed a perfect place to camp. The only disconcerting element was the bleached white skull of a buffalo that lay nearby, with vacant eye sockets and short, curved horns. By the time I had pitched my tent the first sprinkling of rain had started. Until darkness fell, there were intermittent showers. At that altitude the wind kept blowing from different directions and the clouds swept back and forth above the meadows like shadowy schools of predatory fish feeding on a reef. Every time it stopped raining, I tried to light my stove and cook some noodles for dinner but before I was done the drops would start again. Finally, in desperation, I made a temporary kitchen using my umbrella and succeeded in preparing a simple meal.

By the time I finished eating and had washed up at the spring, the lightning began and the rain grew heavier. Sealing up my tent I lay down and waited to see what would happen.

The storm grew steadily louder and the flashes came nearer and nearer until there wasn't a second's gap between each burst of electricity and crack of thunder. I could tell it was striking on the ridge above me, about two hundred feet away. With each explosion the nylon fabric of my tent lit up like a fluorescent dome. Lying inside my sleeping bag I kept expecting the roof to rip open in a blinding arc of light. The ground shook with every blast and the wind bent the tent poles back and forth above my head, like fishing rods straining against a struggling trout. More than ever before I was glad to have a tent that was rated for extreme conditions, though until now it hadn't really been tested. At the same time I kept wondering if the aluminum poles might attract the lightning and whether it was wise to have camped among the oaks. But it was now too late to do anything about it, as the storm pounded the bugiyals. After a while the rain turned to hail, beating against the outer fly of the tent like a Bajgi's drum.

Fear is often the raw material of faith and it takes different forms, from momentary panic to prolonged anxiety. Many times I have felt afraid for no reason at all, an irrational nervousness that makes me keep glancing over my shoulder as I walk through a forest. But that night at Panwali there was nothing ambiguous about the fear I experienced. Each bolt of lightning sent a current of terror through my body and as I lay there in the tent I felt the immediate possibility of death. At the same time there was an excitement to the storm, so powerful it was oppressive and almost erotic, my mind filled with horrifying visions of electricity surging through my body. Worst of all were those moments of anticipation between each thunderclap, waiting for the next flash of light to fuse the earth and sky. My nerves were like copper wires threaded throughout my bones, a circuitry of fear. They ran from the base of my skull between each vertebra in my back and into my joints, through the hollow crater of each socket and down into my toes and fingers. Every time the lightning struck the tension increased, as if my nerves were twisting inside my bones. Lying there on my back with my eyes closed I could understand the terror the gujjar girl had felt the night before, a paralyzing sense of hysteria brought on by the volatility of nature. Even when the storm eventually subsided, more than an hour later, I could not escape the residual fears that kept me awake for most of the night. In the silence that followed the storm I experienced an uneasy reverence for the ferocity of wind and weather.

The bugiyals at Panwali serve as a setting for the penultimate scene in one of Uttarakhand's many creation myths. In his book *Mountain Goddess: Gender and Politics in a Himalayan Pilgrimage,* the anthropologist William Sax has recorded some of the epic songs of Nanda Devi, which are sung by the women of this region. These are versions of myths that are told all across India, part of the shared lore of the mother goddess. Unlike canonical accounts in Hindu mythology that tend to give prominence to male deities, these oral traditions identify the goddess as the source of all creation. Assuming her primal form, Adishakti (original power), she sings, "I created the forests and mountains, I created the trees and plants, I created the rocks and cliffs, I created the pebbles and boulders, I created the Ganga and Yamuna, I created the wishing cow . . . I created the faithful earth. But how can I live without a man?"

This is the cosmic dilemma that faces the goddess in the first age of the world. Though she has brought the earth and the heavens into being, she cannot find a suitable mate. Reincarnating herself as Maya, the mother goddess, allows menstrual blood to flow from her womb and out of this she creates the god Brahma. To Maya's dismay, however, Brahma refuses to have sexual intercourse with her because he is her son. Saddened by his rejection she sings, "How can I give birth to a man? I will give birth to a man from my body. I will produce a tree from my body." (In this case the tree symbolizes a man, who "gives shade" to a woman.) After Brahma's refusal, the goddess generates another male partner from the blood of her womb. He is known as Jatilo Bagyelo—"(The one with) matted locks (who sits upon) a tiger skin"—an incarnation of Shiv. (In other versions of this myth the goddess rubs the dirt off her skin and uses it to form Brahma and Shiv.)

Once again, however, her male counterpart cannot have intercourse with her because of the taboo of incest. Finally, the Devi uses her menstrual blood to create a blacksmith named Kaliya Lohar. The goddess instructs him to forge seven iron knives for her. Carrying these weapons in her arms, the Devi climbs the mountains to the meadows at Panwali. Here she bathes and worships the seven knives with milk and rice before ascending the Path of Bhrigu, beyond Kedarnath. In a final act of desperation, Maya uses the knives to sever her own head from her body. She splits herself in two and her head turns into Shiv, while her body is reincarnated as Gaura Devi, yet another form of the goddess. In this way the problem of self-generation is resolved. Though Shiv and Gaura represent two parts of the same whole, neither is the parent of the other, which allows them to consummate the Devi's passion.

The dominant and aggressive sexuality of the goddess is an integral part of Hindu mythology, but in most conventional renditions—generally recounted by men—the female deity is subservient to the male and her lust is muted. In the songs of Nanda Devi, however, there is a much more complex, vibrant, and "dangerous" image of the goddess. As the story continues, Shiv and Gaura travel to Mount Kailash. Along the way the goddess discovers a buffalo calf that she adopts as her child, against Shiv's protests. He warns Gaura that her son will eventually become her enemy. Ignoring Shiv, the goddess cuts off one of her fingers and feeds the calf with the milk that flows from her wound.

Over time the buffalo grows up to be a demon named Mekhasur who terrorizes the people of Kailash, attacking women when they go out into the forest to cut grass or to fetch water. He even destroys a water mill by trampling on the stone. Finally, after the people complain to the goddess, she agrees to send Mekhasur away to a city called Andhapuri.

The buffalo demon remains safely in exile for many years until Narada, messenger of the gods, starts spreading malicious stories. Mekhasur has been boasting that he plans to make Gaura his wife. At the same time Narada tells Mekhasur that his mother wants to sleep with him. Incensed by these vicious rumors, the goddess and the buffalo demon confront each other in battle. With a wooden pole that is used for pounding grain, Gaura Devi knocks off one of Mekhasur's horns. Out of every drop of blood that falls on the ground, however, another buffalo demon is born. This angry herd appears to be invincible until the goddess finally drinks up all the blood.

A number of variations on this myth have been recorded, from different recitations of the Nanda Devi epic. In some versions the buffalo is merely a sacrificial calf, whereas in others the goddess is ambivalent about her dual role as a mother and a lover. Layers of narrative come together in the myth as these women's voices tell a story of fertility, desire, and betrayal, with characters as human as the gods.

I had been expecting the trail from Panwali to lead straight downhill to the village of Triyugi Narayan but instead it continued along the top of the ridge for at least six kilometers and gained another five hundred feet in altitude before beginning its descent. The morning after the storm dawned gray and misty with a depressing heaviness in the air. I was still uneasy from the lightning and eager to get down off the mountain. Near the dharamshala I met one of the men from Ghuttu who was searching for their mules. He seemed anxious because the animals had wandered off in the storm. Buffaloes were grazing on the meadows, their monstrous black shapes emerging from the mist like threatening apparitions. Though a couple of these beasts shook their horns at me and flared their nostrils they seemed more interested in cropping the wet grass than trampling me underfoot.

For the first hour or two the clouds were so thick that I could see no more than a few feet ahead of me. The path ran along the spine of the ridge but I had no idea what lay on either side. At one point I had to climb straight up through a chimney in the rocks, an uneven staircase leading to a shrouded crag. Pilgrims had erected cairns along this route but other than that there was no evidence that anyone had recently passed this way. After a while I lost all sense of direction in the mist and though I hadn't seen any other trails branching off I began to wonder if I was following the correct path. Just beyond Panwali there were a few chaans but after that no sign of habitation, not even the sound of cowbells in the mist.

Patches of hailstones appeared along the path and farther on these turned to snow, hardly an inch deep but just enough to whiten the ground and make the trail slippery. Eventually I came to the highest point on the ridge. Though the clouds engulfed me there was an unmistakable sensation of standing on top of the mountain, a feeling of emptiness all around. A few minutes later my instincts were confirmed when the mist suddenly parted, drifting aside and revealing the surrounding contours of the mountain. From where I stood the ridge dropped away several thousand feet to my right, snowfields melting into grassy slopes. Far below me lay a forest of fir and cedar. To my left the drop was even more precipitous though interrupted by rocky promontories that leaned out over the cliffs like flying buttresses. Now that I was able to see where I had come from, I looked back at the meadows of Panwali and saw the dharamshala and chaans clustered on a saddle of the ridge. To the west I could see the Khatling Valley and the village of Gangi far below. The Bhilang River looked like a delicate white thread stitching together the folded seam of the mountain. Directly in front of me, the lower halves of the snow peaks above Kedar-nath were visible as well as a section of Chaukhamba—a massive iceberg in a sea of clouds.

The ridgeline was exceptionally sharp, the trail weaving back and forth between serrated cliffs. One of the stories of the Pandavs describes how they chased Shiv across these mountains as he kept disappearing in and out of the rocks, an image that easily came to mind. There was no level ground at all but in a notch of the ridge I came upon an abandoned grass hut, which looked like a giant bird's nest. Lower down there were shepherds' chaans and on the north side of the ridge I saw a herd of goats. Three dogs began to bark at me though they were five hundred feet below, their hoarse baying carried on the wind. Glancing down I noticed footprints in the snow, a single pair of shoes leading the way ahead of me. I followed these for half an hour before they turned off the trail and disappeared into a gully between the cliffs.

The snow began to melt as I descended off the far end of the ridge, but soon I came to an ice bridge in a sheltered ravine. This was all that remained of the past winter's accumulation and the surface was gray and speckled with debris, like a miniature glacier. A good-sized stream flowed out from underneath the ice, which looked precariously thin, though I could see where others had crossed. Using my umbrella as an ice ax I made my way over the slippery surface, averting my eyes from the drop below. Farther on I had to cross two more of these bridges and just before I reached the last one, I met a sadhu coming up the hill. He was walking barefoot, with a glazed look in his eyes. *"Jai Shiv Shankar,"* was all he said. As I kicked footholds in the ice bridge with my boots I tried to imagine what it must be like to walk this trail with nothing to protect my feet.

On entering the forest once again, I felt an immediate sense of relief. Despite the swarm of gnats that greeted me as I passed through a grove of rhododendrons and sorbus shrubs, I was glad to leave behind the exposed rocks and icy trail. Though the meadows at Panwali and the dramatic views from the ridge were beautiful, I was still haunted by the violence of the storm. Ever since I'd met the gujjars, a wary, restless feeling had come over me, a sense of uncertainty and premonition.

Halfway down the hill, at a place called Maggu, were the ruins of a dharamshala. From there the pilgrim trail continued a steep descent to Triyugi Narayan, which lies above the main road to Kedarnath. When I reached the village I was directed to the temple, an ancient stone structure that stood in a depression surrounded by other buildings. The architecture of this temple is characteristic of the Kedarnath Valley and quite different from the wooden temples near Yamnotri or the shrine at Gangotri, built by the Gurkhas. When I asked how old the temple was the priests told me that it had stood there "since the beginning of the world." A more probable estimate would be that the temple dates back to sometime near A.D. 900, when Shankaracharya began mapping out the holy sites of Uttarakhand. The present structure must have been rebuilt several times in the intervening years, though it has the appearance of great antiquity.

Triyugi Narayan means the god of three eons and the primary deity here is Vishnu. The most popular myth associated with this temple, however, is the marriage of Shiv and Parvati (yet another form of the goddess). It is here that their cosmic nuptials were sanctified in a ceremony attended by the gods. Unlike the songs of Nanda Devi that celebrate the preeminence of the mother goddess, the stories told at Triyugi Narayan portray her as the submissive bride of Shiv. Very different from the all-powerful Adishakti, the sexually aggressive Maya, or the fearsome Gaura Devi who fights with buffalo demons, Parvati instead presents an image of docile domesticity. Hers is the story of a stereotypical Hindu bride, a subservient partner whose husband has become the dominant and domineering head of the household.

The temple at Triyugi Narayan was crawling with priests and I was told that I would not be permitted to enter the precincts unless I performed a pooja. The panda who had attached himself to me as soon as I entered the village was a pushy, garrulous man who guided me to a shop near the entrance to the temple. Though I kept protesting that I only wanted darshan at the temple, he insisted that I purchase a pooja tray, offering me a cut-rate thali for eleven rupees. Seeing as it was the only way that I was going to be allowed into the temple I finally agreed. Removing my boots I followed the priest into the courtyard. He first led me past a series of stone cisterns that were half full of water. One of these tanks was called Bhrahm Kund, another Rudra Kund. Each had an attending priest who demanded a donation and I was reminded of what Bihari Lal had said about vested interests. After I reluctantly paid off the priests we went to the site of Shiv and Parvati's marriage. This is located outside the main temple and consists of a shallow, circular trough carved into one of the flagstones. The panda and I sat cross-legged as he intoned a sequence of prayers and instructed me on what to do, first offering a few grains of rice, followed by flower petals and water, then finally smearing the rocks with vermilion. When the ceremony was complete he looked at me and nodded in encouragement.

"Now you can donate whatever you wish," he said. "A hundred, two hundred, three hundred rupees."

"But I thought the pooja cost only eleven rupees," I said.

"That was just for the thali," replied the priest. "You must also give an offering of your own free will."

He frowned in disapproval as I placed ten rupees on the tray but grudgingly got to his feet. When I asked if I could go inside the temple now, he shook his head.

"Wait. First you have to pray to Ganeshji," he said.

As if on cue another priest appeared and hustled me over to a stone image of the elephant-headed deity—the son of Shiv and Parvati, who was ensconced in his own private shrine to one side of the temple. Here I was instructed to pour water over the idol and sprinkle it with rose petals. In many ways it was like working my way through a celestial bureaucracy, from one deity to the next. At each step in the process, a different priest demanded an offering, urging me to hurry up before the temple closed for lunch.

Finally, I was taken inside the main sanctuary. Just beyond the entrance, in the center of the room, was a fire that burns in perpetuity, two enormous logs smoldering in a stone hearth. The beams and ceiling of the temple were blackened with soot and the smoke rose up through cracks in the masonry. The head priest, wearing a crisp white dhoti, impatiently guided me to the threshold of the inner sanctum. The deities were hardly visible, with only a couple of oil lamps flickering in a shadowy vault. Silver masks and ornaments glinted in the darkness. There was a stone image of Vishnu reclining on a serpent and the idols of Shiv and Parvati, arranged like figures in a wedding portrait. Once he had shown me the deities and I had paid my respects, the priest took a pinch of ash from the fire and smeared it on my forehead, then opened his palm expectantly.

# PATHWAY TO PARADISE

TWO WEEKS BEFORE I REACHED KEDARNATH, THE
famous Hindi screen idol Amitabh Bachan made a pilgrimage to
this temple. Though he seldom acts in films these days, Bachan
remains one of India's most popular celebrities, and his yatra led
to enormous excitement both in Garhwal and elsewhere in the
country. The primary reason for Bachan's Kedarnath pilgrimage was to offer prayers for the success of his son's first film,
which was about to be released. A good deal of ritual and ceremony surrounds the making of movies in India and prayers to
Hindu deities are regularly offered on the first day of shooting,
as well as on the opening day. In an unpredictable industry
where millions of rupees are at stake with the release of each
film it is customary to propitiate the gods. Bollywood's studios
have always produced films on religious themes as well as more
secular fare. Some of the earliest Hindi movies were mythological extravaganzas and there is an enduring intersection of religion and cinema in India, where celluloid myths blend with
Sanskrit lore.

Amitabh Bachan is best known as an action hero, starring in
blockbusters like *Sholay, Kalyug,* and *Coolie.* He usually plays the
part of an invincible, athletic crusader for justice who rids the
world of evil, much like the heroes of Hindu epics. His exploits
on the screen, aided by a generous amount of trick photography,

include flying karate kicks and roundhouse punches that knock out half a dozen villains in a single blow. Bachan's popularity extends well outside of India, from Cairo to Moscow and beyond. He is a tall, lanky figure with sleepy, sensuous eyes. Equally adept at dancing and singing, Amitabh Bachan can also turn on the charm as a romantic hero. Even at the age of sixty, with a handsome gray beard, he is immediately recognizable and just the rumor of his presence can draw a crowd in seconds.

The day after he visited Kedarnath, most of the newspapers in India printed front-page photographs of Amitabh Bachan setting off on his yatra. Ironically, for a hero who displays no signs of fatigue after defeating a dozen adversaries in single-handed combat, or whose characters can sprint uphill and somersault from rock to rock, Bachan was shown seated in a dandie, hoisted on the shoulders of four Nepali porters. Instead of walking the last fourteen kilometers from the road head at Gaurikund to the temple at Kedarnath, Bachan was ferried up the path by relays of men and followed by a huge parade of his fans. In many ways it was not unlike the processions taken out each spring at the opening of the Kedarnath temple, when a doli containing the deity is carried up the same path. Though Bachan had come to offer obeisance at the temple — along with a sizable donation — he could not help but assume the role of an idol himself.

Walking down the pilgrim trail from Triyugi Narayan to Sonprayag, I began to hear the sound of bus horns blaring and engines revving in the valley below. The forest was so thick that the motor road was hidden from view and only when I came to the final turn in the path could I see the line of vehicles waiting to go up to Gaurikund. This last stretch of the road is particularly narrow and the police have introduced a gate system for one-way traffic. However, the rules of the road are not always enforced and often an impatient bus driver will force his way through in the opposite direction, causing a traffic jam that can extend for several kilometers.

After crossing over the ridges at Panwali, where I had met no more than a dozen people in two days, it was a shock to descend into the valley and find myself surrounded by a cavalcade of buses and taxis, each of them overloaded with pilgrims. Even on foot it was difficult to weave my way through the lines of vehicles as I had done at Gangotri. In several places the buses were wedged so close together that I wasn't able to squeeze between them and even the margins of the road were blocked. For sections of the route I had to negotiate my way around the outside of the buses, with less than six inches to spare between the vehicle and the cliffs that fell away into the river below. The bulky pack on my shoulders made it all the more difficult and once or twice, as I edged past, the bus suddenly lurched forward and nearly toppled me over the side. What made it even worse were the black clouds of diesel fumes that billowed out of exhaust pipes. The other threat I had to dodge, as I made my way through the traffic jam, was the spitting of pilgrims. Without warning a gob of phlegm or a jet of red betel juice spewed from the open windows of the buses above me and I narrowly missed being hit on several occasions.

The Mandakini River, the main tributary that flows down from the glaciers above Kedarnath, passes through a precipitous and thickly forested gorge. At places the valley is hardly a hundred feet wide, a deep canyon that cuts between the ridges. Where the motor road ends the gorge widens slightly, though there is still a feeling of confinement about the valley, accentuated by terraced parking lots crammed with pilgrim coaches.

Gaurikund—pool of the pale goddess—is famous for its hot springs, which have been diverted into large, rectangular tanks where pilgrims bathe before beginning their ascent to

Kedarnath. These thermal baths wash away the sins of thousands of Hindus every day, a collective immersion that precedes prayers at the temple. What was once a natural phenomenon, a sulfurous stream bubbling out of the rocks, has been transformed into lukewarm soak pits where the faithful immerse themselves in uninviting tubs of gray-green water.

The area immediately around the hot springs has been completely built up with dharamshalas and hotels on every side. For half a kilometer or more the valley is blocked by two lines of cement buildings. The footpath to Kedarnath goes straight through the middle of this bazaar, the roofs converging overhead like a tunnel. On either side there are shops and restaurants while up above a warren of tiny rooms are available for rent. The density of the crowds at Gaurikund is overwhelming and the smells of mustard oil and kerosene, incense and wet laundry, rotting vegetables and frying samosas made the air catch in my throat. Walking through this market I felt an oppressive, claustrophobic sense of being surrounded by other human beings. All I wanted to do was escape the crowds, to push my way through to the far end of the bazaar, and climb out of the valley, leaving behind the stench and squalor of Gaurikund, the diesel fumes and expectorating pilgrims.

The trail above Gaurikund is paved with cement and runs along the west bank of the river. On either side the Himalayas rise up in defiance of human civilization, dwarfing the pious procession of figures that walk this route. Though the majority of yatris complete the pilgrimage on foot, there are dandies, kandies, and mules available for those who cannot manage the climb. During the height of the pilgrimage season, in May and June, two continuous streams of devotees pass each other going up and coming down. On certain sections of the trail it felt as if I was walking in a queue and there was hardly any room to pass. No clearly defined right-of-way exists but the trains of mules tend to nudge pedestrians aside, their garlands of brass bells jingling as they go by. The majority of yatris who ride on these mules have probably never sat in a saddle before and after the first kilometer or two their discomfort is clearly evident. It is hard to know whether the pain they experience while seated on a mule is worse than the exertion of the climb but when they dismount their faces display a combination of agony and relief. As for the mules, they suffer in silence, plodding up the trail as if they were doing penance for sins committed in a former life. Their owners urge them forward with the help of bamboo switches and maintain a firm grip on their tails to keep the animals from straying off the path.

Dandies are probably the most comfortable form of transport, though their seats are narrow and they look like a flimsy kayak balanced on the shoulders of four men. This slow portage uphill requires a synchronized march-step and the dandies sway up and down in rhythm with the bearers' stride. Coming downhill, however, the porters pick up speed. Racing around the corners they shout, "Side! Side!" to warn anyone who might be in their way. It often seems as if the dandie bearers have lost control and for the passenger it must feel like riding through whitewater rapids without a paddle. Most of the yatris who hire dandies are either very old or seriously overweight and from the looks on their faces, as they careen down the path, it must not be very good for their hearts.

In comparison kandies are the slowest and least dignified mode of conveyance—a conical bamboo basket with a seat fixed in the middle. One side of the kandie has two ropes attached that fit over the porter's shoulders. The other side is partly open, so that the passenger faces backward with his or her feet dangling out of the basket. Kandies are usually reserved for children but sometimes adults will also ride in these. Most of the kandie porters are Nepalis and they often use a strap that goes across their foreheads to help support the heavy load they carry. Climbing up the steep switchbacks these porters stare intently at the ground, perspiration streaming off their faces and bare feet shuffling forward one step at a time. It is painful to watch their progress and I couldn't help but wonder what value there was in a pilgrimage, when one human being is forced to carry another.

The standard rates for conveyance are clearly posted on signboards at Gaurikund—900 rupees for a mule, 1,500 rupees for a dandie, and 750 rupees for a kandie. These prices are open to negotiation, however, and there is endless haggling at the transport depot near the foot of the trail. Hundreds of mules are lined up along the side of the hill while the dandies and kandies are stacked together in heaps as porters wait their turn. Even with the swarms of pilgrims heading up to Kedarnath there seems to be an excess of mules and porters, which leads to competition. Several of the men I spoke with complained that they had been sitting idle for two or three days. When they did finally get a fare, often they had to accept less than the standard rate.

All along the route up to Kedarnath there are shops selling tea, snacks, and cold drinks. These are located every two or three hundred meters and at the major stops there are usually more than a dozen tea shops clustered together. Most of these are temporary structures, with roofs made of bamboo poles and plastic sheeting. A few folding tables and rickety wooden benches provide the only furnishings. In some ways the trail above Gaurikund is like an extended bazaar and each of the tea shops competes for customers with colorful signs and banners. Even though there are government sweepers who move up and down the trail carrying long-handled brooms, the path is littered with rubbish and mule dung. When it rains, as it did on my way up to Kedarnath, the gutters overflow with mud and the cement surface of the trail becomes dangerously slippery. Public latrines are located at certain places but these are inadequate for the volume of pilgrims, many of whom relieve themselves at the side of the trail. Wherever water crosses the path there is filth and the streams and springs that trickle down the side of the mountain are reduced to a squelching mire of mud and excrement.

Though everyone was heading to the same destination, there was little uniformity in the procession of pilgrims. Some wore robes of saffron and ocher but the fashions ranged from jeans to loincloths and because of the rain there were plenty of umbrellas and bright colored ponchos. The yatris came from all over India, from Bengal and Maharashtra, Tamil Nadu, Kerala, Punjab, and Orissa. They represented all ages, from toddlers who rode on their parents' shoulders to feeble octogenarians in dandies like patients being taken to the hospital on a stretcher. One group of six widows I passed all had their heads shaved and wore white cotton saris. There were plenty of mendicants, including a blind sadhu who was being led up the trail. A little farther on I passed a man with only one leg, who was hobbling up the hill on a pair of wooden crutches, making slow but determined progress. Some of the pilgrims carried radios and cassette players, which blared out film music and religious bhajans. At one corner of the trail we passed a man who sat in a shallow cave picking at the keys of a harmonium. He too was blind and sang hymns to Shiv and the other gods. Perhaps the most eccentric character was a yatri with a brass trumpet, who stopped from time to time, putting the instrument to his lips and blowing a short serenade. The shrill sound of the trumpet echoed between the ridges, as if the rest of the band was hiding in the trees.

Though I missed the silent, solitary segments of my pilgrimage—the chestnut forests near Belak, the lonely meadows at

Panwali—I grew to appreciate the crowded, frenzied atmosphere along the path to Kedarnath. Looking up from the trail I could see the untrampled slopes of the mountains but here along this cemented lane was an eclectic and vibrant parade of humanity. The voices, the faces, the gestures and attitudes, the laughter and groans of exhaustion blended together as a form of movable theater, a continuous loop of personalities and players that mingled along the trail. Each character assumed a different role, from the humble to the pretentious, from the comical antics of the trumpeter to the tragic self-abnegation of the widows. The pilgrimage was alive with drama but in this case the audience and players were one. All along the route I was aware of being watched by others just as I was watching them. Resting on a rock at the side of the path I couldn't help but stare at an obese man riding up the hill on a swaybacked mule. As he came past me the pilgrim raised a hand in greeting and shouted, "Hello, Foreigner!" Each of us was an oddity, providing entertainment and satisfying the curiosity of others.

Those I met and spoke with told their stories—a textile merchant from Gujarat who was walking to Kedarnath for the third time in his life, two college students from the coast of Kerala, a family from Delhi with three teenage children who tried every shortcut. Their Hindu faith had brought them here but for each of these pilgrims the journey was as much an escape from the routines of their lives as it was a search for truth. They were driven by a sense of fascination and wonder. For most yatris the Himalayas represent a remote and mythical landscape, a place inhabited by gods. Whatever they had imagined these mountains to look like, the pilgrims were now confronted by the imposing reality of Uttarakhand. At the same time, however, the path itself provided a secure and familiar corridor through which they passed. Most of these yatris were city dwellers and except for the steepness of the climb, the trail could just as easily have been a crowded street in Delhi or Calcutta. The pilgrims jostled together like commuters on their way to work. But unlike the impersonal anonymity of a city sidewalk, the yatra provoked a sense of communal purpose. On one level, everyone I passed was a stranger but at the same time people spoke to each other without hesitation, whether shouting encouragement or making anxious inquiries about the distances that remained. All of us were transients, uprooted from our homes and the mundane routines of ordinary lives, but there was no sense of alienation in the crowd. Despite the exertion of their pilgrimage, yatris looked each other in the eye, greeted strangers with folded hands, and sat down together to rest in the shade.

Though the differences in class and caste were clearly evident, from the wealthy businessman urging his dandie porters on with an indolent wave of his gold-ringed fingers to the impoverished old man begging for coins at the side of the trail, everyone was traveling the same route. The only pilgrims who did not have to negotiate the fourteen kilometers from Gaurikund to Kedarnath were a group of state politicians and dignitaries who made the journey by helicopter. As the chugging sound of their aircraft filled the valley, all of us looked up in consternation to see the whirling rotor blades and bulbous fuselage passing overhead like a giant dragonfly.

There was no place to camp along the trail to Kedarnath. The gorge was precipitous and every patch of level ground had been occupied by tea stalls. I kept searching for spots above or below the trail where I might be able to pitch my tent but nothing suitable presented itself. With so many pilgrims I was worried that I would find no place to stay but on reaching Rambara, seven kilometers above Gaurikund, I was able to get a room in the GMVN rest house. It cost four hundred rupees for the night, more than I had spent on any accommodation until this point, but with the rain growing heavier and darkness falling I was ready to splurge.

The next morning I left my pack behind at the rest house and walked the last seven kilometers to Kedarnath without any weight on my shoulders. At points it felt as if I were flying, even with the altitude. Once your body gets used to carrying a load the sense of release is exhilarating and I had to keep myself from running up the path. Deliberately I set out early, just after dawn, and for the first hour there were no mules or dandies and hardly any yatris on the trail. It was much easier walking and I was relieved to see that most of the clouds had lifted, revealing the snow peaks at the head of the valley.

Kedarnath is by far the most dramatic of the four main sources of the Ganga. It stands in a broader valley than Yamnotri, with a panorama of mountains arranged directly behind the temple. Unlike Gangotri, where the glacier has receded out of sight, Kedarnath appears much closer to the source and the cliffs of blue-green ice are visible a few kilometers beyond the shrine. As the trail ascends above the tree line, circling up over a ledge of moraine, the temple comes into view, a tapered dome of gray granite rising above the roofs of the town. Sloping meadows, on either bank of the Mandakini, frame this scene as the river flows directly from the white snowpack. High above the trail I saw flocks of sheep and goats and a gauzy pennant of smoke drifting out of a shepherd's hut. There is an austere grandeur about this valley, as it opens out of the gorge and leads into the heart of the mountains, an awe-inspiring sense of magnitude and serenity. The glaciers are tinted aquamarine, a color that seems almost artificial, and the snow looks fresh and dazzlingly white against the rocks. I was surprised how similar the mountains were to the idyllic scenes painted in the background of religious pictures. These were unmistakably the same Himalayas beneath which Shiv sits in stoic meditation—monumental peaks rising up in sculpted profile, dominating the artist's imagination.

Kedarnath was established by Shankaracharya over a thousand years ago, though the present temple is less than two centuries old. It bears cracks of earthquakes, which probably felled the shrines that stood here before. During winter the priests carry a representation of the deity to Okhimath, a town about thirty kilometers downstream. Though Mount Kailash, which lies across the border in Tibet, is considered the true abode of Shiv, his domain extends throughout the highlands of Uttarakhand. Whereas most of the shrines for Vishnu are located lower down in the valleys, Shiv's temples are generally situated at higher altitudes and more remote. In many ways, he is the least accessible god, preferring the seclusion of the snows.

During the pilgrimage season, however, Kedarnath temple is besieged by worshipers and the lines of yatris waiting to perform pooja stretch from the austere granite steps of the sanctuary, across the courtyard, and through a brightly painted gate into the streets of the bazaar. The town at Kedarnath is not too different from a summer resort except that it exudes an atmosphere of piety. Hundreds of dharamshalas and ashrams are built one against another, with signs advertising their spiritual and secular amenities. Hindu tour groups arrive en masse and the various rest houses cater to regional tastes. There were signs for a MAHA-RASTHRA BHAWAN and a DELHI/PUNJAB HOTEL, as well as a large Kali Kambli dharamshala. On the signboard outside was a painting of its founder, an ascetic figure draped in a black blanket from which the institution gets its name. But today, instead of the rough woolen blankets that kept their predecessors warm, many yatris at Kedarnath don nylon parkas to ward off the cold.

Aside from the main temple, which rises above a rusty montage of tin roofs, there are dozens of other shrines including one dedicated to Shankaracharya. He is now revered as a god himself, for many believe that he rescued Hinduism from the pernicious and egalitarian influences of Buddhist teaching. The head priests at this temple still come from Mysore, in southern India, a lasting legacy of Brahmanical reforms that occurred in the ninth century. At the same time Hinduism remains an individualistic, fluid faith and for many of the pilgrims their journey to Kedarnath is an ecstatic experience, closer to the Bhakti tradition of personal communion with god than the austere, hierarchical rituals of Brahmanic worship. Many of the dharamshalas and ashrams at Kedarnath play religious hymns over loudspeakers, a shrill cacophony of static and song.

The idea of self-sacrifice is an inherent part of this pilgrimage and many yatris believe the ultimate goal would be to die en route to Kedarnath, ensuring an immediate release from the cycle of suffering and rebirth. Years ago some of the more fanatical pilgrims would climb to the top of a cliff that overlooks the temple and commit suicide by throwing themselves onto the rocks below. The precipitous path that leads to this site is known as Bhrigu Panth, the pathway to heaven, and the cliff is called Bhairon Jhamp. It is impossible to know how many pilgrims actually have thrown themselves off this cliff in the past but the practice is said to have been stopped by the British in the middle of the nineteenth century.

A short distance beyond the Kedarnath temple lies a small lake that used to be known as Chorabari Tal and is now called Gandhi Sarovar, because a portion of Mahatma Gandhi's ashes were emersed in this lake. As with Shankaracharya there is a tendency to deify the leader of India's freedom movement and popular Hinduism allows for a multitude of icons both ancient and modern.

When the Pandavs sought Shiv's blessing and forgiveness for the death and destruction they had caused on the battlefields of

Kurukshetra, Mahadev refused to grant them darshan. Their determined pursuit through the upper regions of Uttarakhand serves as an analogy for the pilgrimage itself—the hardships and challenges of the yatra route. After Shiv eventually changed himself into a buffalo and escaped into the high pastures near Kedarnath, the four heroes of the Mahabharata came up with a scheme to trap the reclusive god.

Bhim, the strongest of the brothers, planted his feet on either side of the valley while the others drove the herd of buffaloes between his legs. The Pandavs knew that Shiv would never allow himself to stoop in front of anyone and for that reason he would avoid passing under Bhim. Their plan was successful. As the stampede of cattle came down the valley one of the buffaloes refused to go forward and instead of ducking under Bhim's legs the animal buried itself in the ground. Immediately, Bhim and his brothers caught the buffalo by its tail and kept it from disappearing under the mountains. A large rock inside the temple at Kedarnath is worshiped as the buffalo's hindquarters and marks the place where Shiv burrowed underground. Mahadev tried to escape with such force that different parts of his body reemerged at various places in Garhwal. Each of the Panch Kedar (the five main shrines to Shiv) represent the locations where sections of the deity protruded—his navel at Madhmaheshwar, his arms at Tungnath, his face at Rudranath, and the matted locks of his hair at Kalpeshwar. In this way the Pandavs were able to finally worship Shiv and gain absolution for their sins. Like the myths of dismembered gods and goddesses that are found in many other religions, this legend allows the deity to be worshiped in more than one place at the same time.

An interesting variation on this story was told to me by one of the pandas at Kedarnath. He claimed that whenever ghee was poured over the sacred rock that represents Shiv, the same clarified butter flowed out of a lingam at Pashupatinath temple, the main shrine in Kathmandu, four hundred kilometers to the east. This legend reflects the influence of Gurkha invaders on the mythology of Garhwal. In fact, versions of these stories are told all across the Himalayas from Kashmir to Assam.

The central metaphor of the buffalo, as it relates to the legends of Shiv and the mythology of the goddess, is obviously connected with the cultural traditions of mountain herdsmen. This ungainly, temperamental creature represents the chief source of livelihood of most dairy farmers in Garhwal. They depend on it for milk and manure and much of their energy goes into tending these animals, collecting fodder and water. Unlike Krishn's cows, which symbolize the gentle, pastoral life of the plains, buffaloes are viewed with some ambivalence.

In certain parts of the Indian Himalayas, as well as Nepal, buffalo sacrifices are performed to appease the goddess. The animals that are killed are usually young males, which have no real value since they don't provide milk and only a few are needed for stud purposes. Though most of the people I spoke with on my pilgrimage claimed that sacrifices no longer take place in Garhwal it is reasonable to assume they continue at certain, isolated shrines. The influence of contemporary, urbanized Hinduism, carried up to Garhwal from the plains of northern India by pilgrims, discourages this practice. Certainly, at the main dhams like Kedarnath, any suggestion of sacrifice is frowned upon. At some of the more remote temples, however, particularly those dedicated to the goddess, animals are killed during specific festivals and their blood offered to the Devi, ensuring her blessing on the harvest and the well-being of the herd.

Years ago I witnessed a number of animal sacrifices at a temple called Devidhurra, in Kumaon. The festival took place during the monsoon, in mid-August, and also involved a mock battle that re-creates the wars fought between the ancient armies of Garhwal and Kumaon. Villagers came from miles around, each procession led by a team of drummers, who could be heard approaching like the distant beating of hooves. The animals were brought to the temple by individuals who had specific requests of the Devi, goats tethered with a length of twine or chickens in a basket. The worshipers started arriving early in the morning and by noon there was a long queue of supplicants waiting their turn to perform a sacrifice. Most of the killing was a formalized process of slaughter that took place in an open courtyard paved with flagstones. Next to this was a small shrine to the Devi. A larger, newer temple stood above this courtyard, discreetly removed from the blood-stained square. The chickens and goats, some of them still chewing on a mouthful of grass, were brought forward and their necks severed from their bodies with a single stroke of a chopper, known as a mashaal. Within half an hour the courtyard was awash with blood and the carcasses were taken away to be butchered and cooked to feed each group of villagers.

By midmorning there was a crowd of about a thousand people surrounding the temple and the sacrificial courtyard, which stood on a knoll at the end of a broad ridge, about half a kilometer from the village of Devidhurra. Above the temple grew five enormous deodar trees, their roots extending into the crevices of a giant boulder that was broken down the middle. Inside one of the caves, formed by the cracks in this rock, was a small shrine to Shiv. The only way to enter was to crawl through a narrow passageway that opened into a hollow chamber about four feet wide and six feet long. Suspended from the sloping ceiling were dozens of brass bells that set off a shrill ringing when my head brushed against them.

Another larger crack in the boulder provided a natural gateway to the courtyard where the sacrifices were performed. According to the story I was told, this huge boulder was one of the gambling pieces used by the Pandav brothers. Infuriated when he lost a wager, Bhim struck the rock with his mace and split it into several pieces.

After an hour or two of watching goats and chickens being beheaded the crowd of spectators grew restless. Suddenly, from a distance up the ridge, the drumming became noticeably louder and I saw a group of men running toward the temple with a young male buffalo in their midst. Everyone turned to watch as the terrified animal tried to escape but the men kept slapping at its sides and shouting, so that the buffalo was forced to circle around the temple complex before passing through the crack in the boulder. At this point, all but two or three of the men fell back and the intensity of the drumming increased so that the ground felt as if it was shaking. Finding no other route to escape, the buffalo ducked its head and scrambled through the crack in the rock. Waiting on the other side were several men who quickly put a rope around its neck and led it into the sacrificial courtyard. Soon afterward, a man with his trouser legs rolled up to avoid the blood stepped forward with a three-foot-long mashaal. Bracing himself he lifted the blade of the chopper over his head and brought it down on the buffalo's neck. Immediately the animal sagged to the ground and a second man came forward and finished cutting off the head with several clumsy strokes. Later I was told that the first man had been a rajput, whose caste permitted him to kill the animal but not to touch it after it was dead. The second man was a harijan; being low caste he was responsible for disposing of the buffalo's carcass. After the blood had been spattered in front of the Devi's shrine, the buffalo's remains were dragged down the ridge and rolled over a nearby cliff, since none of the villagers would eat the flesh. A flock of vultures waited in the trees and I was told that tigers and leopards often came to feed on the remains.

During the course of one day at Devidhurra three more buffaloes were killed and like the first, each was driven through the same opening in the rock. When I asked about this ritual, I was told that if the buffalo refused to go through the crack in the boulder then its life was spared. As far as I could see, however, the animals had little choice and even when they balked, several of the men stepped forward and slapped their backs to encourage them forward.

Years later when I heard the story of Shiv at Kedarnath the connection became clear. At Devidhurra Bhim's shattered gambling piece has taken the place of the Pandav hero standing with his legs apart and just to make sure that none of the buffaloes is actually a god in disguise, the villagers put them through this test. Not only was the sacrifice a means of propitiating the goddess but also a reenactment of the myth.

The road in front of you, which has been trodden by the feet of millions of pilgrims like you, is excessively steep and incredibly rough; and you, whose lungs have never breathed air above sea level, who have never climbed anything higher than the roof of your house, and whose feet have never trodden anything harder than yielding sand, will suffer greatly. Times there will be, a-many, when, gasping for breath, you toil up the face of steep mountains on feet torn and bleeding by passage over rough rocks, sharp shale, and frozen ground, when you will question whether the prospective reward you seek is worth the present price you pay in suffering; but being a good Hindu you will toil on, comforting yourself with the thought that merit is not gained without suffering, and the greater the suffering in this world, the greater the reward in the next.

These words were written by Jim Corbett in the first chapter of his book *The Man-Eating Leopard of Rudraprayag*. He begins by addressing the pilgrims directly, for many of the leopard's victims were yatris on their way to Kedarnath, walking up and down the Mandakini Valley. Between June of 1918 and April 1926, the man-eater killed over a hundred and twenty-five people, and its "reign of terror" made headlines in newspapers all over the empire. After a number of sportsmen failed to kill the leopard, the British authorities in Garhwal dispatched Corbett to rid the region of this "menace."

Seventy-five years later the man-eating leopard of Rudraprayag has become an integral part of the mythology of Garhwal and its story is told and retold, almost as often as the legends of the gods. When it was alive, this leopard was considered an evil spirit, and Corbett describes a number of conversations he had with pilgrims, sadhus, and priests, most of whom believed that the leopard was a demon and could never be destroyed. Hunting along the banks of the Mandakini and the Alakananda Rivers above their confluence at Rudraprayag, Corbett covered hundreds of miles on foot and spent many sleepless nights sitting up for the man-eater. His book is one of the great classics of adventure literature, full of danger, suspense, and heroism. Unlike many of his colonial compatriots, Corbett voiced respect and praise for the people of this region and recognized the hardship they suffered on account of the leopard.

Both a hunter and a naturalist, Corbett had a deep appreciation for the jungles of India and wrote about the fauna and flora of the Himalayas with a clarity of perception that has yet to be matched. Though he killed many animals it was seldom for sport and Corbett often expressed regret on the death of a tiger or leopard. In later life he turned to photography and produced some of the first films on tigers in the wild. Despite the awards and commendations he received from the British authorities, Corbett was never a part of high-brow Anglo-Indian society. Born in the hill station of Nainital, where his father was postmaster, he had a much greater affinity for the Himalayas than for his ancestral home in England. Because of his class and his birth in India he was essentially an outcast in the colonial hierarchy and it was only his prowess as a hunter that elevated him to a level of uncomfortable celebrity within the British Raj. His editor at the Oxford University Press once described him as "a modern-day dragon slayer," and that is how he is still remembered in Kumaon and Garhwal.

After a lengthy and arduous pursuit, full of danger and frustration, Corbett finally succeeded in killing the Rudraprayag man-eater. When at last he came face-to-face with this predator, who instilled fear in the hearts of villagers and pilgrims alike, Corbett expressed nothing but sympathy for his prey.

> . . . here was no fiend, who while watching me through the long night hours had rocked and rolled with silent fiendish laughter, at my vain attempts to outwit him, and licked his lips in anticipation of the time when, finding me off my guard for one brief moment, he would get the opportunity he was waiting for of burying his teeth in my throat. Here was only an old leopard, who differed from others of his kind in that his muzzle was grey and his lips lacked whiskers; the best-hated and the most feared animal in all India, whose only crime—not against the laws of nature, but against the laws of man—was that he had shed human blood, with no object of terrorizing man, but only in order that he might live; and who now, with his chin resting on the rim of the hole and his eyes half-closed, was peacefully sleeping his long last sleep.

The mango tree, from the branches of which Corbett fired the shot that killed this leopard, still stands by the side of the motor road near the village of Golabrai. A whitewashed memorial marks the spot with a marble plaque that reads:

ON THIS VERY SPOT

WAS KILLED

THE MAN-EATING LEOPARD

OF

RUDRA PRAYAG

BY

JIM CORBETT

ON 1 MAY 1926 AT 10 P.M.

The name of the river Mandakini means "that which moves slowly." Though it begins as a rushing torrent, cascading from the glaciers above Kedarnath and tumbling down the gorge to Gaurikund, the Mandakini eventually becomes a placid river as it approaches its confluence at Rudraprayag. Unlike the Yamuna it does not writhe between the ridges but flows gracefully around sweeping bends in the valley. Of the four main tributaries of the Ganga it is the shortest and least celebrated though it has a gentle beauty that seems implacable compared to the Bhagirathi and Alakananda.

Each river that feeds into the Ganga has its own narrative, recounted by priests and pandas. These competing legends attempt to assert the predominance and purity of one stream over another. Gangotri claims to be the site where the Ganga fell from heaven and the name of this dham is a contraction of the words "Ganga" and "uttri," which means to descend. For this reason the priests at Gangotri assert that the Bhagirathi represents the primary source. In opposition to this story, the Alakananda takes its name from the hair (alak) of Shiv, which cushioned the river's fall to earth. In the Vaishnavite tradition it is believed that this tributary, also called the Vishnu Ganga, flows directly from the feet of Vishnu. The Mandakini, on the other hand, stakes its claim as being the primary essence of the river, for this is the name by which the Ganga is known in heaven before it came to earth. Furthermore, Mandakini is the daughter of Sati Ansuyia and Atari Muni, immaculately conceived through meditation. Despite the conflicting narratives, each of these tributaries and each of these stories eventually flow together and are resolved in the confluence at Devprayag where the river becomes one, known only as Ganga.

The Mandakini Valley is heavily populated with several large towns—Guptkashi, Okhimath, Agustmuni, and Tilwara. Though this region was once thickly forested, much of the timber was cut in the nineteenth century to provide sleepers for India's railways. Huge tracts of pine and deodar were felled by the British and floated down the Mandakini and Alakananda, all the way to Hardwar. When one begins to calculate how many trees it must have taken to support the thousands of kilometers of tracks that run across the subcontinent, the wealth of forest resources in Garhwal and the scale of destruction becomes staggeringly evident. Before the mid-1970s, when the forest department finally stopped giving contracts for felling trees, the Mandakini carried an enormous harvest of timber from these mountains. Throughout the year contractors cut the trees and when the water level rose during July and August, the logs were launched into the river and carried away by monsoon floods.

When I was a boy I remember watching teams of men who would follow the logs downstream, dislodging those that washed ashore or got stuck on the rocks. These men would swim out into the swollen river using inflated buffalo skins to keep themselves afloat. As they shot the rapids like daredevils and skillfully maneuvered through whirlpools and backwaters, the bloated black hides on which they rode looked as if they were alive, tossing wildly on the rapids like untamed river creatures—a cross between a porpoise and a buffalo.

A number of old footbridges span the Mandakini at regular

intervals. Next to several of these bridges are the ruins of dharamshalas and ancient banyan trees that provided shelter for pilgrims in the past. The old bridges are graceful structures with tall twin pylons on either bank and a delicate cat's cradle of braided wires that reach across the river. The curving, parallel lines provide a symmetrical contrast to the perpetually changing current that passes beneath.

Just above the confluence at Rudraprayag is the first of these bridges. On my way down from Kedarnath I spent a night in a rest house that overlooks the confluence. As darkness settled over the valley I sat on the porch outside my room and felt a timeless sense of mystery in that scene. The Alakananda flowed in from the right, a muscular, turgid current that was a shade lighter than the Mandakini, curving in from the left. Their confluence was remarkably calm, in part because the water level was high and most of the rocks were submerged. A delicate chevron of ripples, like a knitted seam, joined the two rivers. The ridge that divides these tributaries tapers down to a point, so narrow that it looks like the prow of a ship. About fifty feet above the confluence stand two small temples built on a rocky ledge. A twisting staircase descends to the water while higher up several more buildings are hidden within a grove of trees. Each of the elements in this scene appear perfectly balanced, the two channels of water that flow together, the rugged cliffs that come to a point where the rivers meet. Even the man-made structures—the temples, the bridge, the staircase—complement the natural contours of the mountains, so that nothing seems intrusive or out of place.

As the sun disappeared behind the ridges the lines began to blur and the water turned to liquid shadows. The sound of the two rivers filled the valley, like a steady rush of wind. Faintly, over the roar of the confluence, I heard the sound of temple bells and the moaning of a conch. An oil lamp was lit in the portico of the temple, though it was now too dark for me to see the priests who performed the evening aarti. From a distance I watched the lamp being waved in front of the deities, flickering like the last spark of a fire. After a while it was carried down the steps, moving slowly in cadence with the ringing of the bells. By the time the lamp had reached the water's edge, the darkness was complete. The two rivers had vanished and only the echo of their mingling currents remained. The tops of the mountains were faintly profiled against the sky—stars were coming out from behind the clouds—but here at the confluence it was impossible to distinguish one ridge from the next. There was no temple, no footbridge, no trees, no rocks—even the porch on which I sat seemed to have disappeared. All that was left was the single oil lamp hovering over invisible water.

# IV
# TRANSCENDENCE

## KEDARNATH–BADRINATH

*May your eye go to the sun,*
*your life's breath to the wind.*
*Go to the sky or to earth, as is your nature;*
*or go to the waters, if that is your fate.*
*Take root in the plants with your limbs.*

RIG VEDA

# VEHICLES OF THE GODS

EACH OF THE HINDU DEITIES TRAVEL ON THEIR
prescribed vahana—the goddess Durga sits on her tiger,
Ganesh on his mouse, Yama on his buffalo, Brahma on his
swan, Shiv on his bull, and Vishnu on the wings of Garud. For
the pilgrims who worship these deities, however, there are more
mundane, mechanized forms of conveyance—Tata buses, Com-
mander Jeeps, and Ambassador taxis, as well as motorcycles
and scooters. Though I have repeatedly complained about the
expanding network of motor roads in the mountains it is only
fair to admit that between each stage of my yatra, I took advantage of the different forms of public transport in Garhwal.

Some of these vehicles are more convenient and comfortable
than others. Coming down from Yamnotri, for instance, after
the first stage of my yatra, I was able to hitch a ride in a Jeep
taxi from Hanuman Chatti to Barkot. It was overloaded with
passengers and the only place for me to sit was on the roof rack
with four other men. As we hurtled around the corners each of
us grabbed onto whatever handholds were available to keep
from falling off. With the combined weight of passengers and
luggage the Jeep picked up momentum going down the hill and
the driver seemed ignorant of the brakes. Several times we
screeched around a corner and I felt sure that all of us were
going to go spinning off into the river. When the engine on this

Jeep suddenly caught fire and we came to an abrupt halt at the side of the road, I was almost relieved to see the black smoke billowing out from under the hood. Passengers inside the vehicle vaulted through the open doors and over the tailgate, while the four of us on the roof leaped to the ground like stowaways abandoning ship. After the driver unlatched the hood we all threw dirt on the flaming carburetor to put out the fire. Though we saved this Jeep from an untimely cremation it was obviously not going to take us any farther and I had to flag down a bus on its way to Barkot.

Five months later, returning from my winter pilgrimage to Gangotri, I rode in another Jeep from Harsil to Bhatwari. This time I was grateful to get a seat inside, for it was bitterly cold and all of the passengers squeezed together for warmth. The driver of this Jeep was relatively cautious, though he had an unnerving habit of letting go of the wheel and blowing into his cupped hands as we coasted around the bends. Beside me sat an elderly man who turned out to be the owner of the Jeep. A wealthy farmer from one of the valleys near Uttarkashi, he had recently bought the Jeep as an investment. The driver was his employee and after we had gone ten or fifteen kilometers the old man ordered him to stop, taking the wheel himself. Initially I wasn't concerned until he stalled the Jeep three times in a row before he got it going and then weaved back and forth wildly as we picked up speed. It was obvious that the owner didn't know how to drive and when he finally got the gearshift stuck in neutral while veering straight for the parapet wall, I let out a yell and told him to stop.

We came to a jarring halt about two inches from the edge — fortunately he did know where the brake pedal was — and the old man looked at me with a hurt expression. I told him that this was no place for him to learn to drive, pointing out the cliff that dropped away to our right and the blind corners up ahead.

From the inside pocket of his coat the owner produced a driver's license and waved it in my face.

"Look," he said. "Of course I can drive."

Two or three of the other passengers took my side for it was obvious to all of us that the owner of the Jeep was sure to run it off the road. Finally, with great reluctance, the old man moved aside and let the driver back behind the wheel. The rest of the way to Bhatwari he sat beside me in angry silence, his pride severely wounded.

On most of the motor roads in Garhwal it is impossible to go much faster than fifty or sixty kilometers per hour but with the narrow, winding stretches of the highway, these speeds feel much faster. I saw several accidents — a truck and a taxi that had collided on a hairpin bend, the front end of the car crumpled into a mangled mass of steel; a pilgrim bus that had plunged headfirst into a deep ravine, its wheels in the air; a minivan that had slammed into the hillside after its brakes had failed. At one of the tea shops where I stopped for breakfast there was a young man with his head wrapped in a turban of white gauze and bandages on both arms and legs. His face was badly bruised and he told me that he had been riding in a truck that had gone over the side of the road the day before. Fortunately nobody was killed but later, when I passed the site of this accident, the wreckage of the truck was being winched up the hill and seeing how badly it was damaged I couldn't believe that anyone had survived. In towns like Barkot, Uttarkashi, or Rudraprayag there are repair shops where the remains of these vehicles are beaten and welded back into shape. Looking at the twisted chassis and shattered bodies of the vehicles it is hard to imagine that they will ever run again but even the most badly damaged Jeep or truck is often back on the road within a month or two.

Each summer, during the height of the pilgrimage season, there are dozens of accidents in which yatris are killed. With the

number of drivers who come up from the plains it is surprising
that more fatalities don't occur. Never having driven in the hills
before and unfamiliar with the steep gradients and sharp corners, these drivers often lose control and the passengers constantly put their lives at risk. At various points along the
highways there are small roadside shrines, commemorating the
victims of past accidents. On one level people take a fatalistic
approach to these tragedies and some would say that the pilgrims were predestined to lose their lives. Because they died on
the road to Yamnotri, Gangotri, Kedarnath, or Badrinath, their
souls are released from suffering. At the same time there is
something unforgivable about the recklessness displayed by
many of the drivers who take to the roads of Garhwal and I was
far more afraid while riding in Jeeps or buses than I was while
walking even the most precipitous trails.

Some of my journeys by motor road produced less harrow-
ing but equally unpredictable experiences. During the yatra
season it is difficult to get a ride. Often I would have to hop
aboard whatever vehicle I could, to get from town to town, and
this meant riding in the back of trucks, squeezing into crowded
buses, or sharing cars and Jeeps with other yatris. On my way
down from Kedarnath, for instance, I got a seat in a taxi that
took me from Guptkashi to Tilwara. Eight of us were crammed
into a space intended for five people. As it turned out, one of the
passengers was a snake charmer and there was immediate panic
when the others learned that he was carrying a cobra in the basket on his lap. The driver, who seemed the most frightened of
all, wanted to throw him out of the car but we had already gone
a few kilometers. After a heated argument the snake charmer
was allowed to remain in the taxi as long as he promised to keep
the basket securely closed. While the rest of us were pinched
together, sitting in each other's laps, the man with the cobra sat

comfortably at the other end of the seat with plenty of room to spare. He was going as far as the town of Agustmuni and when we stopped to let him off, he began to unfasten the lid on the basket. Immediately two of the passengers bolted out of the taxi and the driver shouted at him as if he had threatened our lives. Taking advantage of the situation, the snake charmer apologized and explained that the only way that he could pay his fare was to open the basket since that was where he kept his money, safely guarded by the cobra. The driver knew that he had been tricked but he was also terrified of the snake and in the end, after a good deal of cursing and complaining, the snake charmer was allowed to disembark without paying his fare.

Several times I rode in vehicles that were carrying animals—miserable-looking chickens in bamboo baskets or a goat that was tethered to the seat of a bus and calmly fell asleep despite the jostling roar of the diesel engine. At one roadside village I watched a buffalo being unloaded from the back of a Jeep. The driver had to park the vehicle with its front wheels halfway up the side of the hill so that the huge, ungainly beast could be tipped out onto the ground. As soon as the buffalo slid free and got to its feet it shook its horns and urinated on the spot, as if expressing indignation.

Toward the end of my yatra, I rode in a bus from Srinagar to Tehri and found myself seated on a bench at the front, shoulder to shoulder with three men and a young boy who had a pet parakeet. The bird was still a fledgling and the boy told me that he had taken it from a nest several weeks earlier. It was extremely tame and sat calmly in the boy's hands nibbling at his fingers with its beak. Once the driver of the bus started the engine and we headed off the boy placed his parakeet on the dashboard, allowing it to sit there and look out through the windshield. Much to the amusement of the other passengers the tiny green bird kept staring at the road, cocking its head from side to side. It remained like this for several hours as the bus roared back and forth around the corners.

The driver was a gruff, impatient man who shouted at the passengers every time he stopped to let them off, complaining that they were wasting his time. He seemed to be in a great hurry to reach Tehri even though it was a local bus and had to stop at every village along the way. But the driver too was fascinated by the parakeet, who looked up at him with curiosity every time he wrestled with the gearshift or accelerated around a corner. Eventually, as the morning wore on, the sun was shining directly through the windshield and the inside of the bus grew uncomfortably hot. Without any warning the driver suddenly pulled over near a spring that was flowing across the road. While the rest of us waited he jumped down from the bus, filled a tin cup with water, and brought it for the parakeet to drink. Though he had shown no patience for his other passengers when they needed to stop, the driver seemed to have all the time in the world for this tiny bird, who casually lowered its beak into the cup and took one sip at a time, raising its head to let the water trickle down its throat.

The vehicles of the gods are as much companions as they are modes of transport. Ganesh's mouse scurries about at his feet and nibbles at the crumbs of sweets that the portly god consumes. While Shiv sits in meditation on Mount Kailash, Nandi the bull lies complacently nearby, chewing his cud. And the tiger who carries the goddess on his back looks very much like a huge pet cat, fawning over his mistress. Each of these images suggests the animistic traditions out of which Hinduism was born but they also imply the vital connection between man and other species.

The mistreatment of animals in India is often a source of

concern and consternation. There is no doubt that many creatures suffer at the hands of cruel and vicious masters—mules
that are beaten with a stick when they refuse to carry a heavy
load, dogs that are kicked and pelted with stones, chickens that
are crowded into pens so small they can hardly turn around.
These are things that nobody should condone and examples can
be found in almost any village or town. But the relationship
between human beings and other creatures is far more complicated than it may appear to an outside observer. For one thing,
in rural areas like Garhwal, people live in greater proximity to
animals and for the most part these are not pets but a source of
income, transport, or protection. Most village homes have a stable on the ground floor where cattle, horses, and mules are kept,
while their owners live in the rooms above. Dogs and cats are
usually relegated to the balcony of a house or kept outdoors,
where they serve a useful purpose. Though a certain amount of
affection may be expressed for these animals each of them has a
definite role to play within the household, whether it be providing milk, catching mice in a thatch roof, or chasing away monkeys in the fields. Under circumstances where life is hard, as it is
for most villagers in Garhwal, there is little room for sentimen-
tality when it comes to animals. At the same time, the conscious
mistreatment of these domesticated beasts is not in the interests
of the owners, who depend on them for their own survival.

Hinduism is often described as a religion in which all forms
of life are sacred but it is also a pragmatic faith, with as many
exceptions as it has rules. Cows are usually treated with inordi-
nate respect and in towns all along the pilgrim route wealthy
benefactors have endowed gaushalas. At these bovine rest
houses the cows are fed and cared for with greater hospitality
than most human yatris receive. Other creatures, however, must
fend for themselves.

Often there seems to be a kind of purposeful neglect when it comes to animals in Garhwal, particularly dogs who appear ill kept and starved. They are certainly not pampered like the parakeet in the bus but fed a few scraps from time to time and allowed to scavenge for whatever food they can find. If their owners had the luxury of giving them regular meals and brushing their coats I'm sure they would. But a family of subsistence farmers, struggling with their own poverty, are unlikely to provide for a dog before themselves.

Here I have to admit my own bias and ambivalence for I have a pet dog who is fed twice a day, allowed inside the house, regularly visits the veterinarian, occasionally sleeps on our beds, and is taken for a walk every morning. All this for an animal who serves no practical purpose except companionship. Though our dog is the size of a wolf, with a mixed lineage of labrador and German shepherd, she has never barked in her life and would gladly welcome even the most threatening burglar into our home by licking his hand and rolling onto her back.

Over the course of my trek I encountered any number of dogs, from skeletal mongrels cringing in the streets of Rishikesh to fierce bhootia mastiffs guarding sheep and buffaloes on the high pastures. More than once I was attacked by dogs that came at me with their canines bared, ready to tear my ankles to shreds. Most of them presented a ferocious demeanor at first but were soon wagging their tails and trying to charm me into throwing them a biscuit or a crust of bread. One particularly vocal bhootia outside a village near Yamnotri barked and barked on my arrival. But later that night, as I slept on the porch of his owner's house, he came and curled up at my feet.

Camping at Lanka, on my way down from Gangotri in December, I was setting up my tent behind the sadhu's hut when I was startled by a cold, wet nose pressing up against my arm. Turning around I saw a brown and black dog that had crept up behind me. Her fur was matted and her tail was full of burrs but she had a face as beautiful as any I've ever seen. In her moist brown eyes there wasn't the slightest hint of ferocity though she was strongly built with a thick red mane of hair around her neck. Unlike most mastiffs who have dull, vicious features, her face was expressive and full of affectionate curiosity. Her muzzle was a pale tan color and inching closer she nudged me once again with her black nose.

She lived with the sadhu and he told me that her name was Rani, which means queen. He said that he had adopted her a year ago when she was still a puppy, left behind by a passing group of shepherds. Though the sadhu did not let Rani come inside his hut, he fed her at the door and she slept in a sheltered burrow at the back. As it was winter, there were leopards in the forest and the sadhu said that another dog who used to live at the Army Signal depot down the road had been killed a few weeks earlier. That evening, as we sat in front of the fire, I suddenly heard Rani start to bark. Taking my torch I went outside and shone it into the trees behind the hut. She was standing absolutely still, her hackles raised and her tail coiled like a spring. Flashing the torch farther up in the woods I saw the eyes of a fox, two yellow beads reflected in the beam of light.

Later, as I fell asleep in my tent, I kept worrying that Rani might be taken by a leopard but in the morning when I got up she was waiting to greet me. I gave her a couple of Gluco biscuits, which she ate with relish, whimpering and sniffing at my knees when they were done. As I began to take down the tent she kept circling around me and nosing playfully at my arms. She could tell that I was about to leave and when I started to roll up the tent Rani kept putting both of her front paws on the fabric, refusing to let me continue. Finally, the only way I could break camp was to distract her by throwing a biscuit ten or fifteen feet away, then quickly rolling up my tent and groundsheet.

After I said good-bye to the sadhu and set off down the road,

Rani followed me. Several times I tried to shoo her back and even though she turned and pretended to go the other way, as soon as I set off again she was immediately at my heels. By the time I'd gone a kilometer or more, I was beginning to get worried. Reluctantly, I picked up a small rock and tossed it in her direction. She gave me a heartbroken look and put her tail between her legs, then started to slink away. Twice again I had to throw a rock at her, for she was persistent and each time I went around a corner, a few minutes later Rani appeared behind me. I had no intention of hurting her and my stones missed by several feet each time but it was clear that if I didn't throw them at her she would have followed me all day. Finally, after the third rock, Rani gave up and retreated in the direction of the sadhu's hut. Continuing along the road, I felt guilty for chasing her away and kept looking back to see if she was there.

In the final episodes of the Mahabharata the five Pandav brothers and Draupadi take darshan of Shiv and receive his blessing. After this they begin their journey into heaven, climbing up through the high Himalayas. Along the way they are joined by a dog who follows after them and keeps them company.

Eventually they reach the glaciers and snowfields of Swargrohini, the mountain of heaven. As they ascend higher and higher, each of them succumbs in turn, first Abhimanyu the youngest, then Draupadi, followed by Sahadev, Nakul, and Arjun. Even the mighty Bhim collapses along the trail and dies, leaving only the eldest brother Yudhistar and the dog. Struggling upward through the snow and ice these two companions approach the summit of Swargrohini.

All at once, Indra, the lord of heaven, appears in front of them, riding in his celestial chariot. He greets Yudhistar and tells him that Draupadi and his brothers have already reached heaven and it is only his mortal body that is holding him back.

Indra then invites Yudhistar to take a seat in the chariot and ride with him to paradise. Before accepting this offer, the eldest of the Pandavs requests that the dog, who has shown such loyalty, should also be admitted to heaven but Indra refuses, saying that the animal is unclean and will pollute his chariot.

"If this dog cannot enter swarg then neither will I," says Yudhistar, refusing to abandon his companion.

When he hears these words Indra is pleased, for the dog is actually Yudhistar's father, Dharma, in disguise. As a final test for his son, Dharma had been asked by the gods to assume this form, to see if Yudhistar was worthy of heaven. Together they climb aboard Indra's chariot and fly up to swarg where Yudhistar is reunited with his brothers and Draupadi. In this way the great epic of the Mahabharata ends with a disarming allegory about the relationship between man and dog.

# Shiv's Navel

From Kedarnath there are several different routes that pilgrims can follow to Badrinath. The highest of these leads directly over snow-covered passes but even though the trails are outlined on some of the tourist maps and religious brochures of Garhwal, this route is only accessible to experienced mountaineers. Nevertheless, there is a persistent, popular mythology about these upper regions of Uttarakhand and I was told on more than one occasion that sadhus who performed extreme tapasya were able to walk barefoot across the snow peaks and glaciers at elevations of eighteen to twenty thousand feet. In many people's minds these high-altitude crossings represent the ultimate pilgrimage, which can only be accomplished through acts of severe austerity and yoga, a transcendental passage through realms of snow and ice. One of the yatris I met on the trail to Kedarnath insisted that if you climb high enough into the mountains it is possible to walk from Yamnotri to Badrinath in a single day, touching down at Gangotri and Kedarnath en route. He seemed to believe that all of the trails converged at the apex of the Himalayas, like diffuse beams of light refracted through prisms of ice.

At the beginning of my pilgrimage I made a conscious decision not to carry any maps with me, partly because it was unnecessary, but also because it seemed that I would be traveling through a region that defied the staid conventions of cartography. Whenever I looked at the framed Survey of India map on the wall of my office, I could easily trace the walking trails that linked the tributaries of the Ganga, but the more I stared at the intricate filigree of contour lines, the blue veins of rivers, the mottled colors in the paper, it seemed less certain and undefined. Whenever I removed my finger from the twisting lines of ink I quickly lost my bearings and it was difficult to regain perspective. In many ways this map was an optical illusion, like one of those psychedelic drawings where everything seems to be a jumble of abstract patterns but if you fix your eyes on it for long enough, suddenly a disconcerting image appears.

On earlier journeys I had learned to distrust most depictions of the Himalayas. Between each stage of my pilgrimage, when I consulted maps and guidebooks there were always discrepancies. Distances were wrong, the names and positions of villages reversed, the trails misleading, sometimes nonexistent. There was also the perpetual confusion between miles and kilometers, meters and feet, so that it often seemed as if these charts and diagrams were intended to confuse rather than assist a traveler in finding his way. A few of the older accounts, like Atkinson's *Gazetteer*, gave distances in "chains." Some of the maps that I consulted were like elaborate riddles or a maze that tested my perseverance. To have carried them with me on the pilgrimage would only have led to frustration. Instead I preferred to ask my way from one village to the next or to use my own judgment when confronted by a fork in the trail. As a result, several times I took a wrong turn and wandered off my route but in none of those situations would a map have aided me.

Projecting a mountainous landscape onto a flat piece of paper is bound to create distortions and inaccuracies. Though I have always had a fascination for maps, I have learned not to believe the stories they tell. In the bazaar at Kedarnath plenty of brochures and maps were available for pilgrims but none of these presented a particularly reliable image of the terrain. In fact most of the maps were more like mythological diagrams with schematic lines and points transposed against the celestial scenery of the mountains. The general position of each temple or pilgrimage site was indicated by a sketch of the shrine or a portrait of one of the gods. Shiv appeared above the temple at Kedarnath, levitating over the valley like a cloud formation. Ganga streamed across the sky in the form of a rainbow and the glacier at Gaumukh was portrayed as if it were literally the head of a cow carved out of ice. In this way a pilgrim who consulted these maps was constantly reminded of Uttarakhand's religious lore. Juxtaposed against such colorful images, the motor roads and footpaths were a rigid web of lines—the distances between each point printed with mathematical authority, undermined by an artist's spiritual fantasies. The rivers too were marked on the maps—not so much as physical features but as abstract blue lines that flowed together off the page.

The more I walked through Garhwal the more I understood that this landscape is as much a part of the pilgrim's imagination as it is a factual, finite world. What some might call inaccuracies on a map to others would reflect a greater truth, an internal vision of the mountains rather than an external representation of the landscape. At points I drew maps in my own journals to remind me of certain places and paths but looking at them later I could see that they bore less resemblance to the terrain itself than to my imagination of it.

A careful surveyor might well be able to establish the exact altitudes and distances between two temples but for a devotee on his way to the sacred sources of the Ganga these details are meaningless. Instead, the geography of Uttarakhand must be perceived in the context of a much larger cosmology, a fluid world in which scale and magnitude are less important than the changeable layers of dreams. In this landscape it is possible for a single event to occur in two places at once, or for the past to become the present. Here paradox serves as the rule rather than the exception. Two paths can lead in opposite directions but reach a single point. Natural phenomena cannot be measured by ordinary instruments. To travel through this region is to suspend our spatial and temporal assumptions. At the same time, however, it is not a completely fanciful landscape—the pilgrim experiences hardship and exhaustion but these are part of a journey that lifts us above the plateaus of reality and into the highlands of faith.

A pervasive sense of dislocation accompanies the pilgrim along these trails. The names of places are often repeated, so that "Phool Chatti" can be found not only five kilometers beyond Rishikesh, but eight kilometers below Yamnotri, and at several other locations in between. The approach to virtually every major temple in Garhwal is guarded by a shrine to Bhairon Devta and as a yatri proceeds along this route, he must propitiate the same deity again and again, as if the trail kept doubling back on itself. Adding to this confusion, certain places have more than one name, reflecting different myths and conventions—Chorabari Tal and Gandhi Sarovar, or Buda Kedar and Tati Tatur, are one and the same. Even something as basic as the pronunciation of Hardwar is in dispute—known as Haridwar by the followers of Vishnu and Hardwar by those who offer allegiance to Shiv.

Though the sequence of the Pandavs' journey through the Himalayas dictates the order in which a pilgrim must visit the various shrines there are a number of anomalies. For example, Swargrohini, the mountain the Pandavs climbed on their way to heaven, is actually located northwest of Yamnotri, whereas the route they followed leads to the east. On a much grander scale, however, the Char Dham Yatra itself is open to dispute. Many would argue that Badrinath may represent the ultimate destination in northern India but the other three dhams are not located in Garhwal, but at the cardinal points of the subcontinent — Puri in the east, Kanyakumari in the south, and Dwarka in the west.

Hinduism has always had a predilection for sacred diagrams in which the cosmos is depicted as a complex geometrical pattern, a carefully constructed mandala that represents the symmetry of the universe. At the same time, however, various traditions, both ancient and modern, distort and compromise this orderly scheme of lines and shapes. Primal myths of snakes and tree sprites, river goddesses and buffalo demons, seep through the codified layers of Brahmanical narratives and undermine established hierarchies. On the other hand, current headlines and the superstitious whims of today's political leaders give precedence to certain shrines. During an electoral battle, the ballot symbols of open palms, lotus blossoms, and even the hammer and sickle are plastered on the walls of dharamshalas and temple complexes, blurring the lines between sacred and secular.

Traveling throughout Uttarakhand, over a millennium ago, Shankaracharya attempted to bring order to this chaotic mountain region. He identified the Panch Prayag, the five main confluences in Garhwal; the Panch Kedar, the five main shrines of Shiv; and the Panch Badri, the five main temples of Vishnu. In this way he attempted to achieve a balance between the landscape and the collective imagination of Hindu beliefs. Though this overarching structure has survived and remains the organizing principle behind most pilgrimages in Garhwal, disputes have arisen over the exact location of certain shrines, not to mention the relative importance of one site or another. At many destinations, for instance, there is often a relatively new temple as well as an older shrine located a short distance from each other. With the Panch Badri there is an ongoing controversy as to whether one of these temples is actually located at Adi Badri or at Urgam, almost a hundred kilometers apart. In an effort to cleanse Hindu traditions of the polluting influences of Buddhism and other cults, Shankaracharya ordained a limited pantheon of deities, largely ignoring the goddess as he established a male hegemony in Garhwal. But the resilience of female shakti could never be subdued and all along the pilgrimage routes there are temples to the goddess, at places like Kalimath or Ansuya Devi, which attract considerable crowds.

Essentially these conflicts are a result of priests competing over the reputation and renown of their ancestral domain. However, for most pilgrims the subtleties of these disputes are insignificant and they enter this sacred terrain with a limited concept of the spatial relationships between each shrine. For every opinion there is always an opposing point of view. As someone who was schooled in the efficacy of maps, I have always presumed that certain absolutes of topography existed, but over the course of this pilgrimage I came to understand that in Garhwal there is never a single line between two points and every claim can be contested. One evening I had to sit up until midnight listening to a fellow pilgrim vociferously postulating that instead of four dhams there were actually five, while a week later another yatri tried to persuade me, with equal conviction, that only three existed.

From the town of Guptkashi I crossed the Mandakini River and followed a trail that led to Madhmaheshwar, the second of the Panch Kedar. At this site Shiv's midriff and navel emerged from the ground, after he buried himself in the earth to escape the Pandavs. A detour of thirty kilometers in each direction, the temple at Madhmaheshwar lies northeast of the main pilgrimage route to Badrinath. As with most shrines dedicated to Shiv, it is only accessible on foot and lies at an altitude over ten thousand feet.

There are several approaches to Madhmaheshwar but the path I followed from Kalimath, by way of Lank and Ransi, is the most common route. Climbing steadily through a scattered pine forest, I eventually came in sight of the Madhmaheshwar Ganga, a tributary of the Mandakini. For most of the year this stream is not particularly large or swift but during the monsoon it collects a considerable amount of water from all of the ravines and gullies that funnel into the valley. The lower ridges on either side of the Madhmaheshwar Ganga have suffered extensive erosion over the past ten years. On entering this valley I was immediately confronted by an enormous landslide, directly across the river from the village of Lank. The entire facade of one ridge had collapsed, going up to a height of five hundred meters. At its base the landslide was close to a kilometer in width and from a distance it looked as if a whole section of the mountain had been bitten off and chewed up into dirt and gravel. In many ways the destruction reminded me of the wasteland created by the Tehri Dam. The exposed gash of earth and rock had nothing growing on it, though the forest extended right up to the crumbling edges of the landslide, a thick jacket of trees that suddenly gave way to empty space. Looking at this landslide from across the valley I was suddenly aware of the instability of the mountains. While walking up the trail from Kalimath I had no reason to doubt the solidity of the earth but now it seemed that the ridge I was standing on might collapse at any moment.

This feeling of uncertainty grew stronger as I made my way toward Lank. At several places the trail crossed broad channels of rock and debris, where monsoon rains had loosened the surface of the hill. Much of the soil was clay, a silvery gray color, the consistency of freshly mixed cement. Dozens of springs seeped through crevices in the rocks, so that it felt as if the mountain was gradually flowing away beneath my feet. Most of the plants that grew on these eroded sections were weeds such as stinging nettle and marijuana, which was coming into bloom. Scattered trees still clung to this slope but seemed in danger of losing their grip, leaning precariously to one side or the other with their roots exposed. It was not difficult to imagine that within a few years the entire surface of this ridge would sheer off like the opposite slope.

Lank (pronounced *Leynk*) is a sizable village of roughly fifty houses, all of which are in imminent danger of being swept away in a landslide. Many of the terraced fields that surround this village have already been furrowed by erosion and several of the houses are situated only a few feet away from the edge of crumbling ravines. The runoff from the rains has cut ragged scars down the entire length of the ridge, as if a pair of giant claws had ripped open the surface of the mountain. The houses, with mud walls and slate roofs, look fragile and exposed. Just to live in these homes, particularly during the violent onslaught of a monsoon storm, is an act of courage. Every day the people of Lank must face the reality that their village will soon be destroyed and yet they have not abandoned their homes. Though it seems reckless and foolish to remain, as one villager said, "Where else will we go?" For people who have lived on these slopes for generations and farmed the land for as long as they can remember, the instability of the mountains must seem a harsh betrayal.

As I passed through Lank and came to the other side of the village the true scale of destruction became evident. The scree from the landslide on the opposite slope had blocked the Madhmaheshwar Ganga, creating a dam that backed the water up for almost a kilometer. On the near side of the valley there was another enormous slide that looked like a glacier of rocks and stone, undercutting the north face of the ridge on which the houses of Lank are perched. Buried beneath this landslide is a village called Pondar, which was completely destroyed in 1998.

All of the inhabitants and their cattle were killed without a trace, entombed beneath a wave of dirt and rubble.

When I spoke with people in Lank and other nearby villages I was given different numbers for casualties, with figures ranging from a thousand dead to less than twenty-five victims. Nobody seemed to know for sure, but everyone agreed on the sequence of events. During the first weeks of the monsoon, two years earlier, there had been more rain than usual and the ridge to the north of Lank, directly above Pondar, began to show signs of collapse. A couple of minor flash floods had come down the valley, strewing boulders and mud near the village. Some of the inhabitants grew worried and took shelter on higher ground but most of the villagers remained in their homes. One night, after several days of constant rain, a section of the ridge sloughed off and poured down into the valley, burying Pondar beneath twenty or thirty feet of debris. The sudden force of this landslide blocked the Madhmaheshwar Ganga and as the water level rose it triggered a second landslide on the opposite shore. One of the villagers at Ransi, five kilometers upstream, said that he had woken up to the sound of this catastrophe and thought it was another earthquake, like the one that struck Garhwal in 1991. He said that the ground shook and the valley echoed with a muffled roar like thunder.

As for the causes of the landslide it was clear that the ridges above Lank and Pondar had become severely deforested, which must have contributed to their instability. The recent earthquakes too had probably loosened the foundations of the slope so that the heavy rain turned the soil into a slurry of clay and rock that broke loose like an avalanche. There was also a new motor road being built, from the valley up to Lank and on to Ransi, though everyone I spoke with denied that its excavation had anything to do with the disaster. In fact, work on the road was continuing even though a large section had been buried underneath the slide and the new motor bridge across the Madhmaheshwar Ganga had been washed away. Just as I was leaving Lank, I heard the dull thud of dynamite, as a crew of laborers were blasting boulders. With each explosion I could feel the ground tremble and looking up at the fragile slopes of exposed earth I had to wonder at the wisdom of those detonations.

Serious catastrophes like the earthquakes in 1991 and 1993 or the landslide that buried Pondar are often understood and explained as acts of God. The violence of these natural phenomena suggests a powerful and judgmental force that wreaks vengeance on the human population. Even when the immediate causes and effects may be self-evident in the environment there is a tendency on the part of many people to blame the failure of religious practices or the disgruntlement of presiding deities.

As I was filling water at a spring that flowed down the center of the landslide, a man came around the corner of the path and greeted me. He was in his late thirties and introduced himself as Puran Singh, saying that he was employed as a day laborer working on the new motor road. It was late afternoon and he was on his way home to the village of Lank. As we spoke it became clear that Puran Singh was somewhat simpleminded, cheerful but slow-witted—the sort of person who used to be uncharitably known as a village idiot. After a while I asked him about the landslide and the fate of Pondar. Immediately Puran Singh's smile vanished and he scowled with disgust.

"The people of that village deserved what they got," he said. "They were harijans, neech jatis, untouchables. Because of them the whole ridge is crumbling and now our homes are threatened."

Confused by the spite and vehemence of his words I asked Puran Singh to explain.

"This whole region is sacred ground, the home of Shivji,

Mahadev," he said. "But these harijans, they refuse to show respect. A group of them came to our village and polluted the temple and drank tea in a hotel. You may not understand these things, but when a harijan drinks tea from a glass it has to be left untouched for three days and then washed with cow's urine to purify it. There are places in these mountains that are so sacred, if a harijan goes there, his breath will stop and he will die. But these bastards, they defied the laws of caste. That's why their village was destroyed and now our homes and fields are going to be swept away."

Puran Singh ranted on like this for several minutes and as I listened to his irrational babble it was clear that he was simply spouting the prejudices of others. He himself was an upper-caste Rajput but being mentally retarded it seemed unlikely that he could have formed these opinions on his own. Obviously he had heard someone else say that the harijans of Pondar were to blame, passing judgment on those who could no longer speak out.

Two days later, as I was returning down the valley after visiting the temple at Madhmaheshwar, I followed a different path that led me across the lower end of the landslide a kilometer below Lank. As I made my way over the rocks and rubble, I tried to imagine exactly where the houses of Pondar must have been. There wasn't the slightest sign of habitation, the entire village completely wiped out in a matter of seconds. Recalling the crazed and desperate anger in Puran Singh's voice I couldn't help but feel the oppressive weight of this tragedy. Not only were the victims buried somewhere beneath my feet but they had been crushed by the bigotry and intolerance of those who survived.

When the landslides occurred in 1998, not only was the village of Pondar destroyed but most of the Madhmaheshwar Valley was completely cut off and the government had to send helicopters with relief supplies and food. Throughout Garhwal the river valleys provide the only link with the outside world. Whenever flash floods and landslides occur these tenuous channels of trade and transport are severed and isolated villages have to wait for weeks until bridges and roads are repaired. In fact, the day after I set out for Madhmaheshwar, there were several landslides along the footpath up to Kedarnath, which left thousands of pilgrims stranded for three days.

Despite a number of rural development schemes and government projects intended to improve the lives of people in Garhwal, the steep and unstable terrain, as well as the scattered and often nomadic population, makes it difficult to provide even the most basic of modern amenities. Indoor plumbing is an unknown luxury in many villages, where women are often forced to carry water in vessels on their heads over distances of two or three kilometers. Electricity has been made available in the more densely populated areas of Garhwal, usually along the motor roads, but the supply is erratic and, once again, landslides or falling trees can cut off power for weeks on end.

The upper reaches of the Madhmaheshwar Valley have never had electricity, though a recent government scheme provides villagers with the means of tapping solar energy—photovoltaic cells, batteries, and fluorescent lamps. As I was walking up the path to Ransi I passed three separate groups of women who were hauling huge batteries on their backs. Each of these weighed close to a hundred pounds, twice the load that I was carrying. The women were sharing the burden, trading off in shifts, as they slowly worked their way up the trail. One group of three were resting at the top of a climb and returned my greeting with cautious smiles. The battery—a dull industrial black with stubby terminals—was the kind used in trucks, at least three times the size of an ordinary car battery. It was partly wrapped in a folded gunnysack with ropes that ran over the woman's shoulders.

"How far have you been carrying it?" I asked.

"From Mansuna," one of the women replied, pointing to a small town on the opposite side of the valley, about eight kilometers away.

"Why don't you use mules?"

"There aren't any available this time of year," she said, with a shrug of frustration. "All of our mules are at Gaurikund, carrying yatris up to Kedarnath. What can we do? For a whole year now we've been waiting for this 'solar' to arrive, then suddenly we get word it's been delivered and we have to go and collect it immediately."

In Ransi at least a dozen of the photovoltaic panels had already been assembled and erected on the balconies and slate roofs of the houses. When I arrived the sun had just gone down behind the ridge and it was growing dark. One of the villagers eagerly invited me inside his house to show me a lamp that he had hooked up the day before. He told me that he had paid one thousand five hundred rupees for the complete set, which is provided by the government at a subsidized rate. His two young sons and a couple of neighbors gathered around to watch as he connected wires and pressed the switch. The lamp flickered on and off with a blinding white pulse, then filled the room with ghostly brightness that reflected off the mud walls. The six of us blinked at each other in bewilderment and grinned as if we'd just seen a magic trick. Most of the houses in the village were still illuminated by kerosene lamps and the orange glow of firelight, but one of the wealthier families had already bought a television set, which had been connected to a battery charged by solar power. Several dozen people were crowded into one room, all of them seated on the floor. Though the reception was poor because of the surrounding ridges, from the doorway I could just make out the fuzzy gray image of a meteorologist in Delhi announcing the progress of the monsoon.

The next morning it was wet and foggy, a dense mist lying over the valley, like gray felt. As I set off from Ransi, some of the villagers were already herding their cattle into the forest to graze. I made my way slowly past the lines of cows and goats walking single file along the trail, their bells ringing in the mist. After a short distance I came upon two of the women who had been carrying the battery the day before. By this time a light rain had started to fall and they nodded to me from under the hooded borders of their woolen shawls. Each of them was carrying a dry piece of smoldering cowdung they would use to light a fire once they got their cattle safely into the forest. Smoke from the burning dung drifted through the damp air, a sour-sweet fragrance that promised warmth.

From Ransi I had expected the trail to keep climbing but instead it pitched down into the valley for six kilometers before reaching another village called Gondhar where the final ascent to Madhmaheshwar begins. With the rain and mist it was difficult to get my bearings but from time to time the clouds parted and I could see the ridges ahead of me and occasionally the white summit of a snow peak far above. After passing through a forest of long needle pines I descended into a dense oak jungle, the branches of trees knotted together overhead. Banks of ferns and other monsoon plants hemmed in the path, their moist, grassy odors emerging with the rain. Most of the tree trunks were covered with moss and one of the oaks below the trail was draped in purple orchids. Earlier in my trek I had seen one or two of these flowers growing like a rare corsage on the wrist of an inaccessible branch but here they erupted in profusion from every limb of the tree. There seemed to be no explanation why this single oak, instead of all the others in that valley, should have been decorated with orchids, an eccentric whim of nature. Amid the shadowy tangle of green foliage the tree looked almost garish, like purple frill on a dark velvet cloak.

The farther into the valley I went the more I felt as if I were entering a protected sanctuary. Instead of the exposed and vulnerable slopes above Lank and Pondar, here the mountains seemed to be held together by the matted roots of ringal bamboo, the dense webbing of ferns, and a solid scaffolding of trees. Rather than opening out into broad, bare contours the ridges folded into each other and the sheltered ravines and gullies seemed closely guarded. As I approached Gondhar the trail dropped steeply into a gorge and I crossed a bridge over one of the streams that runs into the Madhmaheshwar Ganga. Just above the bridge a slender waterfall dropped into a circular pool that had been hollowed out of the rocks. Compared to the open wounds of landslides that I had seen the day before, where the unrestrained force of water had scarified the land with a brutal and merciless hand, here there seemed to be a perfect balance in nature. This delicate stream, which spilled over a moss-covered ledge, had gradually carved the rocks into a sheltered chamber. The pool, which was twenty feet across at its widest point and about ten feet deep, was still and undisturbed except where the waterfall creased its surface in concentric rings. Looking down from the bridge, surrounded by trees and mist, I felt as if I were peering directly into the mountain's womb.

A short distance beyond Gondhar is a confluence at a place called Buntoli, where the Madhmaheshwar Ganga is formed out of two separate streams that come down from the mountains on either side. The path to Madhmaheshwar goes directly up the center of the intervening ridge, a climb of ten kilometers and close to three thousand feet in altitude. The day before, a tea shop owner in a small village below Ransi had warned me about this climb. He said that every year he joined a procession that carried the idol up to the temple. Like so many of the other deities in Garhwal, the image of Shiv at Madmaheshwar spends the winter months at lower elevations.

"In Baisakh, at the start of spring, we carry the doli up to the temple," said the tea shop owner. "Each of us takes turns bearing the weight on our shoulders and at that time you do not feel tired because Mahadev gives you strength. However, when we have to climb up there after Diwali to bring the doli down, we feel exhausted and the trail seems to go on forever."

The path is steep and almost as long as the climb from Ghuttu to Panwali. There are a few seasonal settlements along this route and a couple of makeshift rest houses where tea and biscuits are available. The majority of pilgrims who undertake the journey up to Madhmaheshwar are Bengalis; of the dozen yatris I encountered along the way, all but two of them were from Calcutta. Nobody could give me a satisfactory reason why this was the case but the tea shop owners in the valley have obviously latched on to this trend and many of their signs were written in Bengali, even though the language is not spoken in Garhwal. Near the chaans at Nanu, about five kilometers beyond Gondhar, I passed a family of four yatris. The husband introduced himself as Ashok Dey and told me that he was a schoolteacher from Calcutta. We walked together for a short distance, while his wife and twelve-year-old daughter struggled behind us up the hill. Their youngest child was riding on the shoulders of a Garhwali porter who had a bundle of luggage strapped to his back. Ashok Dey explained that his school was on holiday and he had brought his family to Garhwal for a two-week pilgrimage. They had already been up to Kedarnath but found it too crowded and despite the steepness of this climb he said that he preferred coming to Madhmaheshwar so that he and his family could "enjoy the beauty of nature."

The forest opened out again as we climbed above Gondhar

and there were grassy cliffs and precipitous terrain but none of the dangerous erosion that threatened the valley lower down. Ferns and wildflowers grew in profusion, especially spirea bushes with cascading white blossoms, like unpruned hedges along the trail. Above and below Nanu I passed through groves of anyar trees (*Pieris ovalifolia*), which are common in the Himalayas at altitudes up to eight thousand feet. At this time of year these trees were also flowering, with strings of pendant white blossoms that looked like plastic beads. The leaves of the anyar tree are poisonous and unlike oaks, which are lopped for fodder, these remain untouched even in the vicinity of seasonal chaans.

Unlike the footpath to Kedarnath, the trail to Madhmaheshwar is unpaved, though it is well maintained. Halfway up the hill I came upon two men who were employed by the PWD to dig water channels across the trail so it wouldn't wash away during the monsoon. The two of them were taking a rest when I came by, their pick and shovel abandoned in the middle of the trail. One of the men was lounging on a flat rock, smoking a bidi, while the other was knitting a child's sweater out of bright green and purple yarn. Soon after passing them, I flushed a monal pheasant, its brilliant plumage almost the same color as the wool. By this time the rain had stopped and I could see the mountains all around me, with forests of fir and pine giving way to the bugiyals higher up.

After what seemed like an endless zigzag up the ridge the trail finally leveled off and emerged from the trees onto a broad meadow that formed a basin below the high snow peaks. Most of the mountains were still obscured but in the muted light that filtered through the clouds these sloping fields of grass took on an eerie hue, like glowing moss. The Madhmaheshwar temple lay at the center of this meadow, a solid stone structure with a tapered spire. Next to it was a two-story dharamshala, a couple of tea shops, and another rest house. Scattered over the meadows on either side were flocks of sheep and goats, as well as buffaloes, their black shapes floating in a sea of grass.

A group of three pilgrims had arrived about an hour ahead of me and they were preparing for a pooja in the temple. One of them said that this was his third visit to Madhmaheshwar and he preferred this temple to all the others in Garhwal because it was a peaceful, secluded place. It was true that there was none of the clutter and noise of Kedarnath. The priests were not as aggressive as those I'd met at temples like Triyugi Narayan. They allowed me to enter the shrine for darshan along with the other yatris and did not insist that I purchase a pooja tray.

The rain was falling once again, as I removed my boots at the edge of the courtyard and walked barefoot across the wet flagstones to the entrance. Though there wasn't much of a breeze it was cold and gray, the light having faded in the afternoon. The blocks of stone out of which the temple is constructed were dark and lifeless, though there was a patch of color above the door, where the image of a tiger is carved into the lintel and painted bright orange and red. Immediately inside the temple was a rectangular room with a dozen or more brass bells hanging from the ceiling. In the center of this chamber, on a stone pedestal, stood a brass image of Nandi the bull facing the inner sanctum.

The head priest at Madhmaheshwar was an elderly man with a white beard and uncombed hair that fell to his shoulders. Over his dhoti he wore a woolen bathrobe and looked as if he had just got out of bed. He and his assistant instructed the yatris on what to do, while lighting incense and presenting their pooja trays to the deities. The entire procedure was performed with a certain amount of distraction and at several points the priest had to interrupt his Sanskrit prayers to warn the yatris not to turn their backs on the gods. One of the group had a video camera and wanted to record the event but the priests shook their heads emphatically and made him take it back outside. As with so many temples the images were obscured in shadow and it was hard to make out which gods were present.

The rituals of worship and devotion at these shrines are often perfunctory, even when there is no queue of yatris. Little time is spent in meditation or reflection. After having walked for hours to reach a temple the pilgrim often gets only a fleeting glimpse of the idols, their silver eyes glimmering in the faint light of oil lamps. Most of the priests perform their duties with undisguised impatience, setting aside the trays of rice and coconuts after the briefest gestures of oblation to the gods. Longer and more elaborate rituals are conducted at these temples but only when generous offerings are made. The entire pooja at Madhmaheshwar took less than ten minutes and it concluded with each of the three yatris writing the names of family and friends on slips of paper and placing these, along with money, in a wooden offering box. Once they had finished, I also stepped forward and took Shiv's darshan, folding my hands and bowing in front of the stone lingam. After I put ten rupees in his box the head priest smeared a yellow tilak across my brow.

At the edge of the open courtyard in front of the temple is a stone channel lined with slabs of slate. Through this tiny canal a spring of clear water flows out of the meadows and splashes onto the flagstones where pilgrims can drink and bathe. Unlike at many other religious sites in Uttarakhand, there is neither a glacier nor a lake and the water emerges directly out of the earth. It is cold, pristine, and tastes of minerals in the soil. Though the course of this umbilical stream is governed by a man-made channel the spring appears to flow naturally into the temple precincts.

More than any other shrine I visited in Garhwal the temple

at Madhmaheshwar seems to exist in harmony with the landscape, as if placed there by God rather than human design. But
just as I had discovered at so many other pilgrimage sites the
exact location of this shrine was somewhat ambiguous. Though
most yatris come and pray at the present temple, believing it to
be the specific spot on earth where Shiv's midriff and navel
emerged from the ground, there is an older site on the ridge
above that is known as Buda Madhmaheshwar. The name itself
suggests greater antiquity and perhaps even authenticity, though
the newer temple retains its prominence.

After drinking a steaming glass of goat's milk tea at the
dharamshala, I set off for Buda Madhmaheshwar. The owner of
the tea shop had directed me, pointing out a faint path that
climbed up through the meadows to a ridge obscured by dark
clouds, which looked like fistfuls of kneaded clay. It was raining, but not heavily, a fine mist that beaded my hair and beard. I
had no trouble finding my way to the top of the ridge, though a
pack of four shaggy mastiffs came barking in my direction and
forced me to take a detour off the trail. The dogs were guarding
a flock of goats and sheep but once they saw that I posed no
threat they quickly retreated to the shelter of a shepherd's hut.

It took me about half an hour to climb to the top of the
meadow where the path suddenly disappeared. There were no
other human beings nearby, only a few buffaloes grazing on the
lush pastures. Looking down I could see the blurred outline of
the temple through the mist and rain. For a while I wandered
back and forth along the crest of the ridge casting about for the
shrine. On the other side lay a heavy oak forest and farther up I
could just make out a spine of granite crags, like twisted verte-
brae. The clouds kept shifting all around me and I felt a sense of
vertigo, as if the ground was swaying beneath my feet.

Eventually, by accident, I came upon the Buda Madhmaheshwar shrine. It was much smaller than I expected, little more

than a cairn of rocks. Several flat stones were propped against each other to make a simple shelter three feet high. Inside of this was a lingam, a smooth, oblong stone about eight inches in length, daubed with vermilion. The only other symbol was a handful of primulas that someone, probably a shepherd, had picked and left there as an offering.

I found myself moved by the simplicity of this shrine. It was a place where nothing stood between me and the spiritual elements of nature. Unlike the brief darshan I had performed at the temple lower down, here I could meditate in front of the shrine as long as I chose. Nothing was hidden from view—no lamps and shadows, no smoke and mirrors, no priests performing a sleight of hand. I noticed the lichen on the rocks, the irregular colors in the stone lingam, the bruised petals on the primulas. Garlands of mist trailed out across the meadows.

It is hard to say how long I stood there, at least a quarter of an hour, before I suddenly felt the air grow colder as a breeze picked up. Within seconds the clouds were swept aside and straight ahead of me appeared Chaukhamba. One of the largest snow peaks in Garhwal, this broad massif stands over twenty-two thousand feet above sea level. Though I have often seen Chaukhamba from a distance, part of a familiar panorama of snow peaks, this was the closest I had ever been. The mountain looked out of proportion, like an impregnable citadel of rock and ice. Compared to the small, stone cairn in front of me, Chaukhamba was infinitely larger and more impressive. But at that moment the size and scale seemed irrelevant and in my mind's eye both the mountain and the shrine became one.

# CHIPKO

FOR THREE DAYS NOW THE RAIN HAS BEEN FALLING steadily, from daybreak to dusk. At night the sky clears but each morning I wake up to the same gray light, as if wet ash were sifting through the clouds. My clothes are soaked and my boots caked with mud, mildew growing on the tongues. Even my sleeping bag is damp despite its waterproof cover. The tent keeps out the rain but the air is sodden and moisture condenses on the inner fly, dripping down the sides. Until now my umbrella has served me well. I have used it as an ice ax, as a weapon to fend off vicious dogs, as a shield against the sun, as a windbreak and shelter for my stove, as a cane to steady myself on precipitous paths, even as a stake to tie down the guy ropes on my tent. But when it comes to protecting me from the rain the umbrella is all but useless for the drops blow in from the sides and water leaks at the seams, dribbling off the metal spokes. There is nothing I can do, except to keep walking and hope that sometime soon there will be a break in the weather.

At Chopta, a roadside stop above Ukhimath, I take shelter in a tea shop as the rain grows more intense. Six hours drag by as I sit and wait for the storm to ease, making myself as comfortable as possible on a low wooden bench. The rain batters against the thatch roof and there are leaks all along the rough-hewn beams, leaving a wet line of pitted spots on the mud floor.

Fortunately I am not alone. A dozen men have taken shelter in the tea shop and all of us are huddled together behind the fire. Its meager flame offers little warmth but from time to time the wind blows in and nearly asphyxiates us with billows of damp smoke, the raw odor of unseasoned oak. After an hour or two our conversations drift into silence. We all have had as much tea as we can drink though the proprietor keeps offering to make more, as if suggesting that we should pay for taking shelter in his shop. Like waterlogged castaways we sit together and wait. Three of the men are shepherds who have been stranded here since morning, their animals grazing on the high pastures above Chopta. One man runs a hotel at Tungnath and he has a load of supplies that are piled in the corner behind us—sacks of rice and flour, a canister of mustard oil, three brand-new quilts that have been delivered by Jeep. Earlier he negotiated with a couple of the men to carry these up to Tungnath, five kilometers ahead, but with the rain continuing there is nothing to be done.

For the first time on this pilgrimage I can feel myself getting sick, my sinuses blocked and a raw, painful burning in my chest. Smoke from the fire and bidis, which the others light up with regularity, makes me cough and I feel feverish in my wet clothes. If only I could sleep but there is no room to stretch out on the tea shop floor. Even though this is the last stage of my trek—another week and I'll be in Badrinath—I feel discouraged and depressed, wondering if there is any point in going on. My hopes of seeing the dramatic vistas of snow peaks along this route have been hampered by the clouds and rain. Other than my brief glimpse of Chaukhamba, the high Himalayas remain elusive. For three days now I have been able to see no more than a hundred feet ahead of me, sometimes less, as the mountains vanish in swirls of mist. The men in the tea shop offer little encouragement, telling me that many of the motor roads are now blocked and even sections of the walking trail may be impassable. There are rumors of flash floods and bridges washed away. Thousands of yatris at Kedarnath and Gaurikund have been stranded for three days as the PWD clears landslides along that route. Added to my uncertainty about the journey ahead is a nagging fear that once I reach my destination there may be no way out. I can picture myself trapped at Badrinath waiting for the motor roads to be cleared, sick and miserable, wanting only to find my way home.

On the far side of the fire sit the tea shop owner's four young children, watching us with cautious but curious eyes. The eldest is a girl of seven or eight and the youngest, a baby boy who is just a year old. Their grandmother is looking after them and I am amazed how patiently they sit together, confined by the rain. For at least two hours they play quietly among themselves without toys or books, passing the baby from one to the next, as if he were a doll that keeps them amused. Finally, one of the men beside me takes a handful of sweets from his pocket and offers them to the children. They hold back until their grandmother signals her approval. Quickly, the three older ones dart forward and take the candy, unwrapping the bright cellophane and popping the sweets into their mouths. This gesture breaks the barrier between us and now the children move freely about the tea shop, the older girl holding the baby on her hip. The middle brother and sister scramble over to where I am sitting. They are still cautious but begin to ask me questions. "Where have you come from?" "What are you carrying in your pack?"

Building up courage they touch the shoulder straps and aluminum frame. When I do not stop them the boy reaches out and fingers the zipper on one of the outer pockets. He pulls it open, then quickly closes it again. After a minute his older sister tries, leaving the baby to crawl about at our feet. The children test each of the zippers in turn, fascinated by the way in which the nylon teeth mesh together. When they open one of the pockets I reach in and take out three chocolate toffees, which delights them. The other men are watching the children explore my pack, laughing at their persistence, egging them on. For a few moments we forget about the rain and our discomfort. The grandmother picks up the baby, who has made his way toward the fire. Standing to one side she warns the children not to damage anything but her voice is gentle, without reproach. Once they grow bored with the pack the children turn to me. The younger girl touches the sleeve of my sweatshirt and announces that it is wet. They inspect my clothes and are fascinated by my boots, the laces, and the ridged pattern on the soles. Each of them is barefoot. The girls wear dark cotton skirts with matching blouses and they have sleeveless sweaters over their tops. The older sister has a string of pink plastic beads around her neck. The boy is dressed in a pair of khaki trousers and a green long-sleeved sweater. All of their clothes are heavily worn and patched in places.

As they grow bolder the children finally touch my hand, reaching out, then drawing back, as if they've scalded themselves. "Gorey" is the word they use to describe the whiteness of my skin, brushing it with their fingertips. I remain completely still, amused by their antics and questions, wondering what they will ask me next. My wedding ring catches their eye and the older girl touches it to see if it is real. "Is it gold?" she asks and I nod my head.

After they have completed their inspection the children retreat to a far corner of the tea shop and from a small tin trunk the two girls take something out to show me. It is a white dress, with elaborate smocking on the front and plastic pearls sewn on at different places, a party frock with frills and lace. Though slightly worn and rumpled, it is a costume fit for a princess. The older girl holds the dress up to herself but it is obviously too small for her. Having outgrown it now she hands it to her younger sister and both of them laugh.

Late in the afternoon the rain finally seemed to taper off and after saying good-bye to the children and the others in the tea shop at Chopta I set out for Tungnath. This is the highest of the major temples in Garhwal and stands at an altitude of eleven thousand feet. A steady drizzle was still falling and the light was bleak. As I climbed through a forest of oaks, streams of water were flowing down the path. After so many hours of sitting in a cramped position my joints were stiff and sore. Though I was relieved to be out of the smoke-filled hut and to breathe clean air again, my sinuses and throat continued to hurt. I could feel the fever just under my skin, as if all of my nerve endings had been brushed with stinging nettle. The climb from Chopta to Tungnath was only five kilometers and I figured it would take me an hour and a half at the most.

Soon after I left the tea shop, however, the storm picked up again. The disheartening stammer of rain falling against oak leaves made it seem as if all of the trees were trying to speak at once. Again my umbrella offered only the pretense of protection as I splashed my way uphill. There was no point in turning back.

Above the oaks were open meadows and I passed a couple of chaans where I might have taken shelter but the sagging thatch roofs and a surrounding mire of dung and mud discouraged me. Besides, I wanted to reach Tungnath before it got dark and the storm now seemed to be gathering momentum once again. Keeping my eyes on the path I trudged on, trying not to calculate the distances I had covered or what remained. The pilgrim route ascended the ridge in a winding series of switchbacks. Engulfed in clouds I lost all sense of direction. Along the way I passed only one other person, a shepherd who was crouched under the lee of a rock. Two of his buffaloes were grazing ahead, oblivious of the rain.

Until the last kilometer I made reasonable progress but as the trail circled around a flank of the ridge the wind grew stronger and the rain began to lash at me with unexpected vengeance. Already sick and exhausted I found it hard to stay on my feet, particularly as the ground was slick. With each step I took the wind seemed to intensify and my umbrella was buffeted back and forth until it suddenly turned inside out. Struggling to close it in the rain I pushed the spokes back into place and used it as a walking stick. As the wind briefly swept the clouds aside, I could see Tungnath ahead of me, the stone temple and cluster of dharamshalas not far away but seemingly inaccessible.

The waterproof cover on my pack fitted over the frame but the sides had come loose. With the wind in my face this nylon envelope was filled like a parachute and held me back. Several times I felt as if a fierce gust would lift me off the ground and send me sailing into the valley. The only way that I could rest was to turn my back to the gale. Each time I felt the wind subside I staggered up a few more feet. With the altitude the air had grown much colder and sliced through my wet clothes like icy shears. The final five hundred meters must have taken half an hour and in the end I crawled up the steps to the first dharamshala, collapsing on the narrow veranda.

Two young men were sitting beside a fire and they came out to help me, opening one of the rooms and dragging my pack inside. Too cold and tired to speak I stripped off my wet clothes and boots then climbed between several layers of heavy quilts. The room was hardly eight feet square and the two wooden beds were pushed up against the walls, leaving only a narrow gap near the door. There was a leak in one corner and a wet stain that reached to the floor but I didn't care. Outside the wind continued to howl against the shutters.

As soon as I got under the quilts my whole body began to shake, rattling the bones from my knuckles to my knees. Teeth chattering and huddled naked under the heavy pile of bedding I lost all control of my body. Muscles twitched with involuntary spasms and for a while it felt like an epileptic seizure. The two young men had been alarmed by my appearance and they brought me tea, though I could not drink it, my fingers unable to hold the glass. Slowly the warmth began to return to my limbs and the shivering stopped, though even after I was finally able to lie still, a sudden spasm would come over me from time to time, as if someone were shaking me by the shoulders. Through all of this my mind felt strangely disengaged from my body though gradually the two were fused again, and drifting into sleep I was aware of the regenerative bond between my physical and my conscious self.

At the heart of so many twentieth-century myths about the Himalayas lies a conflict between man and nature, an ongoing battle for survival in the face of inestimable odds. This is particularly true in stories of mountaineering, as climbers struggle to reach a summit. Our heroes are those who overcome the challenges of nature, pitting their bodies against the dangerous obstacles of altitude, weather, and terrain. The adventure of climbing involves a degree of detachment from the land, in which the indomitable alpinist fights to defeat the mountain, as if it were a dragon or some other evil beast. Often it is a matter of life or death and the Himalayas are littered with the frozen corpses of climbers who have been killed in this pursuit. Inevitably, their tragic deaths are described as noble and courageous, as much an inspiration as a warning to those who might dare to follow.

Without taking away from the skill and perseverance of these mountaineers, I am forced to question the way in which their stories affect us all. To begin with, these myths are part of a larger, colonial narrative in which expeditions of white men carry burdens up a hill in order to achieve honor and renown. Some of that has changed with climbers from other parts of the world, including India, scaling these Himalayan summits. But the story itself remains essentially the same. Despite the cliché we must acknowledge that nobody ever climbs a mountain "just because it's there." Our motives are much more complex and serve to justify the superiority of certain races, nations, and traditions. It is a sport, a competition, in which nature is given the role of adversary and opponent. The thrill of reading about Maurice Herzog's classic ascent of Annapurna, Hillary and Tenzing's conquest of Everest, or Reinhold Messner's solo assaults on Himalayan peaks is often translated into our own experiences. These legends of survival on the rooftops of the world tend to depict the mountains as a remote, cold, and inhospitable landscape. This may be the case above twenty thousand feet but how many of us will ever climb that high? It is like imagining the ocean only as waves.

Moreover, the rhetoric of mountaineering often prescribes certain adjectives to heighten a sense of risk and fear. Himalayan landscapes are seen as "unforgiving," "vengeful," "treacherous," "terrible," and "haunting," so that the mountains are transformed into symbols of demonic proportions. Reading over some of my own descriptions of this pilgrimage, including the trek up to Tungnath, I find myself instinctively falling back on this vocabulary. Even though I would never claim to be a mountaineer, my vision of the Himalayas is colored by those myths of conquest and adventure. The danger here is neither frostbite nor snow blindness but the numbness and myopia that come from believing in the hostile conflict between man and nature. If we are always going to struggle against the elements then we will never truly comprehend them.

As I look back on my trek to Tungnath—what might have been an easy ramble in fair weather—I realize that I allowed my frustration with the rain to turn this climb into a frontal assault on the mountain. Instead of doing the wise thing and taking shelter in one of the shepherd's chaans, I fought against the weather, unwilling to concede. It was foolhardy, especially as I was sick, but my decision to carry on was driven by more than just stupidity and stubbornness. I was acting out those heroic myths and legends that inspired me as a boy, pretending to be Sir Edmund Hillary, or more likely George Mallory, who disappeared on Everest over sixty years ago, his body discovered only in 1999.

As I lay there under that mountain of quilts, shivering like a helpless child, it was easy to blame my condition on the "fierce" storm, the "ruthless" wind, and the "bitter" cold, claiming that I had survived the ordeals of nature and thereby gaining the sympathy and perhaps even the admiration of my readers. In fact the only place to lay the blame was on myself.

Unlike mountaineers, who engage in mortal combat with Himalayan peaks, a pilgrim attempts to become one with this terrain. The Hindu concept of tapasya is difficult to translate but essentially involves austerity and meditation, as well as a process of surrendering to the land. The pilgrim who performs tapasya retreats to the mountains in order to reflect upon God and nature. Through solitude, yoga, penance, and prayer he survives on whatever the forest provides. Tapasya involves severe hardships and acts of denial but these are not seen as a conflict between man and his environment, rather an effort to overcome the weaknesses of the human spirit, so that we can transcend the physical barriers of this world.

Even the gods perform tapasya. Directly above Tungnath temple is a peak called Chandrashila, where Ram is believed to have sat in meditation, donning the robes of an ascetic before reclaiming his celestial identity as Vishnu. Chandrashila (which means rock of Ram Chandra) is about a kilometer's distance from the temple, an exposed crag that overlooks a complete panorama of the Garhwal Himalayas. Though the snow peaks were hidden by clouds while I was there, the lower portions of these mountains were visible, like a white hem beneath a skirt of gray. The rocks on which Ram sat in meditation looked rough and black against wet, green grass. With the overcast sky it was a forbidding landscape, the ridges dropping away into the valley, their contorted shapes like sooty fingers of wax melting from a candle. Unlike the day before, however, when I had struggled up these slopes against the driving wind, the air was calm and still. For the first time in three days the morning had dawned without rain. My fever had also lifted and I felt stronger. Though the clouds hovered so close above me that I felt as if I could reach up and brush my fingers through the lowest layer it seemed as if the storm had finally ended.

Looking down from above the Tungnath temple I could see another rocky crag known as Ravanshila. About a thousand feet lower than the site where Ram once sat in meditation, this promontory is said to be where the demon Ravan performed tapasya. Though he is considered a rakshish, the antithesis of divinity, Ravan still commands respect and he is worshiped by certain sects. In this way the paradox of good and evil is resolved through acts of abnegation, wherein the two great adversaries retire to the mountains and meditate on the sanctity of nature, in order to gain strength and liberation.

Though the stories of Ram and Ravan lead us to Tungnath, the temple itself is dedicated to Shiv and marks the spot where his arms emerged from the ground. In certain instances the myths become entwined, and there is an account of Ravan's confrontation with Shiv, whom he meets along the trail. Having assumed the form of a dwarf, Shiv suffers the ridicule of Ravan, then squashes him beneath his toe. As the third of the Panch Kedar shrines, the main temple at Tungnath is somewhat smaller but similar in design to the structures at Kedarnath and Madhmaheshwar, with a flagstone courtyard and porticoes for lesser deities. Though the facade of the temple is decorated with carvings it remains unpainted and blends into the rocks on the ridge, as if it were a part of the mountain. Near the entrance to the temple are several pieces of slate, engraved with images of Bhairon Devta, the goddess, and Nag, the cobra. These carvings look ancient, as if the shapes had been weathered into the stone, rather than chiseled by a human hand. But the image that caught my eye was a more recent icon, which had been etched onto a piece of slate. It was the simple outline of a musk deer, immediately recognizable from its stooped shape and the two small teeth that emerged from its mouth.

In one of his many forms Shiv is referred to as Pashupati, protector of animals. The slate image of the deer at Tungnath must have been placed there by conservationists from a musk deer farm that used to be located nearby, along the motor road between Ukhimath and Gopeshwar. Supported by the forestry department, this was an effort to breed these rare animals to protect them from extinction. Similar projects have been attempted in China with some success, but in 1998 the farm near Tungnath was closed after most of the captive animals died. Seeing the image of the musk deer outside the temple, I couldn't help but wonder if the only hope for its survival lay in some form of divine intervention.

Though my legs still felt weak from the fever, I carried on from Tungnath to Gopeshwar. Fortunately the trail was downhill most of the way, beginning with a steep descent of five kilometers. At one point I was losing altitude so quickly that my ears popped and suddenly I was aware of the sound of rushing water all around me. After three days of rain, every ravine and rivulet was overflowing. Added to this chorus of streams were dozens of different birdcalls that greeted me as I dropped below the tree line. Laughing thrushes and babblers were keeping up a raucous conversation in the underbrush, while yellow-cheeked tits and bulbuls chattered and whistled as if celebrating the end of the storm. The birds seemed unconcerned by my presence and at one point I passed a red vented bulbul perched on a twig a few inches above my head. His black and white feathers and exaggerated crest made him look like a tuxedoed crooner with a pompadour. At that moment the bulbul wasn't singing, however, for he had a bright orange raspberry in his beak.

The sky remained overcast for most of the day and there was even a sprinkling of rain but my spirits had lifted. Though one of the men at the dharamshala in Tungnath had told me of radio reports that the route to Badrinath was closed by landslides it no longer worried me. Following the trail downhill, I felt more optimistic about completing my pilgrimage and returning home. After several hours of trekking I came to a watchtower built by the forestry department. At this time of year there was no danger of fires but the tower provided a spectacular view of the Alakananda watershed into which I was headed. Climbing up the metal rungs of the ladder to an open platform on top, I could see a network of valleys draining into the Ganga. Most of the upper Himalayas were hidden by clouds but there was a patch of blue sky to the east and there in the distance stood Trisul and Nanda Devi, two of the highest peaks in Uttarakhand, their summits covered in fresh snow.

As I followed the pilgrim trail down the ridge I came upon several old milestones that gave distances to Gopeshwar, Chamoli, Joshimath, and Badrinath. These were relics from the past, their lettering and numbers obscured by moss and lichen. Overgrown with monsoon weeds, the old markers reminded me of gravestones in a neglected cemetery. Unlike the freshly whitewashed kilometer posts along the motor road, they seemed to measure the passage of time instead of the length of the trail.

The farther I descended into the valley the thicker the forest became. Most of the trees were oaks but there were also maples, chestnuts, firs, deodar, and ash. The different shades of green were pleated together like curtains of foliage. I felt as if I was tunneling through verdant chambers draped with moist layers of leaves, penetrating deeper and deeper into the shadowy labyrinth of the forest. For much of this route the mountains were completely hidden from view and except for the contours of the trail I had no real sense of the terrain. I began to feel as if the earth had been consumed by trees, their presence overpowering and pervasive.

Eventually, when I emerged from the green folds of this jungle, the trail passed through a forestry department nursery above the village of Mandal. On either side of me were terraces full of seedlings—pines and deodars about six inches high, growing in thick beds. After having been surrounded by full-sized trees it was disconcerting and I felt as if I had suddenly grown much taller, the forest reduced to a miniature scale, no higher than my ankles.

At Mandal I rejoined the motor road for a short distance, then again found the pilgrim trail, which led me on to Gopeshwar. For much of this route there were no trees at all and the mountains seemed exposed and vulnerable. Ahead of me I could see Gopeshwar town, spread over the south face of the ridge. The final two kilometers of the trail went straight up a barren hillside and from a distance it looked as if someone had scratched a zigzag line onto the surface of the mountain.

Headquarters of the Dasholi Gram Sabha, a nongovernmental organization devoted to rural development in Garhwal, lies in the center of Gopeshwar's main bazaar. It is a gray institutional building, with two floors of cramped offices. When I climbed up the steps to the reception area I found the electricity was off and the rooms were in darkness. There seemed to be nobody about but after a few minutes I heard voices above me. Ascending another flight of stairs I came upon three men seated on the flat cement roof, pouring over files and ledgers in the bright morning sunlight.

One of these men I recognized as Chandi Prasad Bhatt, a prominent leader of the Chipko movement. Dressed in handloom cotton, with a graying beard and self-effacing manner, Bhatt presents the characteristic image of a Gandhian activist. He has received widespread recognition for his work on social and environmental issues and he is a recipient of the Magsaysay Award, Asia's most prestigious prize in the field of development and social work.

Through the efforts of leaders like Chandi Prasad Bhatt and Sunderlal Bahugana, Chipko has become an essential part of the contemporary mythology of Garhwal. A spontaneous, grassroots uprising against the felling of trees by timber contractors, this movement has inspired conservationists throughout India and around the world. Though a number of agencies and institutions like Bhatt's Dasholi Gram Sabha are associated with Chipko there is no single organization that can claim to represent the movement as a whole. As with most myths there are differing versions but in essence the Chipko narrative celebrates the role of indigenous people, particularly women, protecting the forest resources that sustain their way of life.

Though I arrived unannounced, Chandi Prasad Bhatt graciously interrupted his paperwork to talk with me about the Chipko movement. As we sat on the roof the sounds of the Gopeshwar bazaar filtered up from the street, film songs playing on a transistor radio, the cries of hawkers, and the rumble of buses arriving and departing from the central square. Like many Gandhian activists, Bhatt speaks a formal, Sanskritized Hindi, punctuated by occasional words or phrases in colloquial Garhwali.

As he told it, the story of Chipko began on April 14, 1972, in the village of Mandal, which I had passed through on my way down from Tungnath. For years the farmers in this valley had lived a hand-to-mouth existence, depending on the surrounding forests to supplement their crops. As in most Garhwali villages the women were primarily responsible for collecting water, fuel, and fodder. Though they enjoyed relatively free access to the trees and pastures in the vicinity of Mandal, the forestry department controlled the land. This had led to some friction over the years but it was only after contracts were issued for the felling of trees near Mandal that the problem came to a head. The villagers resented the arrival of teams of men from the plains, carrying saws and axes. A virgin stand of ash trees near one of the springs where village women collected water had been marked for felling. Ash is primarily used to manufacture sporting goods and the trees were destined to be turned into hockey sticks and badminton rackets. Assisted by corrupt officials the timber contractors regularly exceeded quotas set by the forestry department and many of the oaks and other trees were in danger of being cut illegally.

Fearing the erosion caused by deforestation and the loss of firewood and fodder, several women from the village of Mandal tried to persuade the contractor to spare the forest. When their pleas were ignored they wrapped their arms around the trees and refused to let them be cut. This simple act of resistance succeeded, for the contractor's men dared not touch the women or try to pry them from the trees.

As the conflict played out over several months the forestry department and the contractor made repeated efforts to cut down the ash trees but each time the women of Mandal held their ground. Eventually, the movement began to spread and a number of political figures and activists like Chandi Prasad Bhatt became involved in the agitation. Two of the women from Mandal, Shyama Devi and Indira Devi, had been working with the Dasholi Gram Sabha and they traveled to other villages in the region and encouraged women to follow their lead. Similar protests were organized in Phata Rampur in the Mandakini watershed and at Reni, a village near the border with Tibet.

The passions that were ignited and the consequences of this agitation have led to a radical change in the policies of forest management in Garhwal. Though it was women who instigated the protests, men like Bhatt and Bahugana helped put pressure on the state and central government, which eventually imposed a ban on the felling of trees in Garhwal. Whereas the forestry department had always looked on its lands as a source of revenue that could be harvested with impunity, the people of Garhwal staked their claim for access to these resources and demanded that the trees be protected. Though it began on a limited scale, with a modest purpose, Chipko—which literally means "cling to" or "grab hold of"—has become a part of the political rhetoric of Garhwal. It has also led to a greater awareness of the environmental threats posed by dams and motor roads, so that over time the message of Chipko has expanded from simply protecting trees to preserving the mountains against all forms of exploitation. Over the past three decades organizations like Dasholi Gram Sabha have made efforts to replant some of the forests that have been destroyed, propagating species of trees that are important to the people of this region.

The hugging of trees, of course, has become a cliché that is not unique to Garhwal. The Chipko story, however, has special significance in a region attuned to myths and metaphors. One of the central images of Hindu tradition is the sacred grove that protects and provides for those who take shelter under its branches. Whether it be the Vedic sages and ascetics who sought refuge in the forest to perform tapasya, or the epic heroes who wandered for years through the jungle, these arboreal landscapes are an essential part of Indian culture and imagination. Proponents of the Chipko movement have always pointed out that deforestation in Uttarakhand has an immediate and direct influence on the watershed of the Ganga. Like the locks of Shiv's hair, the forests of Garhwal help to cushion and restrain the torrential monsoon storms. It is their roots that hold the soil in place and provide a protective layer for the underlying aquifer. The connection between the forests and the rivers is expressed as succinctly as possible in a slogan that I saw painted on a sign near Gopeshwar: TREES EQUAL WATER, WATER EQUALS LIFE.

The central role of women in the Chipko movement is particularly significant because of the female connotations of trees. In the primal mythology of the subcontinent, going back to the terra-cotta seals of the Indus Valley civilization, the mother goddess is depicted as emerging from a tree, her limbs entwined with its branches, her body wrapped around its trunk. This is an image that is repeated in the iconography of the goddess in all her many incarnations. For that reason there is little wonder that the women of the Chipko movement often express their motives in spiritual terms, speaking of their acts of resistance as a form of devotion and worship.

# THE REALM OF VISHNU

JOSHIMATH IS A TOWN FULL OF TEMPLES THAT overlooks the Vishnu Prayag gorge, about sixty kilometers beyond Gopeshwar. In the summer the streets are crowded with pilgrims, many of whom spend the night in Joshimath before driving the last forty kilometers up to Badrinath. Because of the flood of buses and cars during the yatra season there is a system of gates along the motor road beyond Joshimath to regulate the flow of traffic. Within the town the narrow streets are restricted to vehicles going in one direction or the other but in May and June there are endless traffic jams. Approaching the outskirts of Joshimath, I had to maneuver my way through a stalled procession of over a hundred vehicles parked along the two-lane highway. They had obviously been stranded there for hours and some of the pilgrims were taking the opportunity to wash their laundry in a spring at the side of the road, while others had set up kerosene stoves and were preparing meals. Hawkers did a brisk business selling wedges of coconut, pink candy floss, and roasted chickpeas as they wandered between the pilgrim coaches. Despite the long delay there was little sign of impatience among the yatris and the only person who looked harassed was a young policeman trying to get one of the drivers to move his bus to one side. The constable's efforts seemed fruitless for the gridlock and congestion was so complete it appeared as if the vehicles would never move again.

Any number of myths are associated with Joshimath, which takes its name from the eyes (jyotri) of the goddess Uma. These fell out on this spot as the grieving Shiv carried her charred body over the mountains, after she immolated herself. Nine different incarnations of the goddess are worshiped here during an annual festival at the Durga temple. As pilgrims draw closer to their final destination at Badrinath, the spiritual landscape grows more and more crowded with a multitude of deities vying for attention.

Probably the most popular shrine in Joshimath is dedicated to Narsingh, an incarnation of Vishnu. Unlike the more benevolent avatars of Ram and Krishn, Narsingh represents a bloodthirsty aspect of Vishnu, though even in this form he keeps the universe in balance. Half man and half lion, Narsingh came to earth to destroy a daitya, or demon, named Hiranyakasipu who had performed such extreme tapasya that he set the world on fire. In order to put out the flames, Brahma was obliged to give Hiranyakasipu a boon — he could neither be killed during the day nor at night, not by any man or by any animal, not on the ground or in the air. In his arrogance Hiranyakasipu assumed that he had achieved immortality and proclaimed himself a god. Full of his own self-importance, the demon king inflicted all kinds of suffering on his subjects and set out to destroy the three worlds — heaven, earth, and hell.

Hiranyakasipu had a son named Prahlad, who was a devotee of Vishnu. The daitya king became jealous of his son's devotion and demanded that Prahlad worship him instead. When the young man refused, Hiranyakasipu attacked him with poisonous snakes, rampaging elephants, and a malevolent witch. However, because of Prahlad's virtue and devotion to Vishnu, he was protected. The serpents' fangs were broken and their hoods burst into flames; the elephants failed to trample him and their tusks were shattered; the spears of lightning that the witch threw at his heart were scattered in fragments. Eventually, in frustration, Hiranyakasipu smashed one of the pillars of Vishnu's temple. Immediately, the avatar of Narsingh appeared and attacked the demon. A ferocious battle ensued between the man-lion and the daitya king, which lasted for one whole day of Brahma, which is equivalent to 2,160,000,000 years on earth. At the end of that day, just as the sun descended halfway below the horizon, Narsingh lifted Hiranyakasipu onto his lap and tore him apart with his claws and teeth. In this way the seemingly invincible demon was defeated, neither during the day nor at night, not by any man nor by any animal, but a combination of the two, and neither on the ground nor in the air.

The idol of Narsingh that stands in the temple at Joshimath has one arm that is said to be withering away. According to another legend this represents a wound inflicted by an ancient king of Garhwal who mistook Narsingh (in the guise of a Brahmin) for his wife's lover. It is believed that when the arm of Narsingh's idol finally breaks off the mountains on either side of the Vishnu Prayag gorge will collapse and seal off the valley above Joshimath. At this point the dham at Badrinath will be shifted to a site called Bhavishya Badri (the future Badri), which lies to the east, along the Dhauli Ganga. Currently there is a small temple at Bhavishya Badri but it is seldom visited by pilgrims, awaiting the moment when geological forces will shift the focus of devotion to that site. Just as the arm of Narsingh is growing thinner and thinner with time, the volume of water flowing from a spring at Bhavishya Badri is said to be increasing, as if to suggest that the source of the Alakananda will change as well.

The valleys and ridges near Joshimath are located along a

fault line that has generated a number of earthquakes in the past and it is possible to interpret these myths in terms of the seismographic history of the mountains. In 1851 most of the temples at Joshimath were destroyed in a severe earthquake and it is likely that earlier tremors flattened the original shrines constructed by Shankaracharya over a thousand years ago. Despite claims that he planted a mulberry tree that still stands near a cave in which Shankaracharya is believed to have lived, Joshimath and the surrounding region has probably changed beyond recognition since the ninth century. It is far more significant, however, that the myths of this region allow for cataclysms of nature, and these stories acknowledge the unstable terrain.

Man has also inflicted dramatic changes on the landscape and nowhere in Garhwal are the scars of motor roads more evident than in the valley below Joshimath. Here the procession of pilgrim buses and taxis crawl down a series of hairpin bends that drop into the Vishnu Prayag gorge. The face of the mountain, all but denuded of trees, appears to be crumbling into the river and several large landslides have left sections of the ridge exposed like festering lesions that ooze gray mud. Adding to this destruction is a hydroelectric project on the opposite slope, where roads for construction vehicles have been gouged into fragile cliffs. Dump trucks and bulldozers work their way back and forth along treacherous inclines, carrying loads of rubble and shoveling mounds of earth and rock into the Alakananda, so that it looks as if the Himalayas are being eaten away by mechanical termites.

In addition to serving as a pilgrimage center, Joshimath is the headquarters of the Border Roads Organization, a special engineering unit of the Indian army responsible for keeping strategic routes open to traffic. Their bright blue vehicles and uniformed road crews work throughout the year clearing landslides and avalanches that block the road. Though the highway leads up to Badrinath it continues on to Mana, the last village in India before the border with Tibet.

From Joshimath the walking trail descends straight down the ridge to Vishnu Prayag. Along this path I encountered many more pilgrims traveling on foot than I had seen before. Some had walked all the way from Rishikesh while others obviously came this far by bus but had given up waiting for the traffic jams and were hoping to catch a ride farther on. In addition to the Hindu yatris, many of whom wore saffron robes and had their heads shaved, I met a large number of Sikh pilgrims as well. They were headed up to Hemkund Sahib, a separate shrine to the east of Badrinath. The sacred lake at Hemkund, also known as Lakshman Kund, is revered as the site where Guru Gobind Singh, one of the founders of the Sikh religion, meditated in a previous life. In 1936 a gurudwara was built on the shore of this lake, after it was discovered by a noncommissioned Sikh officer in the Indian army, Havildar Sohan Singh. Over the years this high-altitude lake, surrounded by seven snow peaks, has become one of the most popular destinations for Sikh pilgrims in India and a new and much larger gurudwara has been erected at Hemkund.

Though I started walking from Joshimath quite early in the morning, many of the yatris had already set out ahead of me, and I could see them on the trail below, a scattered line of figures moving slowly down the slope. There were others coming up the hill, their faces contorted with exhaustion and streaked with sweat from the unrelenting climb. Having attained the goal of a lifetime and completed their pilgrimage they were now heading home and for them the path must have seemed so much longer going in that direction.

Near the bottom of the trail, about three hundred feet above the confluence, I passed an aged Sikh who was walking barefoot down the path. The old man's legs were bowed, as thin and knotted as the twisted staff on which he leaned. His gaunt features were framed by a feathery white beard. The turban that he wore was loosely tied and on top of it was balanced a small cloth bundle that contained his belongings. Though the trail was extremely steep and littered with stones and rocks, the old man was carrying an open prayer book in one hand and reading to himself as he walked along. I followed him for a short distance and with each step he took I held my breath, expecting him to stumble and fall. Though he kept his eyes focused on the book, mumbling prayers in a hoarse whisper, his feet moved slowly but confidently forward, as if guided from one step to the next.

A little farther on, I came upon another elderly Sikh who was blind. He too was walking barefoot but held the arm of a younger man who greeted me with an enthusiastic *"Waheguru Sat Nam!"*—God's name is truth. When I asked how far they had walked, the young Sikh told me that their party had set out from the Golden Temple in Amritsar two months earlier and had traveled by foot all the way. He estimated that it would take them another four days to reach Hemkund. The blind man said nothing but simply folded his hands in greeting as they paused to let me by.

In the gorge below Joshimath, the Vishnu Ganga and the Dhauli Ganga come together to form the Alakananda. Vishnu Prayag is not so much a confluence but a collision of water. The two rivers plunge into each other with an angry, tempestuous force that seems to carry the full weight of the mountains. It is a frightening sight, especially when viewed from the old suspension bridge that arches over the Dhauli Ganga like a fragile trapeze. The sound of the rapids is deafening, amplified by the cliffs converging in a narrow Y that funnels the two streams into a single current. Much of the turbulence is caused by enormous boulders that have tumbled into the gorge so that the water rears up in boiling waves as it crashes against these rocks. Looking down from the footbridge I couldn't help but think of the churning of primordial waters from which the gods emerged.

A line of cement steps leads down to the riverside ghat at Vishnu Prayag but during the monsoon the force of the water is much too fierce for anyone to bathe. As I watched from the bridge, however, a lone sadhu wearing only a loincloth descended as close as he dared. Standing ten or fifteen feet above the Dhauli Ganga he let the spray wash over him before retreating back up the steps. Some believe that the confluence at Vishnu Prayag must claim the life of one pilgrim each year, by drowning in the churning whitewater.

From this point until the valley finally opens out at Badrinath, high walls of rock enclose the river. As with the final approaches to Yamnotri, Gangotri, and Kedarnath there is a sense of constriction, as if the mountains were standing shoulder to shoulder, pressing in from either side. At places there seems to be no room for anything but the swift waters of the Vishnu Ganga as it cuts a deep groove through layers of granite. The cliffs are so steep that there are hardly any trees, except for isolated pines and cedars that have found purchase in the crevices of rocks. Beyond Vishnu Prayag the motor road follows the alignment of the old pilgrim trail, which disappears for the last time. A single-lane highway has been blasted out of the cliffs and crosses the river over military bridges, as it snakes its way up to Badrinath. Convoys of buses, cars, and trucks move back and forth along this road, shuttling thousands of yatris over the final stage of their pilgrimage. Walking by the side of the motor road I often had to stop and lean against the hillside to let the vehicles race past. Fortunately, at intervals between the one-way gates, there was a lull in traffic and the clouds of diesel exhaust dispersed. The guttural roar of engines was replaced by the sawing of the river, a sound like the deepest notes on a double bass.

At Govindghat, eight kilometers beyond Vishnu Prayag, the trail to Hemkund Sahib cuts off to the right and Sikh pilgrims part company with the majority of Hindus. Though people of these two faiths regularly visit each other's shrines there is a symbolic bifurcation here that leads in distinctly different directions. Over the past two decades divisions between Hindus and Sikhs in India have become much greater than ever before, because of political animosity and religious fundamentalism on both sides. The Sikh separatist movement in the seventies and eighties culminated in the Indian army's attack on the Golden Temple at Amritsar. This was followed by the assassination of Indira Gandhi and communal riots, which exacerbated tensions between Hindus and Sikhs. While the two separate pilgrimages to Badrinath and Hemkund Sahib coincide in a generally amicable atmosphere there is no denying that the fork in the trail at Govindghat marks a recent divergence between these two religious traditions. Fortunately, the mythic geography of Uttarakhand has always allowed for differing interpretations of terrain and one can only hope that extremists in either faith will avoid making confrontational claims.

A couple of kilometers farther up the valley lies the village of Pandukeshwar, which traces its origins back to Raja Pandu, father of the five heroes in the Mahabharata. Pandu was once king of Hastinapur, a powerful and wealthy man. Soon after marrying his two wives, Kunti and Maadri, he was hunting in the forest and came upon a mating stag and doe. Pandu immediately shot the stag with an arrow but then, to his horror, discovered the two deer were actually a rishi and his wife who had changed form in order to engage in loveplay. When the distraught wife of the rishi regained her human form she cursed

Pandu, saying that he would die the next time he enjoyed the pleasures of either queen's bed. Full of remorse Pandu took a vow of abstinence and relinquished the throne of Hastinapur to his blind brother, Dhritarashtra. He then retreated to the Himalayas with Kunti and Maadri. After wandering through the mountains they established a hermitage on the site of the village that is now known as Pandukeshwar. Though the former king of Hastinapur successfully controlled his desires for many years, his first wife, Kunti, had been given a secret mantra that summoned various male deities with whom she and Maadri conceived their five sons—Yudhisthar, Bhim, Arjun, Nakul, and Sahadev. Though he remained an ascetic, Raja Pandu accepted these boys as his heirs. In the end, however, Pandu finally succumbed to his passions, when he could no longer resist the beauty of his wife Maadri. She then committed sati on her husband's pyre and left her two sons in Kunti's care.

Many years later, after the epic battle of Kurukshetra, the five Pandav brothers followed after their parents and passed through these same gorges. At several places the cliffs are scarred with geometrical patterns that are believed to be the lines drawn on the mountains by the Pandavs as they gambled for the last time on earth before ascending to heaven. Today Pandukeshwar is a good-sized village, with over a hundred households. Within the confines of the valley there is not much arable land and most of the residents depend on pilgrim traffic to support themselves. The temple at Pandukeshwar is known as Yoghdhyan Badri, one of the five main shrines of Vishnu, dedicated to a meditative form of the deity. It is an indication of the significance and potency of natural phenomena that even a god as great as Vishnu would retreat to the Himalayas and perform tapasya. This suggests that the contemplation of nature gives power and spiritual resonance not only to the anonymous pilgrim or rishi but to the celestial deities themselves.

During winter a silver image of Vishnu, seated in lotus position, is carried down from Badrinath to Pandukeshwar and housed in the temple there, while the rawal, or head priest, retreats to Joshimath and presides at the Narsingh shrine. In this way the responsibilities and privileges of the yatra route are apportioned among those who live in the valley. The priests and pandas share in the divine presence of the gods as well as the generous donations left by pilgrims. Over the years various temples along this route, particularly the shrine at Badrinath, have accumulated a considerable amount of wealth. Some is spent on charitable institutions, including dispensaries and dharamshalas for pilgrims, or turned into gold and silver ornaments for the gods, but much of this revenue goes into the pockets of priests. Their power and influence have always been a part of the political and economic equation in Garhwal. According to nineteenth-century accounts the maharajahs of Garhwal often borrowed from the priests at Badrinath to support military campaigns. In exchange these kings ceded the revenues from villages in their domain and until 1947 the rawal collected tribute and taxes from surrounding districts.

The last stop along the pilgrim route to Badrinath is a place called Hanuman Chatti, which is located at a bend in the river, overlooking a cataract where the river falls fifteen or twenty feet through a trench in the rocks. It is also the confluence of the Vishnu Ganga and the Khir Ganga, a small stream that flows down from Nilkanth peak. There are several dharamshalas at Hanuman Chatti, where pilgrims traveling on foot can spend the night before making the final ascent to Badrinath. At the side of the road is a modern temple with a life-sized image of Hanuman carved out of marble. The majority of pilgrims do not disembark from their buses, taking darshan through the windows of the vehicles, while priests walk down the aisles collecting donations and distributing prasad from this drive-by shrine.

Vishnu is the most accessible and human of the Hindu triad, a benevolent god who reigns supreme in the imagination of his devotees. Unlike the violent and tempestuous Shiv, who retreats into austere meditation amid the snows of Mount Kailash, Vishnu reclines peacefully on a coiled bed of serpents, recumbent lord and master of the universe. Brahma hovers within a cloudy, indistinct world of abstraction—an aged, reclusive figure, shielded by the petals of his lotus. In contrast, Vishnu is a youthful deity full of emotion and charisma—a god of action. When aroused from pleasurable dreams, Vishnu takes on the role of a hero—Ram of Ayodhya, or Krishn, the divine charioteer. He also assumes the forms of animals—the avatars of Matsya the fish, Kurma the tortoise, and Varaha the boar. Though the goddess Devi, in all her multiple incarnations, is probably the clearest representation of earth's fertility, Vishnu is also a deity of nature. He is the gentle cowherd who leads his cattle to the sacred grove and plays a reed flute as they graze on the banks of the Yamuna. He is the passionate, blue-skinned lover who seduces Radha and her companions in a perfumed forest. His complexion mirrors the colors of monsoon clouds and his lovemaking is as exhilarating as the first rainfall of the year. In the Puranas his dance of seduction is described as insatiable and Krishn makes love to thirty-three women for thirty-three days. The Bhakti poets, who were part of a charismatic resurgence of Hinduism in the fourteenth century, described Vishnu as a god of love and their adoration ranged from the erotic to the sublime. Though Brahma may be the most ancient of gods and Shiv the most powerful, Vishnu is clearly the deity who encompasses the greatest variety of human passions and inspires ecstatic devotion. At Badrinath he is worshiped by all of the other gods, who descend on the shrine during winter, after the pilgrims depart. While the valley is cloaked in snow and the temple doors are locked, an image of Vishnu remains, so that members of the Hindu pantheon may worship at his feet.

By tradition, the rawal or head priest at Badrinath is a Namboodri brahmin from Kerala, a descendent of Shankaracharya. This lineage goes back over a thousand years and provides an enduring link between two geographical extremes — the tropical Malabar coast and the rocky, windswept heights of the Himalayas. It would be difficult to find two regions of India with greater contrasts than Kerala and Garhwal, whether it be the climate, the topography, the culture, the language, or social norms. Yet the connection between orthodox Brahmanic traditions of the south and these remote shrines and sanctuaries in the north has lasted much longer than any dynasties or empires. It is remarkable that this line of priests has officiated at Badrinath for over a millennium despite centuries of political and social upheaval. From the time that Shankaracharya first established the temple at Badrinath, before A.D. 900, and installed one of his acolytes as rawal, the map of India has changed dramatically. A steady stream of invaders have come and gone. Religious and social movements have risen and fallen. Buddhists, Hindus, Muslims, and Christians have all gained and lost power while the land has been divided and subdivided into a complex array of states and territories. Regardless of these changes, however, the Namboodri priests continue to worship at Badrinath, performing many of the same rituals they practiced a thousand years ago.

Some would argue that this is a testament to the tenacious and exploitative legacies of caste — the stranglehold of Brahmanic orthodoxy. Others would claim it is proof that India's unity is grounded in the bedrock of Hindu traditions. The resilience of this link between south and north, between the sea and the mountains, between Dravidian and Aryan cultures, may be interpreted as a historical bond, the invisible glue that holds India together, but these explanations are deceptive and incomplete. When one thinks of the distances that Shankaracharya and his followers traveled, from the coconut groves and green estuaries of the Kerala coast, across the blazing heat of the Deccan plateau, fording great rivers like the Cauvery and the Narmada, passing through jungles and deserts, until they reached the Himalayas, it is difficult to explain their motives except in mythological terms. Undoubtedly, Shankaracharya set out to rescue Hinduism from the egalitarian influences of Buddhist teaching but his story is more a tale of pilgrimage and discovery. As a brahmin he obviously believed in the hierarchies of caste and must have seen himself and his fellow Namboodri priests preserving their power and prestige. But the driving force behind his journey and the traditions of pilgrimage that he established in Uttarakhand was undoubtedly something much greater and more powerful—inspired by an image of the river Ganga flowing out of glaciers and snow peaks in the Himalayas. It was a quest for the ultimate source, the purest essence of life. This has always been the central metaphor at the heart of Sanskrit scriptures, not only in the epics but in the Vedas and the Puranas. These texts describe a landscape of overwhelming beauty, a sanctuary where nature captivates the imagination and symbols become unnecessary. The Himalayas that Shankaracharya discovered and the watershed of the Ganga that he traversed a thousand years ago must have been a magnificent and unspoiled world where one could easily believe the gods retreated in meditation. The power and majesty of nature would have been evident in every snow peak and glacier, every stream, every stone, every animal, and every tree.

Badrinath takes its name from an obscure plant, the berries of which are said to have sustained pilgrims in the past. Some claim that the fruit of the badri plant was eaten by Vishnu when he performed tapasya in this valley. Others have suggested that it could be the common buckthorn (*Hippophae salicifolia*), which grows elsewhere in Garhwal. Whatever the truth, there is an element of mystery about the exact identity of this plant now said to be extinct in the Alakananda Valley. In many ways it seems appropriate that Badrinath should recall the name of a plant that no longer exists. Here is a place where the lines between mythology and nature are blurred, where the eternal enigmas of Hindu tradition take root in the rocky soil of the Himalayas.

Most of the glacial bed through which the Vishnu Ganga flows consists of barren rock and sand, a dull gray color, flecked with mica. Whatever trees there might have been—by some accounts spruce forests stood here when Shankaracharya first arrived—were cut down years ago to provide fuel for pilgrims and priests. As the winding motor road climbs over a ridge of moraine and the gorge opens out into a broad basin, the first view of Badrinath presents a scene of desolation. Even in the monsoon there is little greenery. At places along the highway the forestry department has planted a few saplings of birch and pine as well as juniper and other species of ground cover but these plants struggle to survive and are hemmed in by strands of barbed wire. The only color, besides dusty gray, comes from scattered patches of wild thyme with purple blossoms growing close to the ground.

Snow peaks stand on either side of the valley. The most prominent of these is Neelkanth, an impressive pyramid of rock and ice. Compared to Kedarnath or Gangotri, however, the views are much less dramatic and the barren ridges in the foreground dominate the landscape. If the valley itself lacks grandeur, the town of Badrinath is an even greater disappointment. The largest structure is a sprawling bus stand made of reinforced concrete. It is much the same color as the rocks that litter the valley but exhibits the unnatural contours of modern architecture. Hundreds of public buses and private pilgrim coaches are parked in the rutted fields that surround this building, while a line of vehicles wait for the traffic gates to open. A disorderly collection of hotels and dharamshalas, government offices, shops, and restaurants lie beyond the bus stand. As I walked the last stretch into Badrinath it felt less like a spiritual retreat and more like a frontier town—the highway continues on to the Tibetan border forty kilometers ahead.

Most of the roofs in Badrinath are made of corrugated tin and the buildings are constructed of cement. Despite the pools of water from recent rain, Badrinath had a dry, unwashed appearance. Scraps of paper and plastic bags were blowing about and there were piles of garbage and puddles of motor oil by the side of the road. Even at that altitude the air was full of flies. Drawing closer to the river I found myself in the midst of a crowd of yatris heading in the direction of the main temple, which lies on the west bank of the Vishnu Ganga, about a kilometer from the bus stand.

As I approached the center of town there appeared to be some sort of celebration taking place but when I asked what was going on nobody seemed to know. From all of the hotels and rest houses nearby people were swarming toward the main street that leads down to the bridge across the river. A sudden sense of excitement animated the town and pilgrims were rushing through the lanes and across the rubble-strewn slopes to see what was happening. Still carrying my backpack, I found myself caught up in the gathering mood of anticipation and hurried forward until I reached the main road. At this point the crowds had been stopped by a line of policemen with bamboo lathis.

Coming down the street was a procession of about a hundred people. In the lead were two drummers beating out a frenzied rhythm. Behind them followed a group of women dressed in traditional Garhwali costumes, with long black skirts, embroidered tunics, and colorful headgear. They wore silver jewelry and seemed to be dressed for a festival or performance. Directly behind them was a group of politicians and government officials, most of whom were dressed in Nehru vests with Gandhi caps on their heads. There were also half a dozen men in saffron robes who looked like well-fed sadhus.

Once again I asked what was going on and a man standing next to me replied, "It's Shankaracharya."

"Who?" I asked, completely puzzled.

"Shankaracharya. Can't you see him? He's in the middle of all those politicians."

"Look, there he is," said somebody else in excitement.

At this point I noticed a short, stooped figure wrapped in yards of vermilion fabric who was surrounded by uniformed bodyguards carrying Sten guns.

It took me a while to find out who the dignitary was because most of the bystanders were just as confused as I. Eventually one man explained that this Shankaracharya was the presiding priest from the Kanyakumari temple at the southern tip of India. There are four Shankaracharyas, representing temples at each of the cardinal points of the subcontinent, who act as a supreme conclave of Hindu orthodoxy. With the growing influence of fundamentalism their importance has increased and their roles have become politicized. This Shankaracharya's motorcade had driven up from Joshimath that morning and he had been met by a reception committee of local politicians who were now escorting him to the Badri Vishal temple.

As they walked past the gawking crowds of pilgrims the drummers rattled out a steady tempo, but the procession was hardly keeping pace with their beat. The costumed women were laughing among themselves and glancing self-consciously at the spectators. A few yatris had their cameras out to take pictures of this event even if they didn't fully understand what was taking place. The politicians strolled casually down the hill, chatting with the saffron-clad retinue, smug-looking holy men with well-oiled beards. It was a bizarre scene, particularly because of the commandoes, in bulletproof vests, carrying automatic weapons to protect the political and religious figures from assassination.

Watching the procession, I could only think of what it must have been like over a thousand years ago when the first Shankaracharya came to Badrinath. There would have been no crowds to greet him and instead of the paved street lined with shops and dharamshalas, he must have walked along a simple goatpath, perhaps through a grove of stunted spruce trees. At that time his mission may have been to reform the Hindu faith, to establish Brahmanical power and orthodoxy, but arriving here on the banks of the Vishnu Ganga, Shankaracharya could never have imagined the scene I witnessed. This parade of political and religious power, these security guards and policemen holding the crowds back, this enigmatic figure cloaked in red, surrounded by armed commandoes—in a distorted and unsettling way, it seemed symbolic of the desecration of this valley.

The culmination of any pilgrimage, no matter how successful, is inevitably accompanied by a sense of regret. After completing the Char Dham Yatra a pilgrim is supposed to be transported directly up to heaven but my feet were still firmly planted on the ground. Beyond the tired cliché of a destination that is less important than the journey itself lies a simple truth. The sacrifices and struggles along the trail, the fervor and expectations of the quest can never be completely fulfilled. In the end that moment of arrival, those final steps to the shrine, the physical object of our pilgrimage—all becomes irrelevant because it is only a symbol of something much larger than we can ever imagine and more inaccessible than the remotest corner on earth. The Hindu scriptures teach us that everything we perceive with our human senses is illusion and it is absurd to try and locate the presence of God. A temple, no matter how ancient or beautifully decorated, is nothing but a temporary shelter for our myths. Statues and idols of the gods may embody images of divinity but in the end they remain crude representations made by human hands. Even a sacred stone, sculpted by nature, is nothing but an imperfect lump of ore out of which purer minerals can be refined. And as for the true source of a river, it will never be found. Beyond each glacial stream or mountain spring there is always another point of origin. Every drop of water can be distilled into rain.

Badri Vishal temple lies on the west bank of the Vishnu Ganga. It is the only colorful building in the town, painted with synthetic enamel colors—blue, pink, red, and green. Surrounded by rusty tin roofs the temple looks like a gaudy jewel set in tarnished metal. A domed canopy of yellow and silver rises above an ornate gateway, the entrance to Vishnu's sanctuary. Even from a distance I could see that the courtyard and the steps leading up to the temple were packed with pilgrims, standing in line to worship the deity. During this time of year yatris often have to wait for five or six hours before they can catch a brief glimpse of the idol. Each pooja is performed as if it were a spiritual assembly line, the trays containing coconuts, flower petals, incense, and rice passed from priest to priest, donations collected, prayers recited, and tilaks applied to the forehead of each devotee. There is no opportunity to linger at this shrine and the ceremonies and rituals are perfunctory. After having traveled hundreds of kilometers to reach their destination pilgrims are hustled through the sanctuary in a matter of seconds. Below the temple are a series of hot springs, where water is collected in tanks for pilgrims to bathe. But here too the crush of yatris allows for only a hurried immersion, a quick plunge beneath the steaming surface to cleanse them of their sins.

Whatever sense of relief and accomplishment I felt on arriving at Badrinath was overshadowed by the drab, uninspiring aspects of the town and the mercenary atmosphere surrounding the temple. The Shankaracharya's procession made it impossible for me to approach the shrine and I took my darshan from the east side of the river for the bridge was jammed with pilgrims and policemen. It seemed pointless to fight my way through the crowds and wait for hours until the politicians had departed. After ten or fifteen minutes, I retraced my steps toward the bus stand, feeling disillusioned and depressed. Uncertain what I would do next I trudged past the lines of taxis and shook my head at the hoteliers who offered me a room for the night. Ahead the traffic gate had just opened up for vehicles going down the hill. One of the buses parked in line rumbled to life, its engine expelling a cloud of blue exhaust. The conductor was leaning out of the open door and on an impulse I asked if there were seats available. He gestured impatiently for me to climb aboard and I soon found myself squeezed onto a thinly padded bench between three other yatris. As the bus picked up speed and passed through the police checkpoint I looked back and caught a last glimpse of the town. Despite having walked over six hundred kilometers to reach this place, in the end I spent less than an hour at Badrinath.

# SOLILOQUY

IN THE SUMMER OF 1931 A BRITISH MOUNTAINEER-
ing expedition climbed Mount Kamet in the Zanskar range of
the Garhwal Himalayas, northeast of Badrinath. After successfully conquering this 25,447-foot peak, six of the climbers
decided to explore the watershed of the Alakananda. Instead of
returning by the traditional pilgrim route along the Vishnu
Ganga the Englishmen and their porters crossed over a 16,688-
foot pass into the Bhyunder Valley. The monsoon had just
started and they were caught in a severe storm. Snow and sleet
at higher altitudes turned to rain and mist as they descended.
Coming down from the rocky, ice-covered heights the mountaineers suddenly found themselves in an idyllic green valley
surrounded by hundreds of different species of flowering plants.
For the exhausted climbers it was a magical experience and they
named the place simply "Valley of Flowers."

Frank Smythe, one of the six mountaineers, returned to the
Bhyunder Valley in 1937. He camped there for several months,
collecting bulbs and seeds for his garden back in England. Sub-
sequently, Smythe wrote a book that vividly describes the natural beauty of the valley and the surrounding peaks. His account
inspired one of his readers, Joan Margaret Legge, to travel to
Garhwal in 1939. She was commissioned by the Botanical Gardens in Edinburgh to bring back specimens of Himalayan

plants. At the age of fifty-four, Legge sailed alone to India and reached the valley in late June, accompanied only by her porters. Her visit ended in tragedy, however. While collecting flowers on the cliffs above her camp on July 4, 1939, Joan Margaret Legge slipped and fell to her death. She was cremated by her porters on the banks of the Bhyunder Ganga. Some years later, Legge's sister traveled to the Valley of Flowers and left a marble plaque in her memory, inscribed with a verse from the Psalms, "I will lift up mine eyes unto the hills from whence cometh my help."

Though Smythe and his companions took credit for discovering the Valley of Flowers it was known as Nandan Kanan long before their arrival and regarded as the setting for a number of Hindu myths. By some accounts it was Bhim, in the Mahabharata, who first came to this valley after he was sent by Draupadi in search of the brahmkamal, or Himalayan lotus, a sacred flower that grows in these parts. In other legends the Valley of Flowers is the place where Hanuman, in the Ramayana, uprooted the life-giving herb, sanjivini booti, that healed Lakshman's wounds and brought him back from death. A few kilometers east of the valley lies a lake called Lakshman Kund, or Hemkund Sahib by the Sikhs, who believe that Guru Gobind Singh meditated here in a previous life. There are also a number of folktales about the Valley of Flowers, which is said to be haunted by spirits and ghosts that frighten away shepherds and their animals, allowing the flowers to flourish.

As with so many other places in Garhwal, these layers of narrative converge within the context of a natural landscape. Just as a multitude of flowers bloom on the fertile slopes of Nandan Kanan, a variety of stories have germinated in the rich glacial soil. The history of this valley is a complex blend of legends, wherein the heroes of ancient epics ascend these peaks alongside colonial mountaineers; where Hindu, Sikh, and

Christian verses are inscribed in stone; where flowers can be identified by Sanskrit, Latin, or Garhwali names; where the tragic death of a Scottish botanist, who came here in search of rare plants, resonates with the myth of a Hindu god who flew across these mountains to find the herb of immortality.

Govindghat, thirty kilometers downstream from Badrinath, is the road head for Hemkund Sahib and the Valley of Flowers. At the confluence of the Vishnu Ganga and the Bhyunder Ganga is a large gurudwara and a line of shops selling Sikh religious items, mostly prayer books but also steel bracelets, kirpan daggers, and other spiritual souvenirs. There are restaurants and dharamshalas for pilgrims, as well as terraced parking lots for cars and buses. A narrow suspension bridge across the Vishnu Ganga marks the beginning of the pilgrim trail.

The first fourteen kilometers of the trek to the Valley of Flowers follows the route to Hemkund Sahib, after which the trail splits just beyond the village of Ghangaria. As I walked up the path from Govindghat I must have passed more than a thousand Sikh pilgrims, including a group of army officers and their families, who sat astride military mules that were twice the size of ordinary pack animals used in Garhwal. Though some of the other pilgrims rode on horseback the majority traveled on foot. At Govindghat, the proprietor of a health club had set up a "free massage camp," and all along the route to Hemkund Sahib were banners advertising PREET'S ACU-MAGNETIC MASSAGE AND SLIMMING CENTER in Amritsar. It was a clever marketing ploy, for many of the pilgrims were seriously overweight. While struggling up the steep trail most of them probably took a vow to get in shape.

Hindu pilgrims visit Hemkund Sahib but most of the yatris are Sikhs. Instead of shouting *"Jai Shiv Shankar!"* or *"Hari Om!"* the pilgrims greeted me with cries of *"Sat Sri Akal!"* and

*"Waheguru Sat Nam!"* Villagers in the Bhyunder Valley cater to the Sikhs and all of the tea shops and hotels advertised themselves as PUNJABI DHABAS. Just as the signs in the Madhmaheshwar Valley were all written in Bengali, here the signs were in Gurmukhi.

Ghangaria serves as a base camp for Hemkund Sahib and pilgrims spend the night here before climbing the last six kilometers up to the lake, which lies at an altitude of over twelve thousand feet. Many of the rocks at the side of the trail are painted with signs to encourage the faithful, verses from the Sikh scriptures, as well as English slogans: DIRTY IS UGLY. CLEAN IS LOVELY. Though not as carefully maintained as the trail from Gangotri to Gaumukh, efforts have been made to preserve the natural beauty of this valley. Crews of sweepers work their way up and down the path every day, collecting litter and brushing mule dung off the trail with long-handled brooms.

Though I passed a couple of Europeans along this route many of the pilgrims seemed surprised to meet a foreigner. A few of them teased and taunted me, calling out disparaging names in Punjabi, thinking I didn't understand. Others were much more friendly, shouting a cheerful "Hi!" or "Hello, my dear!" Many of the younger Sikhs called me "Uncle," probably because of my white beard, and they inquired incessantly about where I was coming from. On the final climb from Ghangaria up to Hemkund Sahib, at least fifteen different groups of pilgrims stopped me and asked if I would allow myself to be photographed with them. "Just one snap please?"

The atmosphere of the pilgrimage was festive, though some of the more orthodox Sikhs, dressed in white or blue robes with matching turbans, had a stern demeanor as they strode solemnly up the path. Quite a few of them were carrying swords or kirpans, the martial emblems of their faith. Most of the pilgrims, however, were in a holiday mood. One group of men and women

I passed, about a kilometer below Hemkund, had stopped near a patch of snow. They had brought with them a bottle of bright red syrup that they poured over handfuls of snow and ate like ice cream. For some, however, the altitude and the climb were almost too much and I passed one woman seated by the side of the trail, pressing her fingers to both temples and weeping with exhaustion. Later, I saw her finally reach the top, collapsing in front of the gurudwara that stands on the shore of the lake.

Unlike most Sikh temples, which have domes, the gurudwara at Hemkund Sahib is covered by a steeply pitched tin roof, designed to withstand heavy snowfall in winter. The langar, or charitable kitchen, which is a part of every Sikh shrine, serves large tumblers of sweetened tea to help revive the faithful after they have made it to the top of the climb. Pilgrims do not spend the night at Hemkund Sahib, returning down the hill to Ghangaria where there are rest houses and dormitories.

The lake itself is three or four hundred feet across and reflects the seven snow peaks that ring its shore. Despite the hundreds of pilgrims that crowd the gurudwara and the hymns broadcast over loudspeakers there is a sense of tranquillity and seclusion. As I sat on the shore of the lake I couldn't help thinking of my conversation with Amarjit Singh, the Sikh mendicant I met at the beginning of my pilgrimage, in the forests above Rishikesh. He had talked about Hemkund Sahib and described working here as a volunteer, serving tea to pilgrims.

Quite a few of the men were bathing in the lake, even though the temperature of the water was just a shade over freezing. One of the pilgrims I met was a young businessman from the city of Ludhiana. His name was Dalbir Singh and he was dressed in blue jeans with a Nike T-shirt that said JUST DO IT! Before bathing in the lake Dalbir stripped down to his undershorts, placing his clothes on the rocks beside me. I couldn't help but notice that he was carrying a pistol in the waistband of his jeans, which he hid discreetly under his turban. Striding into the lake without hesitation, he ducked beneath the surface several times, then emerged as if in shock, water streaming from his long hair and beard. Dalbir had a large beach towel with him and as he began to dry himself I saw that it was printed with a colorful cartoon of Winnie the Pooh.

JUNE 10, 2000

I have camped near Ghangaria, on the banks of a stream that flows into the Bhyunder Ganga. The sun has slipped out of sight behind the mountains, which rise up on either side like temples of uncut stone.

This tent has become a second skin for me at night, a nylon blister in which I lie awake and listen to the warbling sound of water running over stones. The darkness is complete, black as the feathers of a chough that whistles at dusk. The stars are hidden by a cowl of mist.

I try to force myself into dreams, memories brushed by sleep, like tangled hairs. Earlier I was exhausted, barely able to set up camp but now it seems I cannot rest, the muscles in my calves twitching with involuntary spasms, my eyes refusing to close though there is nothing more to see. I stare into the void above, knowing that the tent envelops me but unable to trace its outlines, the familiar pattern of seams and struts. Recalling that morning, months ago, when I woke up to see dozens of moths decorating the fabric, I try to retrace the shapes of their wings but they are gone. Tonight there is no rain, not even a breeze and the air is as still as the ground beneath my head.

A strange sense of negative space surrounds me, as if I am suspended in a vacuum. I could be anywhere on earth or nowhere at all. The mountains have vanished, the pilgrims are gone. The sound of the stream is like the blood flowing through my veins. I am aware of nothing beyond myself, nothing to distinguish my presence here from any other presence, an emptiness that is filled with only my thoughts. Gradually the restless sensations in my limbs begin to fade, not with the numbness of fatigue, but with a sense of release. I can feel myself dissolving into sleep and in that brief moment before my eyes close it is impossible to tell where my body ends and the darkness begins.

The next morning I set off at dawn and followed the trail to the Valley of Flowers. A metal signboard marked the entrance to the National Park, established in 1972. It listed some of the species of plants that grow in the valley, along with rules and regulations. No animals are allowed—neither cattle nor mules. No overnight camping. No digging for roots or collecting plants. Entry fees were also posted—Indians 30 rupees, foreigners 350—but there was no one at the checkpoint to collect my money. A little farther on I came to the first of several landslides that blocked the trail and it was obvious that very few people had gone this way in recent weeks. The best time of year to visit the valley is August, when monsoon flowers are in full bloom.

Having left my backpack in Ghangaria, I had no difficulty scrambling across the landslide. The trail entered a grove of fir trees, then dropped down to a bridge across the Bhyunder Ganga. Ahead of me the snow mountains were catching the first beams of sunlight, fretted outlines profiled against the sky and edged with tufts of clouds. To my right, an enormous rock face rose fifteen hundred feet, straight up from the river, and seemed to block the entrance to the valley. The left bank of the Bhyunder Ganga was almost as steep but there were trees on the lower slopes and the path twisted up and around the gorge.

About a kilometer beyond the rock face I could see where the river turned abruptly. The upper end of the valley remained hidden from sight and after negotiating two more landslides I came to a snowfield that extended across the path. Forty or fifty feet wide, the surface was speckled with stones and gravel that had fallen down from above. The snowfield dropped steeply into the valley, about three hundred feet, where it formed an ice bridge over the river. The Bhyunder Ganga passed under this frozen arch, its water a frothy gray.

A single line of footprints had been kicked into the snow to provide a passage to the other side but these markings were at least a week old and rain had fallen since then, leaving a slick glaze of ice. Testing the surface I quickly realized that without crampons or an ice ax any attempt to cross would send me sliding into the river below. Instead I took the safer route, a short detour around the upper end of the snowfield. Looking down from the top I imagined that an experienced mountaineer could perform a graceful glissade, skidding down the slope and across the ice bridge to the other side. Nothing could have tempted me less and after regaining the trail, I was relieved to find that it was broad and level, an easy walk to the heart of the valley.

Along the way I saw a few flowers, bright blue primulas growing in clusters and dwarf rhododendrons. These bushes, with their tiny white blossoms and oblong leaves, reminded me of the elderly widow at Pangari Dondi who used them for incense. Mauve and pink rhododendrons also grew at the side of the path but their season was over and the flowers were withering. Gradually the rest of the valley came into view as the trail circled around to the right. On either side of me the ridges formed a crenellated wall of white-topped crags. Snow softened the profiles of the highest peaks but as the cliffs descended on either side they were scarred by erosion. Over a dozen waterfalls spilled down these cliffs and the sound of splashing streams added a melodic counterpoint to the bass rhythms of the Bhyunder Ganga.

By this time the sun had almost filled the valley, though the ridges to the east remained in shadow. Gradually the light crept down the opposite slope, striking a stand of birch trees, their pale green leaves shimmering like freckled water and their bark a silvery white. I could see to the far end of the valley now, where the glare of sunlight reflected off the south face of Rataban, a notched peak that stands above the glacier from which the Bhyunder Ganga flows. At sunrise and sunset the snow is tinged with red. Rataban is named for the blood-stained arrow of Karna, half brother of the Pandavs and one of the heroes in the Mahabharata. With a single shot from his bow he leveled the army of Raja Rupati. After destroying the enemy Karna's arrow flew straight to the Himalayas, plowing a furrow between the mountains. It is said that the gods were so delighted with this victory that they showered the arrow's path with flowers.

The valley is roughly ten kilometers from end to end, though the main section is only half that length. The surrounding cliffs curve down into a wide trough, with broad terraces at different heights, overlooking the Bhyunder Ganga. Where the river has cut a channel through the rocks there are gashes of exposed rubble and dirt but most of the slopes are overgrown with plants and groves of birch trees. My eye was immediately drawn to a field of bronze that stretched across the center of the valley. At first I thought these were flowers but as I drew closer I could see a swath of new ferns. Their coiled stems were covered with a papery orange casing that reflected the sunlight like burnished metal.

Unlike the bare moraine near Badrinath, where the landscape has been stripped of life, the Valley of Flowers looked as if it were carefully cultivated by nature. The receding glacier has cut a trench between the mountains but the rocky debris is covered with a fragile layer of moss and roots, the crevices between the boulders filled with pockets of humus. From a distance most of the stones are invisible and the slopes on either side of the Bhyunder Ganga have the appearance of meadows. Compared to the bugiyals above Dodi Tal or Panwali, however, the Valley of Flowers does not have a deep cushion of soil. Some writers have referred to it as a rock garden, which is perhaps the most accurate description, though the stones disappear beneath a tangle of foliage in summer and one is only aware of them on leaving the trail.

As soon as I entered the heart of the valley I came upon a sheet of white flowers, like a patch of snow. Going closer I saw that these were anemones, much larger and more abundant than I had ever seen before. White petals with pale yellow centers protruded above whorls of furred green leaves. The anemones grew together, as if planted by design, while the border of this natural bed was fringed with a line of marsh marigolds, like a golden hem. No gardener could have laid out a more perfect pattern and as I carried on up the valley I came upon more and more of these beds.

The waterfalls that cascade from the ridges above cut creases in this expanse of green. One of the larger streams at the foot of the valley used to have a bridge across it but this had been washed away and I had to leap from rock to rock to get across. At other places, tiny springs seeped out of the ground, the water so clear it was invisible except for the wavering reflections of flowers that grew along the bank. Clumps of wild onions, as delicate as narcissus, were sprouting near a stream where I leaned down to drink. The water that I scooped up with my hands was so cold it felt like an icicle going down my throat.

Though the valley would not reach full bloom for several weeks, the early rains had brought on a luxuriant growth of plants. There were still some of the late-blooming spring species—blue irises that opened out in labial shapes, their distended petals like pleated silk. At the lower end of the valley were beds of pink and blue primulas, each cluster of flowers rising on a slender stem, as if it were a miniature bouquet. Dark purple lupins, yellow and green fritillaria, and buttercups grew in patches though these were all but overwhelmed by the abundant leaves of other plants that were just about to bloom — balsam and delphinium, columbine and lousewort. I tried to identify each species but after a while it didn't seem to matter. They grew in such profusion that there was no reason to single out each individual plant. It would have been like trying to separate the threads in an ornate tapestry, or measure each brush stroke in a painting.

No man-made temples stand in the Valley of Flowers, which gives the landscape a different quality than most of the other places I visited in Garhwal. The entire valley is a sanctuary and no single stone or structure is invested with any more value than the rest. Rather than worshiping at a specific spot I was left to wander about and choose my own vantage points. I felt privileged to be alone in this valley and to be surrounded by the magnitude of nature. The only shrine, if you can call it that, is the marble tablet in memory of Joan Margaret Legge. I had no idea where it was located but after I had done a circuit of the valley, I saw a crude flagstaff made from a branch. It was several hundred meters off the path, surrounded by a sea of balsam. Still uncertain what it was I waded through the plants and found a small cairn of rocks that supported the branch. On top of the pile of stones were the remains of the marble plaque, broken into a dozen fragments. These had been carefully pieced together so that the inscription could be read. Tied to the flagstaff were several frayed strips of cotton, and someone had left a handful of white anemones resting against the plaque. The flowers had wilted and the leaves were turning brown. Though I was moved by the simplicity of this memorial, it was the surrounding aura of sanctity, rather than the marble tablet or the words from the Psalms, that made me bow my head.

Reflecting back on my pilgrimage I recalled similar moments, lodged in my memory like facets of crystal embedded in stone. These were the experiences that gave meaning to my journey, an awareness of nature's monuments and shrines, which were far more important than the temples I visited, the kilometers I traveled, or the altitudes I climbed. I remembered the day I set out from Rishikesh, ten months earlier, walking across the suspension bridge over the Ganga, bathing in its floodwaters, and camping that first night on the riverbank at Phool Chatti. Back then I had no clear idea what lay ahead of me, beyond the four main destinations and the names of towns and villages in between, scattered points of reference on an imaginary map. I recalled the rain falling on the surface of Dodi Tal, or arriving at Yamnotri in winter and hearing the sadhus singing at dawn, watching lammergeiers above the cliffs near Kapola and the night I waited for the full moon to rise over the Bhagirathi, the thunder and lightning at Panwali, and the view of Chaukhamba from Buda Madhmaheshwar. Each of these experiences punctuated my memory with a knowledge of the underlying power of nature and that unseen presence that is found only in solitude.

After weeks of walking the pilgrim route and sharing the trail with hundreds of other yatris, I had the entire Valley of Flowers to myself. There wasn't another soul in sight—no shepherds, no sadhus, no pilgrims. Years ago there used to be a forest rest house overlooking the Bhyunder Ganga but it has been dismantled and only the foundations remain, overgrown by grass and plants. At a few places I saw the remains of metal posts, crumpled and rusting into the ground, but the only recent evidence of human visitation was a scrawl of graffiti painted on a rock by a "trekking and culture club" from Delhi who had thoughtlessly inscribed their names in July 1998.

Though I scanned the cliffs for any sign of movement there

seemed to be no animals in the valley and the only bird I came across was a single monal pheasant that burst out of a stand of birches below the path and scared me half to death. Early in the day there were no insects, none of the flies and gnats that accompanied me up the trail from Govindghat. This accentuated the stillness of the scene and later, when a few butterflies appeared, they seemed like interlopers, stealing furtively among the flowers.

I had no clear sense of time but must have wandered through the valley for five or six hours that morning, following indistinct trails until they petered out a couple of kilometers below the glacier. Having completed my pilgrimage I felt no urgency to keep going or to hurry back to Ghangaria. Once I entered the heart of the valley I experienced an immediate sense of closure and contentment. Unlike the restless agitation that came over me in Badrinath, here there seemed no reason to leave or to move on. Part of it may have been the weather, which was perfect. Around noon a few clouds began to gather over the snow peaks but the sun stayed out for most of the day.

Though I was overcome with a sense of wonder and discovery I cannot remember exactly where my mind took me, only that I felt completely at peace. I wandered through the valley without any sense of direction, eventually coming to a point where a field of flowers jutted out over the river. There were several boulders near the edge and after wading through the waist-high plants I clambered upon one of these rocks and sat there for a time. Being impatient by nature and easily distracted, I have never practiced meditation, but somehow the stillness of the valley allowed me to sit motionless on the rock. I felt completely at one with the landscape around me but at the same time totally alone. A hundred feet below me flowed the Bhyunder Ganga. As I stared at the river there were moments when the current seemed to stop, the turbulent rapids froze for a second or two, and the rush of water fell silent as if the sound had crystallized in my inner ear.

Frank Smythe describes experiencing the same feeling of loneliness and revelation in the Bhyunder Valley. He writes:

> For the first time in my life I was able to think. I do not mean to think objectively or analytically, but rather to surrender thought to my surroundings. This is a power of which we know little in the west but which is a basic of abstract thought in the east. It is allowing the mind to receive rather than to seek impressions, and it is gained by expurgating extraneous thought. It is then that the Eternal speaks; that the mutations of the universe are apparent; the very atmosphere is filled with life and song; the hills are resolved from mere masses of snow, ice and rock into something living. When this happens the human mind escapes from the bondage of its own feeble imaginings and becomes as one with its Creator.

For me this was an experience as emotional and illuminating as that moment six months earlier, when I opened my eyes to see the flowering tree on the pass above Kapola. I find it difficult to put my feelings on paper for fear of debasing the enigmatic power of that experience with words that can only approximate the truth. To claim that I felt any presence, other than my own, would be like trying to fashion something solid out of air. All I can say is that whatever I encountered seemed to lie within myself, as if the snow peaks and the waterfalls, the glacier and the river, the rocks and flowers, had been absorbed into my body. In many ways it was the same sensation of negative space that I had experienced the night before, while lying in my tent, except instead of darkness there was light. Though I kept my eyes open and looked around me I could just as easily have been staring back into myself, for everything that I observed—the sun reflecting off the ice, the color and fragrance of flowers, the sound of the river, even the hard, uneven texture of the rock on which I sat—was nothing more than signals from my senses to the nerves within my brain, synaptic illusions that could only hint at those mysteries beyond my skin.

# AFTERWORD

THIS BOOK IS BASED ON FOUR TREKS I TOOK between August 1999 and June 2000. Except for a few short sections, where it was impossible to walk, I traveled the Char Dham Yatra on foot. My objective was to retrace traditional pilgrim trails, many of which have fallen into disuse or have disappeared altogether. The total distance covered was roughly six hundred kilometers and altitudes ranged from four thousand to fourteen thousand feet above sea level. Between each stage of the pilgrimage I traveled back and forth by bus, taxi, Jeep, or truck.

On November 9, 2000, four months after I completed my treks, the new state of Uttaranchal was formed out of the hill districts of Uttar Pradesh. This dramatic change in the political landscape represents the culmination of a struggle by the people of Garhwal and Kumaon, asserting their identity and reclaiming control of the region's natural resources. For the most part, this book does not address these issues directly since my focus is on the mythology and natural history of the Ganga's watershed. Referring to the areas through which I traveled I have used the traditional terms Garhwal and Uttarakhand.

When it comes to myths, legends, and folktales the question of authenticity is inevitably a problem. For every version of a story there will always be several other conflicting accounts.

Recognizing this I make no claim that any of the myths contained in this book are at all definitive. Most of them are stories that I heard recounted by several different individuals and my translations attempt to render these narratives in as clear and coherent a form as possible. Though I have consulted several published works on the subject of Hindu mythology and drawn details from these, none of this should be construed as serious scholarship. In fact, what interests me most are the changeable elements in these legends, their popular interpretations, and ultimately, their unpredictable, undocumented nature.

Those readers who are familiar with Hindu texts may recognize inconsistencies in my transliteration of Sanskrit or Hindi words. I have yet to find a system, using the English alphabet, that effectively conveys the pronunciation of these terms. For this reason I rely on the eccentricities of my own spelling, which seems to be as accurate as any other method of transliteration.

# BIBLIOGRAPHY

Aitken, Bill. *Seven Sacred Rivers*. New Delhi: Penguin, 1992.

Ali, Salim. *Indian Hill Birds*. New Delhi: Oxford, 1949.

Alter, Andrew. "Dancing the Gods: Power and Meaning in the Music of Garhwal, North India." Diss. School of Music, Monash University, Australia, 2000.

Atkinson, E. T. *The Himalayan Gazetteer Vol. II, Parts I & 2*. 1882. Delhi: Cosmo Publications, 1973.

Bose, Subodh Chandra. *Land and People of the Himalaya*. Calcutta: Indian Publications, 1968.

—. *Geography of the Himalaya*. New Delhi: National Book Trust, 1972.

Collett, Henry. *Flora Simlensis: A Handbook of the Flowering Plants of Simla and the Neighbourhood*. 1921. Dehradun: International Book Distributors, 1984.

Corbett, Jim. *The Man-Eating Leopard of Rudraprayag*. 1947. New Delhi: Oxford University Press, 1991.

Dang, Rupin. *Flowers of the Western Himalayas*. Delhi: Wilderness Films India, 1998.

Dimmit, Cornelia, and J. A. B. van Buitenen. *Classical Hindu Mythology, A Reader in the Sanskrit Puranas*. Philadelphia: Temple University Press, 1978.

Dowson, John. *A Classical Dictionary of Hindu Mythology & Religion*. New Delhi: Rupa, 1998.

Eck, Diana. *Darsan, Seeing the Divine Image in India*. Chambersburg, PA: Anima Books, 1981.

Embree, Aislie T.. *The Hindu Tradition*. New York: Modern Library, 1966.

Fleming, Robert L. Sr., Robert L. Fleming Jr., and Lain Singh Bangdel. *Birds of Nepal*. Kathmandu: Robert L. Fleming Sr. and Jr., 1976.

Fuller, C. J. *The Camphor Flame, Popular Hinduism and Society in India*. Princeton: Princeton University Press, 1992.

*Guide Map: The Holy Places of Uttarakhand Yatra*. Hardwar: Randhir Prakashan n.d.

*Hiking in the Garhwal Himalayas, A Guide*. Landour: Woodstock Publications, 1998.

Jayakar, Pupul. *The Earth Mother*. 1980. New Delhi: Penguin, 1989.

Lannoy, Richard. *The Speaking Tree: A Study of Indian Culture and Society*. London: Oxford University Press, 1971.

Mascaro, Juan, trans. *The Bhagavad Gita*. London: Penguin, 1962.

—, trans. *The Upanishads*. London: Penguin, 1965.

Mitchell, A. G. *Hindu Gods and Goddesses*. New Delhi: UBS Publishers, 1999.

Oakley, E. S., and Tara Dutt Gairola. *Himalayan Folklore: Kumaon and West Nepal*. 1935. Kathmandu: Bibliotheca Himalayica, 1977.

—. *Holy Himalaya*. 1905. Nainital: Gyanodaya Prakashan, 1990.

O'Flaherty, Wendy Doniger, trans. *The Rig Veda*. London: Penguin, 1981.

"Pilgrim." *Notes of Wanderings In the Himmala*. Agra: T. W. Brown, 1844.

Prater, S. H. *The Book of Indian Animals*. 1948. Bombay: Bombay Natural History Society, 1980.

Rajagopalachari, C. *Mahabharata*. Bombay: Bharatiya Vidya Bhavan, 1951.

—. *Ramayana*. Bombay: Bharatiya Vidya Bhavan, 1951.

Sax, William S. *Mountain Goddess: Gender and Politics in a Himalayan Pilgrimage*. New York: Oxford University Press, 1991.

Sharma, Man Mohan. *Nandan Kanan: The Valley of Flowers*. New Delhi: Vision Books, 1985.

Singh, Tara. *Sri Hemkunt Darshan*. Amritsar: Singh Brothers, 1982.

Smythe, Frank S. *The Valley of Flowers*. 1939. Dehradun: Natraj, 1987.

Thukral, Gurmeet, and Elizabeth Thukral. *Garhwal Himalaya*. Delhi: Frank Bros. and Company, 1987.

—, and Ruskin Bond. *Himalayan Flowers*. Minneapolis: Roth Publishing Co., 1998.

Wilkins, W. J. *Hindu Mythology*. 1882. New Delhi: Rupa, 1998.

# GLOSSARY

aarti: form of worship using lamp or incense
alak: hair
ameel: buckthorn (*Hippophae rhamnoides*)
asan: yoga posture
ashram: religious retreat
ayurveda: traditional form of herbal medicine
baba: ascetic, master or father
bagh: leopard, sometimes tiger
bhaila khelna: fireworks ritual
bhajan: religious hymn
bharal: blue sheep (*Pseudois nayaur*)
bhoj patra: birch bark
bhootia: of Tibetan origin, also Tibetan mastiff
bidi: hand-rolled cigarette made from bidi leaves
brahmkamal: Himalayan lotus (*Saussurea obvallata*)
burans: rhododendron (*Rhododendron arboreum*)
chaan: cowshed, seasonal shelter made of thatch
channa: chickpeas
chappal: sandal
chappati: unleavened wholewheat bread
charpai: string cot
chatti: shelter or stop along the pilgrimage route
cholai: amaranth plant, eaten both as vegetable and as grain
choola: hearth

choti: single lock of hair at the back of head

chowkidar: watchman

daitya: demon

dal: lentils

damaun: tambourine-like drum

dandie: sedan chair

daranthi: sickle with a broad blade

darshan: to be in the presence of, to view the deity

devi: goddess

dharamshala: rest house for pilgrims

dham: site of religious significance, dwelling place of the gods

dhol: two-sided drum

dhoti: loincloth

doli: palanquin used for carrying a deity or a bride

Gangajal: water from the Ganga

ganja: hashish

gaushala: rest house for cows

ghee: clarified butter

ghoral: goat antelope (*Nemorhaedus goral*)

gram devta: village deity

gujjar: Muslim herdsman

gurudwara: Sikh temple

harijan: untouchable, literally "child of god"

haryali: greenery, foliage

hookah: waterpipe

jadoo: magic, sleight of hand

jhoola: swing, suspension bridge

kabristan: graveyard

kacchi: homebrewed liquor, literally "raw stuff"

kajal: black eye-liner

kakad: barking deer (*Muntiacus muntjak*)

kandie: conical basket used for carrying pilgrims

kanta: thorn or barb

kar sevak: volunteer

karela: small gourd-like vegetable
kavar: pilgrims who carry Ganga water, traveling by foot
khadi: handloom cloth, usually cotton
kheer: rice pudding
kirpan: sword or dagger worn as a martial emblem by Sikhs
kirtan: religious hymn
kurta: longsleeved tunic
langar: charitable kitchen
lingam: stone, phallic representation of Shiv
mahseer: species of fish (*Barbus tor*)
mandir: temple
mashaal: chopper or machete
moksha: salvation
neech jati: derogatory term for untouchable
PWD: Public Works Department
pangar: horse chestnut (*Aesculus indica*)
parantha: fried bread, often stuffed with vegetables
pooja: worship
pradhan: headman
prasad: blessed food or offering presented to worshippers
prayag: confluence
pullav: loose end of a sari, covering shoulders or head
rakshish: demon
rishi: sage
sadhu: ascetic
salwar kameez: loose pantaloons and long shirt
samadhi: release from existence, communion with god, gravesite
samosa: fried pastry with savory filling
sangam: confluence
sanyas: renunciation of the material world
sanyasi: someone who renounces the material world, an ascetic
sari: garment worn by women, made of unstitched fabric
sati: self-immolation
serow: large goat antelope (*Capricornis sumatraensis*)

shakti: power, creative energy, usually related to the goddess

sher: tiger, also lion

suji halwa: sweetened porridge made with semolina

swarg: heaven or paradise

tapasya: act of austerity and meditation

tava: griddle

thali: tray

thar: mountain goat (*Hemitragus jemlahicus*)

tilak: mark on forehead to signify the completion of worship

trisul: trident

vahana: animal that conveys or accompanies a Hindu god

yatra: pilgrimage

yatri: pilgrim

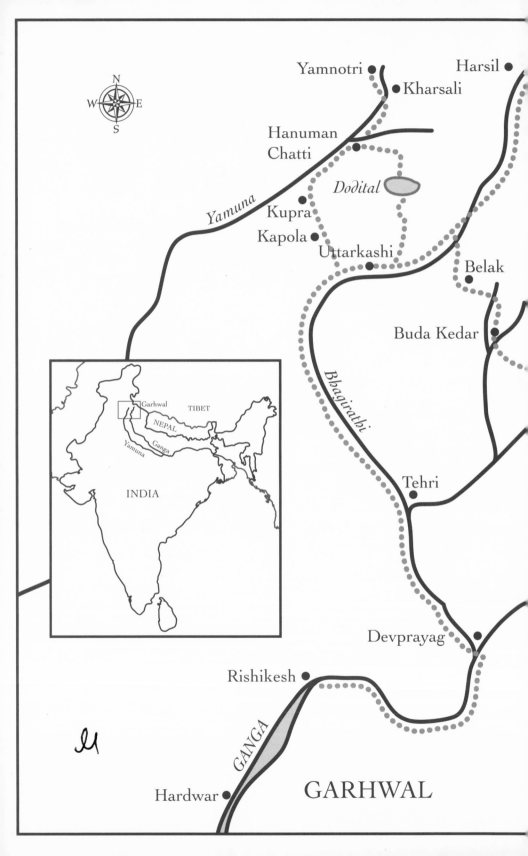